THE
UNARMED
PROPHET

THE

UNARMED PROPHET

Savonarola in Florence

RACHEL ERLANGER

McGraw-Hill Book Company

New York   St. Louis   San Francisco   Bogotá
Hamburg   Madrid   Milan   Mexico   Montreal
Panama   Paris   São Paulo   Tokyo   Toronto

1 2 3 4 5 6 7 8 9 D O H D O H 8 7

ISBN 0-07-019602-8

LIBRARY OF CONGRESS CATALOGING-IN-PUBLICATION DATA

Erlanger, Rachel.
    The unarmed prophet.
        1. Savonarola, Girolamo, 1452–1498.   2. Florence
(Italy)—Intellectual life.   3. Florence (Italy)—
Church history.   4. Reformers—Italy—Florence—
Biography.   5. Dominicans—Italy—Florence—Biography.
6. Florence (Italy)—Biography.   I. Title.
DG737.97.E75   1987   945'.51   87-3212
ISBN 0-07-019602-8

Book design by Kathryn Parise

To Bernie

A NOTE ON MONEY

From 1484 to 1509 the *fiorino d'oro*, or gold florin, weighed 3.45 grams, which would give it a worth of approximately $36 in the 1987 gold market. Since the average yearly wage of an unskilled laborer was 15 florins and that of a skilled worker 33 florins, whatever the intrinsic worth of the florin, to the average Florentine it represented a very large sum indeed. Most Florentines used silver coins, the so-called *piccola moneta*: the *quattrino*, the *grosso* and the *lira*. In 1493 6.7 lire were the equivalent of one florin, and the grosso was the equivalent of one-third of a lira, or 20 quattrini.

ACKNOWLEDGMENTS

I would like to thank those who in one way or another helped me to write this book: Carl Brandt, who worked with me to find a form for the material and constantly encouraged me to keep going; my dear friends Harriette Bressack and Maureen di Biccari, who read each chapter after I finished it; Carole Wasserman, who searched through the libraries of Florence for sources not available in New York; Anna Marie Levi, who helped me with the mysteries of Italian spelling and capitalization; and Tom Miller, who edited the book.

CONTENTS

CONTENTS

x

The people of Florence are far from considering themselves ignorant and benighted, and yet Brother Girolamo Savonarola succeeded in persuading them that he held converse with God. I will not pretend to judge whether it was true or not, for we must speak with respect of so great a man; but I may well say that an immense number believed it without having seen any extraordinary manifestations that should have made them believe it.

Niccolò Machiavelli
The Discourses,
Book I, Chapter XI

If he was good, we have seen a great prophet in our time; if he was bad, we have seen a great man. For, apart from his erudition, we must admit that if he was able to fool the public for so many years on so important a matter without ever being caught in a lie, he must have had great judgment, talent and power of invention.

Francesco Guicciardini
History of Florence, Chapter 16

PROLOGUE

he first confession filled thirty-two pages. It had been signed by the friar, and it was to be read aloud in the Great Hall of the Palazzo della Signoria. The apothecary Luca Landucci, who like so many of the friar's supporters made it his business to be present for the reading, was "utterly dumbfounded" by what he heard. He whom they had held to be a prophet had confessed that he was no prophet and had not received from God the things that he had preached but had made them up "out of a desire for earthly glory."

Just as the Lord had sent the prophet Haggai to Jerusalem to help the children of Israel rebuild their temple, so God had sent him to Florence to help the Florentines build a new order more glorious than the first, the friar had told them after the overthrow of the Medici. And he had promised them that if they followed him, Florence would become a new Jerusalem from which would spring the reformation of all Italy. But now it seemed to Landucci that that whole edifice, that new Jerusalem which was supposed to bring "just laws and splendor and an example of righteous life," had fallen to the ground "on account of being founded on a lie." And even the knowledge that the friar had been suspended from the pulley to make him confess could not ease the heartache and the sense of having been betrayed.

Was it permissible for a prophet and a servant of God to retract even under torture? The notary Lorenzo Violi, who had transcribed so many of the friar's sermons, could not be sure.

"O prophet, now is the time for a miracle!" shouted someone in the vast crowd gathered in the Piazza della Signoria on the May morning when the hangman slipped the noose around the friar's neck and pushed him toward eternity. And soon voices all over the piazza had taken up the cry. Before the hangman could come down from the scaffold, someone had flung a lighted torch on the pile of dry wood heaped below. As the flames shot upward and the firecrackers, which a practical joker had concealed among the tinder, began to crackle and burst, a sudden wind diverted the blaze from its mark, leading some of those who had called for a miracle to believe they were witnessing one and causing a few to flee in terror. But the wind subsided as quickly as it had come; the flames once more shot up toward the gibbet, and groups of boys and young men began hurling stones at the smoldering corpse until "it rained entrails and blood."

"Praise be to God, now we can practice sodomy!" a newly elected member of the Ten of *Balia* was heard to exclaim as he watched the spectacle.

Two of Savonarola's biographers, the marchese Roberto Ridolfi and the Dominican priest Josef Schnitzer, have compared his martyrdom to that of Joan of Arc; and they looked forward to the day when, like Joan, he would be canonized by the church which had sent him to the stake. But if it is possible to find similarities to Joan in his story, it is also possible to find similarities to Ayatollah Khomeini, as well as to Pat Robertson, Jerry Falwell, and the many other apocalyptic preachers throughout our land who are convinced of the imminence of Armageddon and the second coming of Christ. Like the ayatollah, Savonarola became the spokesman for a popular uprising which overthrew the existing government. Like Pat Robertson, he claimed to hold converse with God. Like both Jerry Falwell and the ayatollah, he sought to regulate the inherently private aspects of other people's lives: their dress, their sexual behavior, the way they raised their children. Like apocalyptic preachers everywhere, he was convinced that his was a singularly wicked and corrupt age, that all who followed him would be saved, whereas all who didn't were damned.

"Past things shed light on future ones," said the Florentine historian Guicciardini. "...the same things come back, but under different names and colors." Savonarola's story bears retelling because of the light it sheds on the present. What makes it particularly worthy of notice is that it happened in Florence in the age of the Medici, an age which Voltaire, for one, likened to the age of Pericles in ancient Athens.

How did this homely little preacher from Ferrara, with the hoarse voice and the Lombard accent, manage to convince the people of the most cultured city in Italy that he was God's chosen prophet? And why did so many of them, including Michelangelo and Botticelli, Lorenzo di Credi and Baccio della Porta, continue to be influenced by his sermons long after all that was left of him had floated down the Arno into the Mediterranean? It couldn't just have been charisma. The time and the place must have had something to do with it.

At a time when most of the rest of Europe was consolidating into nations ruled by kings, Italy remained as fragmented as it had been during the Middle Ages—a network of autonomous city-states, the majority of them governed by despots, a few, like Florence and Venice, still clinging to republican forms. The story of Savonarola in Florence is the story of what happened when, as the result of an agreement with one political faction, an apocalyptic preacher became the de facto ruler of the republic—when, in short, religion and politics were allowed to mix. It is also the story of the preacher himself: what George Eliot called his "imperious need for ascendancy" and the compromises he made to keep his hold on the city. Finally, it is the story of the enemies he picked up in the process: from young blades who thought his moral reforms had taken all the fun out of life, to Florentine businessmen whose commercial interests he appeared to threaten, to Ludovico Sforza, duke of Milan, and Alexander VI, the Borgia pope.

Because Florentine history and customs did so much to shape the story, it is necessary to begin with a look at Florence in the years before that day in 1490 when Savonarola walked through the San Gallo gate bearing his message of apocalypse and renewal.

I

LORENZO'S TIME

o Lorenzo dei Medici's erstwhile tutor, the philosopher Marsilio Ficino, the Florentines seemed to be living in "a golden age that radiated its brilliance over the liberal arts so long obscured, over poetry, sculpture, music, the song of the ancient Orphic lyre," all of which excelled at Florence. The wealthy Florentine merchant Giovanni Rucellai thanked God for having created him in "the most beautiful city not only of Christendom but by common consent of the whole world." In that period, wrote the historian Giovanni Cambi, Florence "appeared richer than ever before."

Among other proofs of the wealth and industry of this city of approximately 75,000 persons, the chronicler Benedetto Dei listed 33 banks, 83 silk workshops, 270 woolen workshops, 66 apothecary shops, 54 stonecutting establishments skilled in both intaglio and relievo, 84 wood-carving establishments, 31 ateliers belonging to artists, 26 ateliers belonging to sculptors, 44 jewelers and goldsmiths with shops on the Ponte Vecchio, and an indeterminate number of master builders.

"Men were crazy about building at this time," said Luca Landucci in the summer of 1489 when work on the foundation of the Strozzi Palace filled the streets around his shop "with heaps of stones and rubbish and with mules and donkeys who were carrying away the rubbish and bringing gravel." But the building boom had begun long before that, for Dei mentioned 30 new palaces erected in Florence between 1450 and 1478, as well as 21 loggias, 138 gardens, and over 50 piazzas, not to mention more than 800 villas that went up in the nearby hills and valleys. "A palace with a coat of arms does much honor because it shows more than possessions can do," Michelangelo would later say. The palaces were dimly lit, drafty, and uncomfortable. Nevertheless, everyone who was anyone wished to build one. To make room for all those palaces, whole blocks of workers' houses had to be torn down, so that, complained a government decree, "the people suffered from a lack of accommodations." Unlike the workers' houses they replaced, the palaces were exempt from taxation, since building them gave employment to a host of stonemasons, bricklayers, carpenters, woodworkers, and mosaicists, and added to the beauty and prosperity of Florence.

"Florence is full of all imaginable wealth," said a self-congratulatory inscription on the Palazzo della Signoria. "She reigns over the sea and the land and the whole of the world. Under her leadership, the whole of Tuscany enjoys happiness. Like Rome she is always triumphant."

A series of wars and purchases had given the Florentines hegemony over all the inland cities of Tuscany except Lucca and Siena. The conquest of Pisa in 1406, followed by the purchase of Livorno in 1421, had extended that hegemony to the Tuscan seacoast. By Lorenzo's time, eleven large galleons and fourteen smaller galleons flying the red lily of Florence were bringing raw materials and spices to Porto Pisano and carrying finished goods abroad. The gold florin, with the image of the city's patron saint John the Baptist on one side and the lily on the other, was the most stable currency in Europe. To meet the demand for florins, the *zecca*, or mint, turned out 400,000 new coins a year. There was also a slightly heavier galleon florin in circulation on the high seas and in eastern ports—from Constantinople, where fifty-one Florentine mercantile houses were doing business in 1469, to Alexandria, where the sultan had given Florentine merchants permission to build warehouses in 1421, to Tunis, where Florentines had had warehouses since the thirteenth century.

The stability of the florin made the Mercato Nuovo, in which the Guild of Bankers and Moneychangers had its palace, the financial center of Europe. There, and in the nearby Via dei Tavolini, the money changers sat behind tables covered with green cloth, trading in bullion and precious stones and exchanging coins of all nations from the moment the bell atop their guild residence announced the opening of a new business day until that same bell rang again to proclaim the closing of the money market. There, too, in makeshift shops that rented for 10 or 12 florins a year and employed nine or ten cashiers at annual salaries of 20 florins per cashier, great merchant bankers in ermine-trimmed silk *luccos* dealt in letters of exchange worth hundreds of gold florins each. To make good on the letters, Florentine banks had branches and factors all over Europe. The Medici, whom the French historian Philippe de Comines called "the greatest commercial house that had ever been anywhere," had representatives in London, Naples, Cologne, Geneva, Lyons, Bâle, Avignon, Bruges, Antwerp, Lübeck, Ancona, Rome, Pisa, and Venice. In gratitude for their service to the French crown, Louis XI had given their family the right to stamp the lilies of France on one of the six red balls in its coat of arms. The Medici bank in Lyons handled the savings of an ever-increasing number of French courtiers. The Medici bank in Venice was the center of Florentine trade with the East. Until 1476, and once again after 1483, the Medici bank in Rome handled the financial affairs of the papacy. Because no interest could be collected on the papal debt, the Medici routinely inflated the prices of the relics, tapestries, and paintings with which they supplied the Curia, as well as the finder's fees for the boy sopranos they recruited for the choir of Saint John's Lateran.

Like many Florentine bankers, they also added to their fortune by trading in silk and wool. Lorenzo was enrolled in the guild of the *calimala* (the processors of foreign cloth) when he was 10 and in the silk workers' guild after the death of his father. One Florentine silk merchant boasted that the city's *panni serici*, or silken goods, were unsurpassed anywhere. In silk workshops on the Via Porta Santa Maria and the other streets leading to the Ponte Vecchio and along the Via Maggiore (now the Via Maggio) on the other side of the Arno, 16,000 men, women, and children labored from matins to vespers to produce silk and velvet, taffeta and damask, brocade and cloth of gold to outfit the wealthy in every part of Europe and the Middle East. During the annual feast of San Giovanni, said the historian Goro Dati, "Magnificent silk and gold brocades bearing the emblazoned arms of ten kingdoms whose sovereigns and courtiers were outfitted with the produce of the Florentine silk mills were displayed over the shops and offices of the silk merchants along the Via Porta Santa Maria."

Antonio Pollaiuolo was one of the many artists who provided small sketches to be worked into silk tissue and ornamental cloth by the guild's embroiderers. The guild's laceworkers crocheted gold and silver fringes on everything from ball gowns to baldachins.

Master dyers working for the silk guild, the wool guild, and the guild of the *calimala* boiled cloth in gall to turn it black, and used perse, a brilliant blue obtained from the leaves of the woad plant, as a base for a host of sought-after colors from violet to sanguine (blood red) and burnet (near black). In 1262, a *calimala* merchant had discovered that a reddish-purple dye could be extracted from *oricello*, a white moss growing in the Greek isles. Because Florentine dyers were the only ones who knew how to produce *scarletto d'oricello*, a rich scarlet resulting from the union of *oricello* and madder, the papal court had given the members of the *calimala* the exclusive right to finish the cloth used in the robes of the cardinals.

But the real basis of the city's economy was the domestic manufacture of woolen cloth. In the Via dei Cimatori ("Street of the Shearers"), the Via delle Caldaie ("Street of the Cauldrons"), and the Corso dei Tintori ("Road of the Dyers") and in all the other streets going down to the Arno where lived those involved in transforming raw wool into finished cloth, every residence from the elegant new palaces of the wool merchants to the dingy old palaces known as *casolari*, or hovels, because they had been divided into living quarters for working men, had upright iron bars fitted to its oiled linen windowpanes and wooden crossbars on which great hanks of spun wool and long pieces of woven wool were hung to dry. Because wool from Tuscan sheep was too coarse, raw wool had to be imported from England and Spain. One of Lorenzo dei Medici's numerous diplomatic triumphs was what amounted to a most-favored-nation agreement with Henry VII. In exchange for Henry's promise to land all wool carried on English ships at Pisa, the Florentines gave England the exclusive right to ship wool to the port.

To the poet Angelo Poliziano, Lorenzo was "the laurel of happy birth under whose shade Florence rests joyful and at peace." And Poliziano thought that Lorenzo ought to be called *caput*, or head. In dealing with foreign princes, however, Lorenzo himself was careful to point out that he was not the *signore* of Florence but merely a citizen who, like other citizens, had to be patient and conform to the will of the majority. However, the princes appeared to think otherwise. Louis XI called him "brother" and suggested that he send a confidential agent to the French court. Louis's son and successor, Charles VIII, asked Lorenzo to use his influence with Pope Innocent VIII to obtain a benefice for one of the king's councillors. When the pope was seeking a way out of his entanglement with King Ferrante of Naples, it was Lorenzo that he turned to for help.

Nor was Lorenzo's influence limited to the rulers of Europe. In 1487, the ambassador of the sultan of Egypt arrived in Florence, bringing with him a magnificent striped tent for Lorenzo and a large, tame lion, a "beautiful and graceful giraffe," a goat, and several strange-looking gelded sheep with huge tails and long, hanging ears as gifts for the people of the city. The lion and the goat were consigned to the menagerie behind the Palazzo della Signoria. The sheep found a home on one of Lorenzo's farms. When the weather was good, the giraffe paraded through the streets and marketplaces of Florence, poking its nose into peasants' baskets and accepting apples from children, until one day it struck its head against a lintel post and died. What Lorenzo did with the magnificent striped tent is not known.

Lorenzo was only 15 when his father sent him on his first diplomatic mission. He was only 20 when Piero dei Medici died. Two days later, a delegation composed of 600 of the leading citizens of Florence came to the Medici palace on the Via Larga to ask Lorenzo to take charge of the government as his father and grandfather had done. The proposal was contrary to the instincts of his youthful age, and the burden and danger were great, he wrote in his diary. Nevertheless, he accepted because "it is ill living in Florence for the rich unless they rule the state."

Nothing in the Florentine constitution gave this homely, nearsighted youth with his massive outthrust nose, his wide, shapeless mouth, and disagreeable nasal voice the right to rule the state. Florence prided itself on its republican traditions. The humanist chancellor Leonardo Bruni had called the city the daughter of Rome, founded not by Julius Caesar, as had been believed since Dante's time, but before Rome became subject to the rule of one man. A widely circulated legend held that no less a person than the emperor Charlemagne "had made the commune and the people of Florence for three miles around independent and free."

The new commune changed its laws and its lawmakers so frequently that Dante, who was exiled as a result of one of the changes, thought Florence ought to recognize itself

> In that sick woman's shape
> Who lay down and can do
> Nothing but turn and turn her pain to escape.

If all the people who had been driven from Florence and all those who had been miserably assassinated gathered together, said the Milanese writer Matteo Bandello, "they would populate a city far greater than Florence."

Underlying the conflict between Guelphs and Ghibellines that marked the early years was the conflict between the landed aristocracy, or *grandi*, who were in control of the government, and the wealthy merchants, or *popolani*, who wished to be in control. The conflict ended in victory for the *popolani*. The Ordinances of Justice passed in 1293 destroyed the last vestige of influence the *grandi* as a class still had in Florence by requiring every citizen to enroll in a guild. Those *grandi* who refused to enroll lost the right to vote and hold office. In 1298, the government of the *popolani* ordered the architect Arnolfo di Cambio to build the Palazzo della Signoria as a dwelling place for the officers of the commune and a fortress to protect the people's government from the incursions of the nobles. Henceforth, the only road to political power was via the guilds.

The guilds were of two types: the seven major guilds, or *arti maggiori*, and the fourteen lesser guilds, or *arti minori*. Of the seven greater guilds, the Guild of Lawyers and Notaries had the most prestige. Next came the guilds of the wool, silk, and *calimala* merchants, followed by the Guild of Bankers and Money-changers, the Guild of Doctors and Apothecaries, and the Guild of Furriers. The lesser guilds included all manner of tradesmen and artisans, from butchers, who ranked first in importance, to tanners, leather workers, smiths, stonemasons, retail cloth merchants, dealers in foodstuffs, innkeepers, and bakers.

Wealth was the criterion of worth in Florence. "He who has no possessions is regarded as a mere animal," said Boccaccio. The wealthy merchants, bankers, and professionals who dominated the seven greater guilds and were known collectively as the *popolo grasso* (literally, "fat, or well-fed, people") looked with disdain on the tradesmen and artisans of the lesser guilds, whose world was confined to their grubby shops on the side streets and their even grubbier stalls in the Mercato Vecchio, and sought to reduce their role in the government as much as possible. To the prosperous upper-class apothecary and landowner Matteo Palmieri, it was "lunacy to have a cobbler tell us how civil laws are to be enacted, how the republic is to be administered, how wars are to be conducted." As for the tens of thousands of *sottoposti*, or wage earners who worked as dyers, spinners, weavers, carders, combers, and beaters in the shops of the wool, silk, and *calimala* merchants but were denied a voice in either the guilds or the government because they lacked the necessary property and residence requirements:

> If the lowest orders of society have enough food to keep them going, then they have enough. Those who are lazy or indolent and can offer no just reasons for their condition should be forced to work or be expelled from the commune.

Palmieri's *Vita Civile*, from which these words are taken, was published in 1438, a time when the "lower orders" were relatively quiet, but they had not always been so docile. In 1345, a wool carder named Cinto Brandini was hanged for attempting to organize his fellow workers into a guild. In 1368, a strike of dyers was broken by the threat of a lockout. Ten years later, the workers in the wool shops, led by the washers and carders, or *ciompi*, rioted before the Palazzo della Signoria, shouting "Down with the traitors who allow us to starve!" and demanded the right to organize their own guilds.

After driving the Signoria out of the Palazzo and choosing Michele di Lando, a barefoot carder whose wife and mother sold vegetables in the Mercato Vecchio, as gonfalonier of the republic, they organized three new guilds: the guilds of the dyers, the doublet makers, and the *ciompi*. When the *ciompi* demanded further rights, they were forced to disband by the very gonfalonier they had put into office. The two other guilds became part of a coalition government which has been called the most democratic the city ever had. But the experiment in popular democracy—or *governo popolare*, as it was called in Florence—was short-lived. In 1382, a counterrevolution restored the power of the *popolo grasso*—"the wise and the well-to-do," Guicciardini called them, as if the two automatically went together. And this *governo stretto*, or oligarchy, used the fear of another mass uprising as an excuse to disband the guilds of the dyers and the doublet makers and to reduce the voice of the other lesser guilds in the government.

Government in Florence was a hodgepodge of councils, commissions, colleges, and assemblies headed by the Signoria and its presiding officer, the gonfalonier or standard-bearer of the republic. The members of most of these commissions, councils, and colleges, as well as the members of the Signoria and the gonfalonier, were chosen by lot from *borse*, or leather bags that contained the names of all citizens eligible for office. To become eligible, a citizen had to pass a *squittino*, or scrutiny, which took place every five years. Under the oligarchy and later under the Medici, the gonfalonier and six of the eight priors chosen for the Signoria had to come from the greater guilds, leaving only two priors to represent the more numerous lesser guilds. This 6 to 2 ratio also prevailed in most of the other commissions and councils. In times of crisis, the gonfalonier would summon all the people to a town meeting, or *parlamento*, by ringing the great bell atop the campanile of the Palazzo della Signoria known as *La Vacca*, "the Cow," because of its low mooing sound. Usually, they were asked to approve a *balia*, or special commission, set up to deal with the crisis. Except for the members of a few of these *balie*, no one held office for very long. The gonfalonier and the priors served for only two months.

Although this rapid turnover was intended to give a great number of people a chance to participate in government, Machiavelli found it "no guarantee of the popular will." Rather than being governed in the Palazzo della Signoria, the historian Giovanni Cavalcanti said, "The commune was governed at dinner and desks... many were called to office; but few were chosen to govern." If by chance those who were called took advantage of the secret ballot to vote against a measure favored by the ruling clique, one of the clique's lackeys would immediately demand an open vote to see "who the friends of this regime really are and who are the enemies." It was this sort of bullying that led the wealthy Giovanni Rucellai to advise his sons not to seek public office, for there was nothing he esteemed less or that seemed to him less honorable. The somewhat less wealthy Carlo di Silvestro Gondi, on the other hand, was overjoyed to find his name on the list of those nominated for gonfalonier, not only because he wanted the honor for himself, but because of the "enormous impetus" it would give his family. And Machiavelli's friend, the tavern keeper Donato del Corno, spent a lifetime trying to pass a *squittino* and become *imborsate*, or eligible for office.

One way Lorenzo's grandfather Cosimo kept control of the government after he and his clique unseated the oligarchy in 1434 was by an almost foolproof method for making sure that those citizens who did pass a *squittino* were citizens favorable to the Medici. Besides using the family fortune to reward their friends, Cosimo and his successors also exploited a largely undeserved but assiduously cultivated reputation for being champions of the masses. And they kept the masses happy with what is best described as a program of bread and circuses.

When the people objected to Lorenzo's betrothal to Clarice Orsini, a Roman noblewoman, his father Piero organized two festivals to divert their attention. One of them was conducted with such pomp that, said Machiavelli, "it kept the whole city occupied for many months."

After Clarice married Lorenzo by proxy in Rome, the marriage was celebrated by a mock tournament in the Piazza Santa Croce to which the entire city was invited. The 19-year-old bridegroom entered the lists on a white charger given him by the king of Naples. On his shield gleamed a colossal diamond known as *Il Libro.* Over his velvet surcoat he wore a rose-embroidered scarf upon which the motto *Le temps revient* was written in pearls. Before the combat began, he exchanged his white charger for another given him by the duke of Ferrara, and his gem-studded velvet cap for a helmet topped with three feathers. With the plain speaking that was typical of him, he later wrote in his diary that although he was not "highly versed in the use of weapons or the delivery of blows," the prize was adjudged to him: "a helmet inlaid with silver and a figure of Mars on the crest." The tournament cost Piero 10,000 florins.

After Lorenzo assumed power, he and his younger brother Giuliano formed two companies of young aristocrats who vied with one another in producing tournaments, processions, and festivals. In 1475, Giuliano spent 8000 florins on the costumes for a tournament in his honor held in the Piazza Santa Croce. His helmet had been fashioned by Verrocchio. His standard, which was the work of Botticelli, showed an armed Pallas Athena in a gold tunic looking down on a forlorn Cupid bound to the stump of an olive tree with his broken bow and arrow at his feet.

"Everyone had a different opinion as to why Love had been so pictured," wrote a Venetian visitor. And he found the discussion provoked by Botticelli's work more beautiful than the work itself. In *La Giostra di Giuliano dei Medici,* Poliziano pictured the tournament's Queen of Beauty, Giuliano's presumably platonic love Simonetta dei Vespucci, as Minerva wearing a coat of armor over her robe of virginal white and holding a lance in one hand and a Gorgon's head in the other.

When the beautiful Simonetta died of consumption at the age of 23, she was carried to her tomb with her face uncovered so that those who had known her might gaze on her loveliness one last time. And, wrote Lorenzo, "all the eloquence and wit of Florence were exerted in paying due honors to her memory both in prose and in verse."

To make his own verses more effective, he tried to convince himself that he too had been deprived of his love. Was there any other woman in Florence deserving such honor and praise, he asked himself, picturing the happiness of one "whose good fortune could procure him such a subject for his pen." But the quest for the unattainable lady did not keep him from celebrating more mundane forms of love.

For *Calendimaggio,* the first of May, he and Poliziano wrote a whole series of semierotic verses with which young men might salute the women of their choice, and Lorenzo had them set to music by the music master of the chapel of San Giovanni.

> Welcome to May and its banner of spray.
> Welcome to spring when love is the thing.
> Surrender you belles to amorous spells.

sang the young men as they danced around the maypole and accosted their lady loves on the street.

During the midwinter carnival, Botticelli, Verrocchio, Pollaiuolo, and a host of lesser artists and artisans painted the sides of the *trionfi,* or chariots representing mythological and historical events, and designed the costumes for those who took part in these living tableaux, while Lorenzo and his close friend, the poet Luigi Pulci, devised genre scenes for the *carri,* or carts representing the various trades. Lorenzo also composed a series of *canti carnalschialeschi,* or carnival songs, to accompany both the *trionfi* and the *carri.* In one group of songs for the *carri,* workmen from all over the world described their wares to the women of Florence. "We have bottles as long as your hands," the makers of perfume bottles told the women. And they invited the women to feel the bottles themselves. "Little by little, a delightful smell will spill out right at the center of that little fire."

The most famous of the carnival songs, *The Triumph of Bacchus,* although still suggestive, was considerably more subdued; and it had a lovely lilting refrain that seemed to sum up its writer's philosophy.

> Quant'é bella giovenezza
> Che si fugge tuttavia,
> Chi vuole esser lieto sia,
> Di doman non v'é certezza.
>
> Donne e giovenetti amanti
> Viva Bacco e viva amore
> Ciascun suoni balli e canti
> Ardi di dolcezza il cuore
> Non fatica non dolor
> Cio c'ha esser convien sia.*

It was sung by processions of richly dressed youths on horseback, "sometimes exceeding 300 in number and as many men on foot with lighted torches," who "traversed the city to the accompaniment of music arranged for four, eight, twelve, or fifteen voices, supported by various instruments." The frontispiece of a sixteenth-century edition of the songs shows Lorenzo at the center of one group of masquers, leading the revels in the Piazza della Signoria.

When not party to such revels, the laborers in the cloth factories, the clerks in the shops, the artisans in the *botteghe,* the servants in the palaces, and the vendors in the Mercato Vecchio toiled from sunrise to sunset with one break in winter and two in summer. Layoffs were frequent, and many subsisted on a diet of bread and cabbage, with a bit of oil for seasoning. At midday, throngs of beggars gathered outside the hospitals awaiting their free bowls of soup. But during the carnival season, "everyone

---

* How beautiful youth is
But it goes by so fast
Let he who will be merry
For of tomorrow there is no certainty.

Women and young lovers long live Bacchus
And long live love!
Let everyone sing and dance
Let the heart burn with sweetness
No work, no pain
It's better to be as you want to be.

was made to feel happy and prosperous." And it was because Lorenzo knew how to make them feel happy and prosperous that the masses remained loyal to him at the time of the conspiracy of the Pazzi.

Like the Medici, the Pazzi were a family of wealthy Florentine bankers. Their conspiracy to depose Lorenzo had the blessing of Pope Sixtus IV. It also had the help of one of the pope's nephews and of a number of disgruntled Florentines from other wealthy families. Presumably without telling the pope, the conspirators decided to assassinate both Lorenzo and Giuliano while the two were at mass in the cathedral of Santa Maria dei Fiore on Easter Sunday of 1478. The tinkling of the mass bell would be the signal for the attack to begin.

Giuliano was stabbed to death on schedule; Lorenzo fought off his attackers and retreated to the sacristy with Poliziano and a few other friends, who shut the heavy bronze doors in the faces of their pursuers. Soon afterward, the conspirators' attempt to take over the Palazzo della Signoria was foiled by the eight priors and the gonfalonier. In response to the tolling of *La Vacca*, the people swarmed into the piazza demanding to know what had happened. When Jacopo dei Pazzi tried to arouse them with cries of *Popolo e libertà!* they responded with cries of *Palle!* (a reference to the balls in the Medici coat of arms) and "Long live Lorenzo, who gives us bread!" so that it was all Jacopo could do to escape unharmed. By nightfall, his body and those of nineteen other conspirators were hanging upside down from the windows of the Palazzo della Signoria and the Palazzo della Podesta (now the Bargello). During the next few days, the walls of both palaces were lined with corpses as, one after another, the conspirators were captured and strung up. Later, the body of Jacopo dei Pazzi was disinterred twice, the second time by street urchins who "dragged it through Florence by the piece of rope that was still around its neck."

Florence was a small city. Before the incident in the cathedral, Lorenzo had gone through the streets unescorted and unarmed except for the small dagger which a gentleman customarily wore at his belt. After the conspiracy, the city gave him the right to go around with as many armed retainers as he liked. If this made him seem more like a Roman emperor than a private citizen in a republic, he was too concerned with avoiding similar plots in the future to care. Although like his father and grandfather he continued to deny that he was lord of Florence, the Pazzi conspiracy made him less careful about preserving republican forms, more overtly dictatorial. In 1481, when a new plot to assassinate him was uncovered, he secured passage of a measure labeling any conspiracy against him a conspiracy against the state.

Not long after this law was passed, Luca Landucci noted in his diary that a hermit who had shown up at one of Lorenzo's villas had been arrested because the servants believed he had come to murder their master. Two weeks later, Landucci reported that the hermit had died, "having been tortured in various ways. It was said that they skinned the soles of his feet and then burnt them in the fire until the fat dripped off them; after which they set him upright and made him walk across the great hall of the Palazzo della Signoria. As to whether he was innocent or guilty, opinion was divided."

Lorenzo further strengthened his control of the city by forcing through a change in the constitution which gave most of the real power to a Council of Seventy, which was composed of his henchmen. The council's first step was to appoint a committee of seventeen to revise the tax system. Shortly before the new system went into effect, financial reverses forced Lorenzo to close the Medici bank in Bruges. Three years earlier, he had had to close the Medici bank in London. In consideration of these setbacks, the committee (of which Lorenzo was a member) graciously exempted him from paying the new taxes. When, despite this exemption, he continued to find himself short of cash, he fell into the habit of dipping into state funds to meet his expenses. A document found among the papers of the Strozzi family mentions 74,948 florins paid out to him or his agents in several installments by the steward of the public debt, or *monte*, "without the sanction of any law and without authority to the damage and prejudice of the commune."

The government sought to compensate for the withdrawals by raising taxes and reducing payments on the *monte delle doti*, or dowry fund. This fund had been established to make it easier for fathers to provide dowries for their daughters. For every 10 florins a father deposited in the name of his infant daughter, 100 florins became due fifteen years later. If the girl had died in the interim, her father received half the claimable amount. If she was still alive, the entire sum could be withdrawn, or it could remain in the fund at high interest. In 1490, however, 10,000 florins that should have gone to pay the interest on the state debt went to pay for a cardinal's hat for Lorenzo's 14-year-old son Giovanni. Soon afterward, the government announced that henceforth it would give each girl only one-fifth of her dowry when she married and reduced the interest on the remaining four-fifths by three-quarters of a percent.

No longer assured of a large supply of florins with which to get started in the world, many prospective bridegrooms changed their minds about marrying, leaving their prospective brides with no alternative but to enter a convent. And even the convents thought twice about taking a girl with a marriage portion of less than 100 florins. It was as a special favor to Lorenzo that the convent of Santa Apollinaria on the Via San Gallo accepted Ippolita Baroncelli with a dowry of only 54 florins.

"Whoso wants to do as they wish should not be born a woman," wrote Lorenzo's sister Nannina after her marriage to Bernardo Rucellai. A girl who did not enter a convent generally married at the age of 16 or 17. In a widely circulated treatise on the family, Leon Battista Alberti declared that her first duty was to bear children. And, said Alberti, her beauty ought to be judged "not simply by the grace and gentility of her face but even more by the robust form of her figure, suited to carrying and producing an abundance of beautiful offspring."

People of all classes bet on how long a newly married pair would remain childless and on the sex of the child in utero. When Cosimo dei Medici married Contessina dei Bardi, a French singer asked God to preserve the bridegroom and to arrange that the first night he slept with his bride she might conceive a male child. Women who had difficulty conceiving sought frantically for ways to end their barrenness. One supposedly infallible remedy was to place a poultice on the belly; another was to wear a belt girded on by a boy who was still a virgin; a third was to feed three beggars every Friday. For wives who had no need of such remedies, life was a succession of pregnancies that ended only when they died in childbirth, which was often, or reached menopause. The wife of the Florentine merchant Luca di Panzone bore him fifteen children; Luca Landucci's wife bore him twelve; Clarice dei Medici had ten children and probably would have had more had she not died of consumption at the age of 38.

Rich and poor alike took it for granted that not all their children would survive. *La Moria,* or plague, which in those days meant any infectious disease that reached epidemic proportions, struck most often among the very young and the very old. There were also periodic outbreaks of influenza, as well as a high incidence of tuberculosis, dysentery, smallpox, typhoid, and typhus. Everyone was prone to skin diseases brought on by inadequate diet, even more inadequate hygiene, and rough, irritating clothing. Wool workers and their families suffered from anthrax, painters from arsenic poisoning.

High fever was brought down either by bleeding or immersion in an icy bath. If a headache accompanied the fever, the patient's hair was shaved off, and the bare pate brought close to the fire. If the patient's neck or limbs were stiff, they were washed with a mixture of wine and asafetida. Asafetida, a resinous gum from East Asia with an odor resembling that of garlic and onions, was also a favorite ingredient in poultices applied to the ailing member. For stiff limbs unaccompanied by fever, as well as for most other noncommunicable ailments, a visit to a medicinal spring was strongly advised. After analyzing a sulfur-and-alum spring discovered on the property of Lorenzo's mother at Bagno a Morbo, her doctor wrote that it was "excellent for scabies and asthma," healed "all ills in the body and pains in the joints and nerves," and had many other virtues which he would gladly demonstrate.

Equally effective, in the opinion of many, were appeals to the Virgin Mary and the other saints. As a cure for nosebleed, Luca Landucci advised first "having a Paternoster and an *Ave Maria* said to the sufferer for reverence to the Holy Trinity," then taking the nose with two fingers of the right hand and saying with faith, "On Christmas night Jesus was born, and Christmas night he was lost. On Christmas night he was recovered again. Blood stay in your veins as Christ's blood stayed in his." Like most Florentines, Landucci also placed great faith in a miraculous painting of the Virgin Mary in the church of Santa Maria dell'Impruneta, seven miles south of Florence. Besides having the power to cure the sick, heal the wounded, and drive away evil spirits, the Madonna dell'Impruneta was reputed to have the power to bring rain when there was drought and to halt it when there was flooding, to hasten the delivery of grain to Pisa and Livorno, and to assist Florence in its negotiations with foreign princes. In times of crisis, the Signoria would order the tabernacle containing the sacred picture carried in solemn procession from its resting place in the church to the Porta San Piero in Gattolino (now the Porta Romana) and from there across the Ponte Vecchio into all the streets of the city to hear the prayers of the people and to receive their gifts.

Nor was Our Lady of Impruneta the only miracle-working madonna. In April 1482, a statue of the Virgin in the church of Our Lady of Bibbona reportedly changed from blue to red and from red to black and diverse colors. And, wrote Landucci that June, "this is said to have happened many times between then and now and a number of sick persons have been cured and a number of miracles been performed and quarrels reconciled; so that all the world is running there."

After studying such matters, Guicciardini would conclude that "miracles occur in every religion and prove the truth of none in particular and that all of them may be explained by unknown phenomena of nature." Luigi Pulci also sought to downgrade miracles by declaring that "Moses may well have loosed the floodgates of a fishpond and drowned a few of Pharoah's men," that "Samson might have carried off the door of a summerhouse," and that "Peter had walked on a frozen sea." But such skepticism was limited to a few intellectuals, and even they continued to live their lives within a religious framework.

No matter how pressing his other affairs, every Florentine was expected to attend church services twice a day every day of the year. The more religious considered it a sin not to be present for all seven canonical hours. On holy days, no public business was permitted between early mass and vespers. On fast days, all work ceased; all shops and stalls remained closed, and taverns and inns did not open until midday. Churches, street shrines, and chapels were everywhere; sacred images peered down from every other doorway; all manner of people from Luca Landucci to Lorenzo himself were in the habit of asking God's grace and protection for their every move. The device of the Medici bank was "With the name of God and good fortune"; their bills of exchange closed with the words "Christ keep you." Because Cosimo dei Medici had suffered from what his friend Vespasiano dei Bisticci called "prickings of conscience that certain portions of his wealth...had not been righteously gained," he spent over 40,000 florins to rebuild the monastery of San Marco, commissioned Fra Giovanni dei Fiesole, better known as Fra Angelico, to decorate the walls of the friars' dormitories, and provided the convent with the best library in Florence. Over an altar sunk in the wall of one of the larger cells, Angelico painted a figure of Christ rising from the tomb and surrounded the altar with a semicircular fresco of the adoration of the Magi done in soft pastels and ochers. Cosimo was so delighted with the effect that he decided to reserve the cell for his personal use. As he grew older, he spent more and more of his time there, discussing the sin of usury and how it might be expiated.

To the church, any interest on a loan, no matter how small, was usury. "A sin against the divine goodness," Dante had called it. "Of the Godhead the grandchild, so to say." And he had placed the usurers, each with a money pouch "hung from his throat," in the seventh circle alongside the "accurst spirits of blasphemers and sodomites." In one popular folktale, "an innumerable multitude of men, black as Negroes of Ethiopia, dark and terrible beyond all human imagining, biting and smiting and rending and tearing" carried the usurer off to hell. In another, a fiend wearing a sharp-pointed hat leapt upon the usurer's deathbed, flung himself face downward on the dying man, caught him by the throat, and strangled him. In a third, the wandering ghost of a usurer, "a black smoke, as it were, the shadow of a man," returned to tell his son that he had been condemned to eternal torments.

But what was the point of making a loan if one didn't charge interest? Caught between their desire for gain and their fear of eternal damnation, the merchants and bankers called their loans "exchange transactions," for which a fee might legitimately be charged, and had recourse to a string of other euphemisms from *dono di tempo* ("quick returns") to *avanza* ("unexpected profit") to *ritrangola* ("trifling advance"). Sometimes the due date for a loan was deliberately ignored so that the interest could be collected in the guise of a fine imposed by the lender. At other times, the loan was represented as working capital and the lender made a temporary partner who received a share of the profits. But there was always the uncomfortable feeling that God saw through these ruses. And it was this feeling that led bankers like Cosimo to try to buy their way, if not into paradise, at least into purgatory, by building churches and hospitals. Nor did they perceive any contradiction between their concern for Christian salvation and their mania for pagan books and artifacts.

To encourage the study of Plato, Cosimo sponsored the Platonic Academy which, despite its name, was not a school, but an informal gathering of men interested in knowing more about the philosopher's work. Because so few of them understood Greek, Cosimo asked Ficino to translate the Platonic manuscripts in the Medici library into Latin for them. Ficino grew so enamored of Plato that he repudiated Christianity and addressed his students as "beloved in Plato" rather than "beloved in Christ." Alarmed, the bishop of Florence suggested that he read Saint Thomas Aquinas as an antidote. The combination of Saint Thomas and a serious illness when Ficino was 44 finally convinced him that a philosophy divorced from Christianity could never lead to true salvation. After his recovery, he became a priest and spent the rest of his life trying to reconcile the teachings of Plato with the teachings of Christ. Platonic philosophy was every bit as sacred as the most sacred legends of the church, he declared in one of his sermons. Earlier, he had described Plato as "a Moses speaking Attic Greek," and suggested adding extracts from the philosopher's dialogues to the homilies read in the churches each Sunday.

The effect of all this on his pupil Lorenzo can be seen in Lorenzo's statement that, without a knowledge of Plato, it was impossible to be either a good citizen or a good Christian. He continued the meetings of the Platonic Academy begun by his grandfather, sometimes in the Medici palace on the Via Larga, sometimes at Ficino's villa in the olive tree–covered hills outside Careggi, sometimes beside a flowing fountain in the monastery of the Camaldulese monks. Lorenzo enjoyed playing the role of the philosopher-king, and he could not rest until he had drawn all whose talents he admired into his circle. Voltaire called the men whom Lorenzo invited to participate in the discussions of the Platonic Academy "superior perhaps to the boasted sages of ancient Greece." Others have called them an elitist clique of fawning courtiers, "servile but arrogant beggars."

But if there was a little of the fawning courtier in Ficino, and more than a little in Angelo Poliziano, there was none in the 16-year-old Michelangelo. Lorenzo had found Michelangelo copying the head of a faun in the Medici gardens. Impressed by the youth's talent, he had arranged for him to continue his studies while living in the palace on the Via Larga. A bas-relief of the battle of the centaurs which Michelangelo sculpted during his student days was suggested to him by Poliziano.

Poliziano was an ugly young man with a massive pointed nose, straight, lank hair, bulging eyes, thick lips, and a prominent chin. In a fresco by Domenico Ghirlandaio in the church of Santa Trinità, the artist portrays him gazing worshipfully at Lorenzo. Poliziano had good reason to worship Lorenzo and to play the role of the fawning courtier with him, for Lorenzo had rescued him from the life of unskilled labor to which the poverty of his family would have otherwise condemned him. Besides writing poetry, Poliziano edited the *Pandects* of Justinian for his patron, cared for his library, served as tutor to the Medici children, and taught Greek and Latin at the *Studio Fiorentino*. He had an encyclopedic mind and was in the habit of inserting choice morsels of random information into his lectures, such as the news that the female mouse is "madly lustful." Although he came from the people, he had little use for the common man. In a letter to a friend he complained of the interruptions he met with "from the lower orders of this city and its vicinity." He was forever complaining, forever quarreling with someone. While tutoring the Medici children, he became involved in such a bitter quarrel with their mother that Lorenzo withdrew his patronage for two years. During those two years, Poliziano inundated him with begging letters, poems, and epigrams. "I am yours, O Medici," said one letter. "I am yours forever.... Give back to me my Lorenzo your eyes; give back to me my happiness."

Homosexuality was so prevalent in Florence that the Germans called it "the Florentine vice," and letters like this make it easy to see why Poliziano was accused of being a homosexual. But he did propose to Alessandra della Scala, the most celebrated woman of intellect in Florence. "At last I have found that which I have always sought," he wrote her. "A maiden learned in Greek and Latin, excellent in the dance, skilled in music....I faint, I die for love of thee." And he was both furious and vituperative when she turned him down for a young Greek scholar who, like Poliziano, had once been her tutor.

A very different sort of person was the poet Girolamo Benivieni. Benivieni had planned to study medicine, but a serious illness when he was 16 made this impossible, and he decided to devote himself to poetry instead. One of his first patrons was Lorenzo's brother Giuliano. Giuliano's murder when Benivieni was 25 exacerbated the depression and suicidal tendencies which had first manifested themselves during his illness. Although he would later say that the murder had turned him toward God, it left him with a fear of death which nothing could expunge. "Death terrifies me," he wrote. "Fear presses my anguished mind. Pale my face, frozen my heart in my cold breast." Like Lorenzo and the other members of the Platonic Academy, Benivieni regarded Ficino as his mentor and called him "father." But he was searching for something that neither Ficino nor Plato could provide.

Another member of the academy in search of new horizons was Benivieni's closest friend, Count Giovanni Pico della Mirandola. Unlike Benivieni and Poliziano, Pico had no need of

Lorenzo's patronage, for he had inherited a fortune from his father, the immensely wealthy count of Mirandola and Concordia. As the count's younger son, Pico had been destined for the priesthood since birth. But two years spent studying canon law at Bologna had convinced him that he was unsuited for the priestly life. At the age of 17, he transferred to Padua, where he could study philosophy.

Pico was tall, blond, and handsome. Sir Thomas More, his first English biographer, speaks of "the comeliness of his body... the lovely flavor of his visage," and "his marvelous frame," which "set many women on fire for him." Since their desire kindled Pico's own, he was, says More, "somewhat fallen into wantonness." Apparently, this didn't keep him from spending what he described as "long sleepless nights on the scholastic doctors." He also read Plato, dabbled in magic, and took lessons from Elia del Modigo, a Jewish scholar at the university who translated Hebrew texts for him and instructed him in the mysteries of the cabala.

The cabala is an occult system for the mystical apprehension of God. For the cabalist the words of the Old Testament conceal sublime revelations concerning the meaning and plan of existence. According to legend, God gave Moses the key to understanding those revelations. However the word "cabala," which is derived from the Hebrew word for tradition, did not appear until the eleventh century. In medieval Spain where the study of cabala flourished, the twenty-two letters of the Hebrew alphabet and the ten numbers or *Sephiroth* were considered the thirty-two paths by which the cabalist could expect to arrive at an understanding of holy writ. The *Zohar*, published in the thirteenth century, ridiculed those simple souls who took the Bible literally. Every word of the law held an exalted meaning and a sublime mystery, said the *Zohar*, and it offered a detailed exegesis of the first book of Moses. To Pico, who reveled in the complex and the esoteric, the *Zohar* seemed to provide the most effective arguments he had yet found for proving the divinity of Christ. So that he would be able to study it in the original, he engaged a converted Jew to teach him Hebrew.

In the spring of 1482, he also found time to attend a meet-

ing of the Dominican congregation of Lombardy. Among the
many churchmen at this meeting was the 28-year-old Girolamo
Savonarola, sent there to represent his convent. Pico was a young
man forever torn between an asceticism, which his early training as a priest had taught him to regard as the highest good, and
a sensuality and a love of life, which that same training had pictured as shameful. Rather than being impressed by the arguments of the many learned theologians he had come to hear, he
was impressed by Savonarola's demand for stricter adherence
to the rules of the primitive church. To Pico, Savonarola's uncompromising asceticism—the harmony between what he said
and what he was—made him an unforgettable model of what a
true priest ought to be. But he was not a model that Pico found
easy to emulate.

While Pico was visiting Arezzo a few years later, his sensuality again got the better of him, and he kidnapped another man's
wife. Later, Lorenzo's correspondent in Arezzo would tell him
that the lady, "enamored and blinded by such a fine figure of a
man," followed Pico voluntarily. At the time, however, the people of Arezzo didn't see it that way. In response to the ringing
of the tocsin, the captain of Arezzo assembled more than 200
men. After wounding and killing eighteen members of Pico's
retinue, they returned the abducted woman to her husband. Although Pico and his secretary managed to escape, they were later
overtaken and arrested. Arezzo was under Florentine jurisdiction. In a letter to Lorenzo, the magistrates of the city informed
him that they considered Pico's actions an affront to the entire
people. Although Lorenzo pretended to be sympathetic, he and
Pico's other friends in the Platonic Academy found it hard to
take the abduction seriously. It was the act of a hero running
off with a nymph, not to be judged by the standards of ordinary
mortals, said Ficino. And Lorenzo did his utmost to secure Pico's
release.

After being released, Pico retired to Umbria. His temptations
had been comparable to those of the Anchorites, he told Benivieni, who visited him there. From now on, however, he proposed to lead a life which would erase the memory of his guilt.
His studies had convinced him that "all known philosophical

and theological schools and thinkers contained certain true and valid insights that were compatible with each other and deserved to be restated." To reconcile these divergent philosophies and bring religious unity to humanity, he made plans for a public meeting in Rome at which scholars from all parts of the world would discuss 700 propositions in "dialectics, morals, math, physics, metaphysics, magic, and the cabala." Some of the propositions would be his own; the rest would be taken from the works of Christian, Arab, and Jewish scholars, both ancient and modern. The meeting was scheduled for the early part of 1487, and Pico offered to pay the traveling expenses of the learned men he asked to participate.

While he was in Umbria, he worked on the propositions they would discuss, which by then had grown from 700 to 900. He also prepared an "Oration on the Dignity of Man" with which he planned to open the meeting. Ficino had called man a microcosm, the central figure in the universe, and the one closest to God. With his usual exuberance, Pico went one step further and called man "the molder and sculptor of himself." God, said Pico, had received man as a creature of undetermined nature and, placing him in the middle of the universe, had spoken to him thus:

> I created thee a being neither heavenly nor earthly, neither mortal nor immortal only that thou mightest be free to shape and overcome thyself. Thou mayest sink into a beast and be born anew to the divine likeness. The brutes bring from their mother's body what they will carry with them as long as they live; the higher spirits are from the beginning or soon after what they will be forever. To thee alone is given a growth and a development depending on thine own free will. Thou bearest in thee the germs of universal life.

But Pico never gave this oration; nor was it printed or circulated during his lifetime. As soon as his 900 propositions were published that December, Vatican theologians declared a number of them heretical. An accusation of heresy in 1486 was comparable to an accusation of communism in the United States during the 1950s. Pope Innocent VIII suspended the discussion in Rome and asked a commission of theologians and jurists to examine all 900 propositions. That March, the commission condemned seven of them unequivocally and declared six others of doubtful origin. As a result, the pope ordered Pico tried for heresy. He was condemned on August 5, but the condemnation was not published until the following January. By then, Pico was on his way to France to seek support at the Sorbonne. After escaping capture in Lucca, he was arrested in Savoy and brought to the fortress of Vincennes, where he was imprisoned. His imprisonment caused an uproar all over Europe. Lorenzo, who was suffering horribly from gout and arthritis and had gone to the baths in the hope of alleviating his pain, nevertheless found time to write to the pope, cautioning him against being swayed by his passions. After a series of complex negotiations, Pico was freed and expelled from France. He had thought of going to Germany, but Lorenzo asked Ficino to invite him to "be happy and be Florentine."

Although Pico continued to believe that the different religions were the ways in which various men had translated "the one divine summons," being labeled a heretic destroyed the naive egoism and the limitless confidence that had previously characterized him and brought his latent asceticism to the fore. In Florence, he lived what Lorenzo described to the pope as "a very holy life…[he] recites the Ordinary of a priest and observes the fasts and the strictest continence." But Innocent was not impressed. It was one thing to make one's son a cardinal, he declared, but something quite different to absolve a heretic. Lorenzo must be careful not to be taken in by "the exemplary conduct of the count."

Lorenzo's opinion of the pope had never been high. Now it seemed to him that "ignorant and malicious men" were using the Holy Father as a shield, with the intention of driving Pico to despair and causing him "to lose his head so that he should turn against the pope." In a letter to the Florentine ambassador in Rome, Lorenzo urged him to use all his cleverness to arrange the matter, for "you have no idea how it vexes me." And he continued to press for a settlement all the rest of that year.

Meanwhile, Pico continued his fasts and his prayers. To his

friends, this once-joyous creature appeared obsessed with the imminence of death and the pride and wickedness of those who
would not see the truth. Over and over in his conversations, he
expressed a desire to preach as a barefoot mendicant in the
squares and marketplaces of Italy. At the same time, he felt a
need for religious guidance from someone he could trust and
respect. The most popular preacher in Florence was Fra Mariano
da Genazzano. So impressed was Lorenzo by Mariano's eloquence that he had built a monastery for him outside the San
Gallo gate. Poliziano had at first been distrustful of all the praise
lavished on Mariano but was later won over by the preacher's
"musical voice, his carefully chosen words, and grand sentenc-
es." Rather than wearying men with perpetual admonishments
as other preachers did, Mariano was "moderation itself." But
Pico's self-castigating mood demanded more than grand sen-
tences and moderation. Although it was then almost seven years
since he had heard Savonarola, he could still remember the friar's call for a return to the asceticism of the primitive church.
When they had met at the Dominican chapter meeting, Savonarola had been attached to the convent of Santa Maria degli
Angeli in Ferrara. Soon after arriving in Florence, Pico asked
Lorenzo if it would be possible to have Savonarola transferred
to San Marco.

Ever since Cosimo's time, San Marco had been known as
"the Medici's own cloister." If, as seems likely, Lorenzo spoke
to the prior of San Marco about effecting a transfer, he would
learn to his surprise that Savonarola had been a lecturer at the
convent from 1482 to 1487. He had been a model friar, pious,
chaste, and learned, although not a very successful preacher. The
year before, Lorenzo had expelled a Franciscan preacher for in-
citing a riot against a Jewish banker, and he wanted no more
rabble-rousers. Hence, Savonarola's lack of success in the pulpit was, if anything, reassuring. On April 29, 1489, Lorenzo dispatched a letter to the general of the Dominican order requesting
him "to send here Fra Girolamo of Ferrara."

Lorenzo's arthritis had grown so bad by then that he could
not hold a pen between his fingers. One of Savonarola's early
biographers says that in order to assure Pico that he desired to

serve him, Lorenzo allowed him to write the letter "in which-ever form he pleased." And, continues this same biographer, "it befell Lorenzo as it befell Pharaoh whose daughter saved Moses and fostered him by whose means her father was drowned."

The analogy is labored, but the meaning is clear. By this single, disinterested act, Lorenzo, like Pharoah, prepared the way for the destruction of his own house.

II

ENTER SAVONAROLA

Like all the monastic orders, the Dominican order was a hierarchy in which each member guarded his own prerogatives and was careful not to impinge on the prerogatives of others. After reading Lorenzo's letter, the general of the order passed it on to the vicar of the Lombard congregation. After inquiring about Savonarola's whereabouts, the vicar passed the letter on to the Lombard chapter. Since the chapter did not meet until the first Sunday after Easter of 1490, it was not until the beginning of May that the transfer was finally approved. Savonarola was in Genoa at the time. If he was not then told the reason for his transfer to Florence, he must surely have learned it soon after his arrival at San Marco. But in the explanation of his return he gives in the *Compendio Revelationum*, written in 1495, he alludes to it only indirectly, and he mentions neither Lorenzo nor Pico. Instead, he speaks of a mighty scourge with which God, "seeing that the sins of Italy continued to multiply," decided to cleanse His church.

> And since as the prophet Amos says, the Lord God does nothing without first revealing His secret to His servants the prophets (Amos 3:7), He wanted this scourge foretold in Italy for the welfare of His chosen people so that forewarned they might prepare better to withstand it. Since Florence lies in the center of Italy—God deigned to choose her for

the task of making this proclamation....And so choosing me, useless and unworthy among His servants, for this ministry, He arranged for me to come to Florence.

When he passed through the San Gallo gate at the end of May 1490, he was 38 years old. As a youth growing up in Ferrara, he had never thought of becoming a priest, he would later tell his followers. But he loved two things above all others: freedom and quiet. To have freedom, he never wanted a wife. To have quiet, he fled the world and found refuge in the cloister.

Once again, however, as in the explanation of how he came to be summoned back to Florence and in any number of other instances, he was tailoring the truth to make it conform to the picture he had of himself, the picture he wished to convey to others. In reality, he had fallen in love and had thought to take a wife. The young woman was named Laodamia, and she was the illegitimate daughter of his next-door neighbor Roberto Strozzi. Only a narrow alleyway separated the house of the Savonarola family on Via San Francesco from the palace of the Strozzi. Spotting Laodamia at one of the windows facing the alleyway, the 19-year-old Savonarola leaned across to speak to her. He was planning to ask her father for her hand in marriage, he told her. And what made him think that the great house of Strozzi would consider an alliance with the house of Savonarola, Laodamia wanted to know.

Most of Savonarola's biographers have taken this retort as evidence of her insufferable pride. One of them, however, finds the pride somewhat mystifying because, as he points out, even the ruling house of Este did not hesitate to marry its daughters to sons of the middle class. And the Savonarolas, after all, were not nobodies. Girolamo's grandfather Michele had been one of the leading physicians at the court of Duke Borso d'Este. Young Girolamo was studying medicine at the University of Ferrara with the intention of following in his grandfather's footsteps. But it doesn't seem to have occurred to this biographer, or to any of the others, for that matter, that Laodamia could have been using the social gulf between the Strozzis and the Savonarolas as an excuse: that what really bothered her was the appearance of her would-be husband.

From the descriptions left by Savonarola's contemporaries and the two portraits by Fra Bartolomeo, it is clear that he was exceptionally ugly. When he leaned across to speak to Laodamia, she may have decided that she could not bear to spend the rest of her life with this blushing undersized youth with the jutting lower lip, the flashing gray eyes, and the great hooked nose or have him touch her with those long, thin, semitransparent hands. Since fathers did not normally take the feelings of their daughters into consideration when arranging matches for them, she had to think of a remark sufficiently nasty to discourage this unwelcome suitor from asking for her hand.

Although Savonarola answered her in kind—he is supposed to have asked what made her think that his family would be willing to marry one of its legitimate sons to a bastard—he was crushed by her rejection. As a child, the strongest influence in his life had been his grandfather. "If you wish to serve God, flee the life of the court, for to participate means to endanger your soul," Michele had written. And he had filled his grandson's ears with tales of the wickedness of society and the terrors of hell that awaited sinners. His words so impressed the little boy that when he was presented at court, he is supposed to have fled and refused ever to return. After Laodamia turned him down, all the distrust of the world and its ways that had been drummed into him as a child returned. In the sonnet *De Ruina Mundi*, which he wrote a few months later, he seemed to be echoing his grandfather's advice.

> Flee palaces and meeting places
> Let few men know what you think
> Be an enemy of the world and from it shrink.

"Remaining in this uncertain state for quite a while," says one of his sixteenth-century biographers, "while he was sleeping, he felt a freezing water spill upon his head. This roused him at once, and he woke from his dream. That was the water of repentance, and with it was extinguished the carnal heat of desire, while its coldness froze in him every worldly appetite."

More than likely, he had always had doubts about his ability to attract women. His rejection by Laodamia reinforced his already low opinion of his own attractiveness. By extinguishing the carnal heat of desire, he need never suffer the pain of rejection again. Because the church looked upon sex as inherently evil, he could also feel that in choosing the path of chastity he had chosen the better way. Unlike Saint Augustine, Saint Jerome, and so many others who had chosen the same way, he seldom spoke of the battle to suppress his sensuality. That there was an unending battle seems clear from the extravagant sexual imagery in so many of his sermons and the occasional wistful references to the beauty of young women.

Although his renunciation of sexuality could have only increased his alienation from the world in which he lived, he at first had no thought of becoming a monk. He had been studying medicine at the university, and he continued to study medicine. But the zest with which he had once applied himself to his studies was gone. In those days, he often found himself addressing God in the words of the 143rd psalm: "Cause me to know the way in which I should walk; for I lift up my soul to thee." Then, on a trip to Faenza in 1474, he heard a sermon by an Augustinian friar. A phrase from Genesis—"Get thee out of thy country and from thy kindred and from thy father's house"— impressed him so deeply, Savonarola would later say, that on that same day, he made an irrevocable decision to enter the cloister. But he spoke of his decision to no one; and it wasn't until a year later, while the rest of his family was at the races with which Ferrara celebrated the feast of Saint George, that he mustered the courage to set out for the convent of San Domenico in Bologna.

Returning from the races that evening, his bewildered parents sought in vain for some clue to his whereabouts. They had almost given up hope of ever learning what had become of him when a letter arrived from Bologna. In this letter, addressed to his father, Savonarola tried to explain his reasons for entering the cloister. First and foremost, there was the great wretched-ness of the world, the sins of men: "Lecheries, adulteries, theft, pride, cruel blasphemy...the blind wickedness of the people of Italy." Many times a day, this had caused him to sing, weeping: *Hic fuge crudelas terras fuge litus avarum,"* a line from Virgil translated as "Flee from this cruel land; fly from the shore of avarice."

He had prayed to Jesus to pull him out of this mire, and to God to show him the way, until finally God had done so. "And so, *dulcissime pater,* rather than weep, you must thank Lord Jesus. He has given you a son, has preserved him until his twen-ty-second year and further has deigned to make him one of His champions." And Savonarola asked his father if he did not deem it a great privilege to have a son who was a soldier of Christ.

Apparently, his father did not, for in Savonarola's next let-ter, he berated both his parents for weeping and being "blind fools" who "lie in darkness." "What can I say to you, if you grieve at this if not that you are my chief enemies and even the enemies of virtue?" he asked. And he exhorted them to rejoice that God had made him a doctor of souls (that is, a priest) rather than a doctor of medicine.

There was, of course, a good deal of self-dramatization in both letters, as well as a certain enjoyment of the commotion he was causing. He was the third of seven children. Although he had been his grandfather's favorite, he may very well have felt that his parents had never taken sufficient notice of him. Now, at last, they were being forced to do so. The tone of spiritual su-periority he adopted with them at this time, his indignation at their refusal to accept his decision to enter the cloister, remained with him all the rest of his life.

After she learned of his decision to become a monk, his mother "cried for many years," he told an audience at the time of her death. "And I let her cry. Suffice it that now she must know that she was wrong."

In 1485, when his mother informed him of the death of his father, Savonarola wrote back that since he had chosen the Do-minican order as his family and Christ as his father, she must henceforth regard him too as dead. Nor could he see any reason to be concerned when she informed him that poverty was preventing two of his sisters from marrying. He thanked God for the adversities of his family, he told her that December, for by striking at their worldly possessions, the Almighty was directing their minds to heavenly things, thus preparing for their ultimate salvation. A letter he sent her in 1490 makes it clear that he felt no one in Ferrara appreciated him.

> In Ferrara I have often been told by those who observed my travels from city to city that my order must be lacking for men [that is, preachers], as who should say 'if they use you who are worthless for so many duties, they must indeed lack for men.'

This had demonstrated to him the truth of what the Savior had said: a prophet has no honor in his own country, for even He was not accepted in His own country.

To one so at odds with his family and the society in which he lived, the cloister was a welcome break with the world. Although he had always been an excellent student and had received a degree in philosophy before commencing the study of medicine, his first thought was to abandon all intellectual activity. Rather than become a priest, he wished to tend the garden, sew the brothers' clothes, and give himself to "humble labors in holy places," he told his superiors. When they insisted that he study theology, he meekly accepted their decision. One who knew him then said he was so submissive at this time that "not only his superiors, but the least of the lay brothers could make him come and go at their pleasure."

This excessive meekness was, however, another manifestation of the same imperious need to call attention to himself and impose his will on others that was evident in his letters to his parents. Although the convent of San Domenico was noted for its strict observance of monastic rule, he found the observance mere hypocrisy. Soon he was demanding that the friars emulate him by living more abstemiously, fasting more frequently, and devoting more time to prayer. In *De Ruina Ecclesia*, a canzone he wrote at this time, he lamented the changes that had come over the church: no more did preachers tell the truth boldly; no more did holy doctors shed abroad the light of sound doctrines; no more did saintly contemplatives, devout virgins, and zealous priests and bishops adorn the church with their virtues. He repeated these laments in Ferrara, where he was sent to perfect his theological studies, and at the meeting where Pico heard him for the first time. Either because his zeal impressed his superiors or because an impending war between Venice and Ferrara made it necessary to send the friars elsewhere, at the close of the meeting he was elected to the office of lecturer in the convent of San Marco in Florence.

By then, excessive fasting and mortification of the flesh—the scourge was the best remedy for carnal longing, he would later tell Pico—had given him the gaunt and distracted appearance which, to the Italians of his day, seemed the surest sign of holiness. One of the novices who attended his lectures during that first stay in Florence pictured him coming to class with his eyes filled with tears, having evidently been lost in some divine meditation rather than preparing a lesson. "However," continued this same novice, "he was so learned that he satisfied his hearers exceedingly." Unfortunately, his success in the classroom did not carry over into the pulpit. By his own admission, he had in those days "neither voice, vigor, nor talent for preaching," and his sermons "bored everyone." When he began to preach, he would later write, "few came to listen; only a few simple men on one side and on the other some poor women." Like the apostles, he preached without division in his sermons, says one of the early chroniclers, and his speech was strongly reminiscent of Ferrara. "He used to say *mi* and *ti* and was laughed at for it by everyone, including his fellow monks." In 1484, when he was assigned to preach the Lenten sermons in the basilica of San Lorenzo, his audience kept dwindling until there were only twenty-five people in the pews, and it seemed to him that perhaps he ought to give up his dream of trying to change the world with his sermons.

The year 1484 was a so-called *annus mirabilis*, or extraordinary year, for which astrologers had been predicting some great turning point in the history of Christendom ever since the ninth century. In a commentary on the *Divine Comedy*, Cristoforo

Landino, who, like Ficino, had been one of Lorenzo's tutors and was a member of the Platonic Academy, announced that on November 25, 1484, at thirteen hours and forty-one minutes, there would be a conjunction of Jupiter and Saturn and that this conjunction signified some great change in religion. Since Jupiter dominated Saturn, Landino appeared confident that the change would be for the better and that, as he put it, "Christianity would arrive at an excellent life and organization."

Paul of Middleburg, an astrologer friend of Marsilio Ficino, also foresaw great innovations in religion as a result of the conjunction of the two planets. In his *Pronostic ad Viginta Annos Duratura*, which became an immediate best-seller, he calculated that it would take about twenty years for the changes to be fully realized, and he indicated that they would be preceded by numerous catastrophes, including the advent of a false prophet.

Others foresaw the coming of the Antichrist, followed by the purification of the church, the conversion of the Jews and the Moslems, and the establishment of one universal religion. Francesco Meleto, a Florentine merchant who had visited Constantinople in 1473, reported that a prominent rabbi he had met there had told him in strictest confidence that if the Jewish messiah did not put in an appearance by the end of 1484, all the Jews would convert to Christianity.

On Palm Sunday, 1484, a preacher by the name of Giovanni di Correggio arrived in Rome. Giovanni, who preferred to be known as Mercurius in honor of his mentor Hermes (or Mercurius) Trismegistus, was mounted on a quivering black steed and wore a double-draped, black silk toga, a golden girdle, scarlet boots, and a crown of thorns. After distributing tracts explaining hermetic magic, he called upon all men to prepare themselves for the coming renovation of the church by repenting their sins.

"People were in a mood to expect great things of God," Luca Landucci had written in his diary the previous summer. In July 1484, he reported that an image of the Virgin Mary at Prato had begun to work miracles and that men and women were rushing there from all around the country. In August, the death of Pope Sixtus IV and the ensuing commotion in Rome caused many to fear that the religious renovation announced by the conjunction of the two planets would be preceded by another schism in the church. That Savonarola shared their anxiety is apparent from a laud he wrote in which he spoke of astrologers and prophets who had "foretold the tears of Italy," and a canzone imploring Jesus to "save thy Holy Roman church which the devil is destroying."

It was this frame of mind that was undoubtedly responsible for the illumination in San Giorgio which changed his life. Left alone in the churchyard while a friend visited a sister who was a nun in the convent, Savonarola decided to compose a sermon. Suddenly, there appeared to him at least seven reasons "showing that some scourge of the church was at hand." And, he later told his judges, "from that moment I fell to thinking much on these things." Instead of giving up preaching, he developed the three propositions which he would base his sermons on henceforth: the church shall be scourged, then renovated, and this shall happen soon.

He expected "at any moment a scourge or Antichrist or war or plague or famine," he told his audience when he was sent to preach the Lenten sermons in the town of San Gimignano in 1485. And when he preached there the following year, he chose as his text Matthew 4:17—"Repent, for the kingdom of heaven is at hand"—the same text Jesus had chosen after His return from the wilderness. He was still too uncertain of himself, however, to identify with Jesus, as he would later do, or to claim any direct inspiration from God.

"If you say to me, who are you? Christ? No. Elijah? No. I am not a prophet," he declared. "But I surmise many things from the Scriptures and from past events because the wise man remembers the past and uses it to understand the present and to predict the future." And he cited not seven but eight reasons for believing that "the axe is already at the roots of the tree."

In 1487, he was asked to deliver the Lenten sermons in the church of Santa Veridiana in Florence, but the sermons were abruptly canceled when he was appointed maestro degli studii in the convent of San Domenico in Bologna. After spending a year in Bologna, he was again sent to Ferrara. In 1489, he was on the road once more. In a sermon in Brescia on November 30, he warned that a great scourge was about to descend on the city and that fathers "would see their children slain and shamefully mangled in the streets." He would later say that this illumination had come to him from God, but at the time he cited a text from the Book of Revelation—"the four beasts and four and twenty elders fell down before the Lamb"—as his source. The response of his audience left him exultant.

"When it is time for me to leave," he told his mother in a letter from Pavia that January, "men and women weep and set great store by my words. I do not write this because I seek the praise of men, but to make you understand my purpose in staying away from my own country and so that you should know that I am glad to be away, knowing that my work is more pleasing to God and more profitable to myself and to the souls of my fellow man." Once again, he implored her to take comfort from the fact that one of her children had been chosen for this work.

Italy was filled with itinerant preachers inveighing against the corruption of the church—haggard, lean-limbed men who went from town to town warning the people of the disasters that must precede the final renovation. Had it not been for the intervention of Pico, Savonarola might have continued his peripatetic life indefinitely. Given the way he felt about his mission, it was only natural for him to persuade himself that God had prompted Pico to ask for his return to Florence. As he had done the first time he went to the city, he set out on foot carrying only his Bible and his breviary. Eighteen miles out of Bologna, in the town of Pianora, he grew so faint he could not continue. A stranger who saw him resting by the wayside fed him and, when his strength was restored, accompanied him along the mountain road known as La Futa into the region of the Mugello, and from there to the San Gallo gate.

"Do what you have been sent by God to do in Florence," the stranger told him before departing. It was little more than the conventional formula for taking leave of a friar, but to one so desperately eager to serve God, it seemed yet another sign that God and Florence were in need of his services.

He had been summoned back to San Marco as a lecturer, not

as a preacher. Accordingly, his first assignment was to teach logic to the novices. On Sunday evenings after vespers, while seated beside a damask rosebush in the convent garden, he also explained passages from the Scriptures to all who cared to listen. Pico was usually in the audience at this time, and his presence, as well as his enthusiastic descriptions of Savonarola's exegeses, soon attracted so many other laymen that the garden could not accommodate them all. Perhaps because he still remembered the reception accorded his earlier sermons in San Lorenzo, Savonarola was at first reluctant to transfer the talks to the neighboring church of San Marco. When he finally agreed to do so, the church was filled with people, some sitting, others clinging to the iron gratings in order to see and hear him. So great was the crowd, says one of his early biographers, that scarcely any room remained for his fellow friars who "in their eager desire to hear were obliged to find places on the wall of the choir." As he had done at Brescia, he chose his text from the Book of Revelation.

Although the idea that the world must one day come to an end is to be found in a number of books of both the Old and the New Testaments, including the books of Ezekiel, Daniel, and Matthew, it is in the Book of Revelation that it receives its most dramatic and powerful expression. The author of Revelation was not the John who wrote the gospel and the Epistles but another John, known as John the Divine or John the Prophet. Around the year 69 A.D., this John was exiled to the Aegean island of Patmos for refusing to acknowledge the divinity of the emperor Nero. On this lovely little isle, which to the renowned French historian of Christianity Ernest Renan seemed more appropriate for "the delectable romance of Daphnis and Chloe," John recorded his vision of the Apocalypse.

Like Savonarola, to whom he seems to have been spiritually and mentally similar, John was what Renan calls a *pauvre vertueux*—a poor virtuous creature whose obsession with evil made it impossible for him to see the world as it really was. Instead, says Renan, "he saw with the eyes of Ezekiel and the author of the Book of Daniel, or rather he saw only himself, his passions, his hopes, his resentments....Never did anyone more openly deny the actual world in order to substitute for the harmonies of reality the discordant chimerae of a new heaven and a new earth." To Renan, John's images, while undeniably compelling, were also bizarre, incoherent, and contradictory, "a reflection of the illness he carried in his vitals." Others have thought them simply mad. But during the almost 2000 years since John first recorded his "mad" images for the seven churches of Asia Minor, there have always been those who have taken them literally; living their lives in constant nervous expectation of the Antichrist, the great Beast with seven heads and ten horns which will rise from the sea to harass the faithful until the battle of Armageddon and the 1000-year reign of Christ. And the number of such persons has always swelled in times of social unrest when there appears to be good reason to identify one or another of the rulers of this world as the Antichrist and to accept an apocalyptic view of history.

During the thirteenth century, the intense popular dissatisfaction with the corruption of the church and the worldly life of the clergy produced a vast millennial movement known as Joachism, whose influence was still discernible not only in Savonarola's time but for hundreds of years thereafter. Joachism received its impetus from the writings of another *pauvre vertueux*, a Calabrian abbot by the name of Joachim of Fiore. Among other marvels, Joachim claimed to have found a key to the Book of Revelation. With this key, not only could he detect a meaning in history; he could also prophesy its future stages. History as interpreted by Joachim was an ascent through three successive ages, each presided over by a person of the Trinity. The first age was the age of the Father or the Law, the second the age of the Son, and the third the age of the Spirit, when all the world would be one immense monastery united in singing the praises of God and His son until the last judgment. During three and a half years immediately preceding the final age, Antichrist would reign. Sacrifice and offerings would fail, and the order of the church would be destroyed to such a degree that in the multitude of the people, there would no longer be anyone who would dare openly to call upon the name of the Lord. While Antichrist reigned, a holy pope would preach to the pagans.

Since the majority of thirteenth-century popes were anything but holy, in time Joachim's followers transformed his prophecy of a holy pope into the legend of a *papa angelico,* an angelic pope who would one day replace those worldly and unworthy pontiffs. This angelic pastor would receive his appointment not from the College of Cardinals but from God Himself, and he would convert the whole world to a life of poverty. Side by side with the legend of a *papa angelico* and complementary to it, there arose the legend of a second Charlemagne, a French king named Charles who would cleanse the church, cross the sea to the East, and, after conquering the infidel, unite the world in one flock under one pastor.

Il papa angelico was destined never to come, but over the centuries, both his legend and the legend of the second Charlemagne were kept alive by the popular conviction that God could not possibly allow the corruption in the church to continue much longer. In 1453, when Turkish guns battered down the walls of Constantinople, it was only natural for much of Christian Europe to regard Sultan Mahomet II as the Antichrist and to see his spectacular victory as the final warning to Christendom to reform. In 1480, when the sultan landed his troops at Otranto, even Pope Sixtus IV succumbed to the hysteria that swept over Italy.

In a sermon preached at Genoa that year, a Dominican priest named Annio of Viterbo linked the advent of the Antichrist to various astrological predictions and announced the downfall of the church, followed by a universal union under one pastor. In a tract addressed to the Holy Father, the kings of France and Spain, and the senate of Genoa, Annio stated that this union would be effected by the pope and a future prince working in perfect harmony. And he predicted that the pontiff and his royal ally would destroy the Saracens and usher in the final state of beatitude of the church.

Three years later, 14-year-old Charles VIII ascended the French throne. As was perhaps inevitable under the circumstances, many concluded that this dim-witted and deformed adolescent was the prince for whom Europe had been waiting so long— the second Charlemagne who would conquer the infidel and unite the world in one flock under one pastor. Jean Michel, the king's doctor, had a vision in which Charles appeared to him as the reformer and conqueror of the world. The poet André de la Vigne dreamed that Christendom in the form of a woman implored Charles to rescue her from the infidel. Francesco di Paola, an exiled Calabrian monk who was the king's chief adviser, urged Charles to make the conquest of Italy a prelude to the conquest of the Turks. In "La Prophétie de Charles VIII," Guilloche of Bordeaux predicted that Charles would subdue both Florence and Lombardy before going on to Rome, where he would be crowned king of the Romans and then set out to conquer the infidel.

But during those first years of the king's reign, few outside his inner circle knew of these prophecies; fewer still thought he would ever act on them. Most of Italy, indeed most of the West, was still mulling over the various prophecies associated with the conjunction of Jupiter and Saturn. Whereas humanists like Ficino fastened on the promise of a *renovatio mundi,* a great renewal, which they equated with the revival of ancient learning, it was the catastrophes which would precede the *renovatio* that obsessed the popular imagination. Ragged prophets appeared out of nowhere to announce that first Rome, and later all of Italy, would be filled with the sound of weeping. Using Paul of Middleburg's *Pronostic ad Viginta Annos Duratura* as a model, writers published books describing the final days. Premonitions of an imminent judgment on humanity, forecasts of the overthrow of all existing institutions, and the chastisement of a corrupt clergy passed from mouth to mouth. And in Florence as elsewhere, preachers of trial and tribulation drew immense audiences. Fra Bernardino da Montfeltre, who had been expelled from the city in 1489, was one such preacher. Fra Domenico da Ponzo, who was preaching in the cathedral of Santa Maria dei Fiore when Savonarola began preaching in San Marco, was another. Not long afterward, a Dominican friar with an equally gloomy outlook would occupy the pulpit of Santa Maria Novella.

It was in just such an atmosphere of intense anxiety and preoccupation with the movements of the heavenly bodies, when large numbers of people were convinced that the world was "on the eve of something unheard of," that John the Divine had brought forth his vision of apocalypse. Like a latter-day avatar of the prophet, Savonarola based his sermons on the Apocalypse all the rest of that year and into the first weeks of 1491, relating those lurid and beautiful images to the three propositions concerning scourge and renovation he had preached at San Gimignano.

His heart was more fixed than ever on expounding all the knowledge that God had given him, all for the grace and love of the Almighty and the welfare of those who heard him, he had told his mother the year before. But preaching also satisfied his need to dominate his fellows and provided a release for the frenzy within. If he could always have the same sense of well-being he had in the pulpit, it seemed to him he would never be ill or unhappy or discouraged.

Out of the pulpit, he was still as meek as ever—*un agnellino,* one of the friars called him—a little lamb filled with humility and charity who, no matter what the provocation, never raised his voice in anger. In the pulpit, he appeared larger and more muscular than he actually was, a virile and invincible figure whose fearless denunciations of evil brought to mind the prophets and martyrs of old.

To be another Ezekiel, a Haggai, an Amos, a Jeremiah, or a John was, of course, his dearest wish. Like those early prophets whose words he knew so well, he terrorized his audience with warnings of impending doom. He would later say that he had learned from God much of what he told them. Realizing, however, that their minds were not ready for a "revelation of mysteries," he decided to base his conclusions on rational arguments and parables from the scriptures. Once again, as at San Gimignano, he denied that he was a prophet. He also criticized those "simple people" who cited the prophecies of Joachim of Fiore. He declared that the wickedness he saw all around him was adequate proof that the message of the Apocalypse was soon to be fulfilled. As examples of that wickedness, he cited the depravity of the church, the excesses of the rich, and their oppression of the poor.

This was the period when the Council of Seventy was tink-

ering with the currency and the tax system in order to find sufficient cash to pay for a cardinal's hat for Lorenzo's 14-year-old
son Giovanni. Among other measures intended to bring in the
needed revenue, the council announced plans to revalue the
quattrino at one-fourth more than before and ordered that all
imports and assessments be paid with the new coin. To Luca
Landucci, it seemed ironic that there should be this "little tax
increase to the people…when there was need on the contrary
to relieve them." With tongue in cheek, he concluded that the
increase had been made "with divine permission on account of
our sins because the poor are generally worse than the rich and
the great. Praise be to God!" Although Landucci identified with
the poor, the rise in the price of staples and foodstuffs caused
by the revaluation of the *quattrino* did not really affect him.
But for many of the *popolo minuto*, or little people, it meant
making do on less.

Savonarola's attacks on the inequities of the tax system soon
earned him the appellation "the preacher of the despairing," by
which the Florentines meant not only the poor, but all who despaired of ever ridding Florence of the yoke of the Medici. The
poor were burdened with taxes which went to pay for the palaces and whores of the rich, he declared, whereas the poor no
longer received even charity, so absorbed were the rich in their
sensual pleasures and games. In what many in his audience interpreted as deliberate swipes at Lorenzo, he also excoriated tyrants who, like Nebuchadrezzar, Nero, and Domitian, must
inevitably come to a bad end. But there was never any call to
action in these sermons. Instead, Savonarola pictured the coming scourge and told the poor and the oppressed to bear their
suffering in expectation of divine help. God, not man, would
punish injustice, he declared. Which is probably why Lorenzo
decided there was no need to expel him from the city as he had
expelled Fra Bernardino. "It did not touch him where it hurt,"
said Guicciardini. On the other hand, it might not be a bad idea
to ask the fellow to "speak less of future matters." Rather than
do so himself, Lorenzo sent five of his henchmen to San Marco.
Although the five pretended to have come on their own initiative, Savonarola was not deceived. "You say that no one sent

you here, but I say that someone did," he told them. "Go and tell Lorenzo dei Medici to do penance for his sins, for God intends to punish him and his creatures."

But Savonarola's bold words belied his inner agitation, for not only Lorenzo's henchmen but men of all classes, including some of his own friars, had warned him not to speak of the future. Because of the attention his sermons at San Marco had attracted, he had been asked to preach the Lenten sermons in the cathedral. Although he had already prepared a sermon for the second Sunday in Lent based entirely on his visions, he put it aside. He then spent all of Saturday and the early hours of Sunday fruitlessly searching for another topic. Finally, worn out by the many hours he had lain awake, he began to pray. It was while he was praying that suddenly, in the morning stillness of his empty cell, he heard a voice address him. "O foolish one," it said, "do you not see that it is God's will that you should continue to preach in this manner?" And in obedience to this voice, which he immediately assumed was the voice of God or one of His angels, he returned to his old themes and preached his most terrifying sermon yet. "Bethink you well, O ye rich, for affliction shall smite ye," he warned. "This city shall no more be called Florence, but a den of thieves, of turpitude and bloodshed. Then shall ye all be poverty-stricken, all wretched, and your name, O priests, shall be changed into a terror.... Know that unheard-of times are at hand."

It was thus that Ezekiel and John and Amos and Jeremiah had thundered their warnings to the people after hearing the voice of the Lord. Few doubted that God continued to use both the quick and the dead to warn men of the terrors that lay in store for them. As a child, Savonarola had heard his grandfather Michele tell how in his native Pavia in times of great danger the saints were heard to sigh at night along the streets of the city, and the corpse of a holy nun in the church of Santa Chiara made a noise and lifted up its arms. Ferrara, too, had its prophetic corpse: Beata Beatrice d'Este, who could be heard knocking in her tomb whenever calamity threatened the city.

Nor were the dead God's only messengers. During their lifetime, Saint Hildegarde of Bingen, the abbot Joachim, Saint

Brigitte of Sweden, Saint Catherine of Siena, Saint Vincent
Ferrer, and a host of lesser mystics had all had visions and heard
voices bidding them to announce the disasters to come. In con-
cluding that the voice he had heard was the voice of God,
Savonarola was doing no more than they had done. His urgent
need to be one of God's elect made it impossible for him to admit the possibility of self-deception. That such a possibility was
always there had been emphasized by all the greatest theologians of the church, from Thomas Aquinas to Jean Gerson. Moreover, during Savonarola's first stay in Florence, he had frequently
cited their works to the novices. But when Fra Silvestro Maruffi,
who had been one of his students, reminded him of how critical of prophecy he had once been and accused him of being "mad
and beside himself," he insisted that his prophecies had a solid
foundation. If Silvestro prayed to God long enough, the Almighty
would surely reveal this to him. Or at least Savonarola hoped
that He would, for behind his seeming certainty lurked a persistent but unacknowledged doubt of his prophetic calling that
constantly led him to press the Lord for proof of his election.

Silvestro had been a somnambulist for as long as he could
remember. Since becoming a friar, he had also been subject to
strange dreams and visions. After his conversation with Savonarola, he had several dreams in which the spirits reproached
him for his lack of faith. Because he could not decide whether
these dreams had come from God or the devil, he referred them
to his former teacher, who assured him that God wished him
well. And from then on, not only did Silvestro no longer question Savonarola's prophetic calling; he also brought him all his
dreams and visions.

On Wednesday of Easter week, Savonarola was invited to speak
before the Signoria. Although he compared himself to Christ before the Pharisees and spoke of the need to be more measured
and more urbane than he was in church, he could not resist using the occasion for yet another attack on Lorenzo. All the evil
and all the good in a city depended on its head, he told the priors and the gonfalonier. If the head followed the right path, the

whole city would be sanctified. But tyrants, by whom he obviously meant Lorenzo, were incorrigible because they were proud, because they loved flattery and would not restore ill-gotten gains. The tyrant was wont to occupy the people with shows and festivals in order that they might think of their own pastimes and not of his designs "and growing unused to the conduct of the commonwealth," might "leave the reins of government in his hands." And Savonarola exhorted the Signoria to "remove dissensions, do justice, and exact honesty from all."

Despite the burgeoning taste for gloom and doom, Fra Mariano da Genazzano was still the most popular preacher in the city. To gratify Lorenzo, Mariano announced that his Ascension Day sermon would have as its theme a sentence from the Acts of the Apostles: "It is not for you to know the times or the seasons, which the Father has put in his own power." Since the sermon was obviously intended as an attack on Savonarola's prophecies, Mariano's audience that Ascension Day was even larger than usual. But in his effort to please Lorenzo, the normally moderate Mariano grew so vituperative that he alienated more people than he convinced. To make matters worse, Savonarola then revealed that only the week before, Mariano had praised his sermons and predicted that they would do much good. "Who put it into your head to attack me?" Savonarola asked Mariano from the pulpit. "What made you change so soon?"

Furious because he had been made to look ridiculous, Mariano became Savonarola's lifelong enemy; but Lorenzo, who had acquired a reputation for vindictiveness as a result of his treatment of the Pazzi, apparently decided that this particular vendetta was no longer worth the effort. That July, he did not even bother to protest when the friars chose Savonarola as their prior.

It was customary for a newly elected prior to pay his respects to Lorenzo. Curious to see the man with whom he had been sparring for so long, Lorenzo settled back to await Savonarola's visit. But Savonarola had his reputation as a foe of the Medici to consider. "Who elected me prior, God or Lorenzo?" he demanded when the older monks reminded him of the custom.

"God," was the reply.

"Then it is to God that I will give thanks," he told them.

To Lorenzo, who was accustomed to thinking of San Marco as his very own, such intransigence smacked of lèse majesté. "A foreign monk has come to live in my house and does not deign to visit me," he told his friends.

More curious about Savonarola than ever, he took to strolling in the cloister after attending mass in the adjoining church of San Marco. But since he could not bring himself to ask to see the new prior, Savonarola made a point of not coming out to greet him. And when Lorenzo bestowed a generous gift on the convent, Savonarola in yet another of those splendidly defiant sermons, which his audience had come to expect of him, let it be known that "the good watchdog when a thief throws him a bone or a piece of meat puts it to one side and goes on barking."

Since, as usual, no bite followed the bark, Lorenzo chose to ignore it. Soon afterward, he had his secretary deposit 300 gold florins in the convent alms box. Silver and copper money were quite sufficient for the brethren, Savonarola declared. And he donated the florins to one of the city's charitable orders.

"This is a wily old fox," said Lorenzo after being told of the fate of his gift. Either because he thought it demeaning to be continually finessed by a mere prior or because he had grown weary of the whole business, he made no further attempts to ingratiate himself.

By then, the gout which was the hereditary curse of the Medici had grown so painful that there were times when he felt too debilitated to see anyone or do anything. On August 31, 1491, he went to the baths at Spedaletto near Pisa in the hope that a new water found there would alleviate his pain. Because he was in no condition to ride, he had to be carried there by litter. At various times in the past, he had sought relief at the baths at Poretta, Bagno a Morba, Vignone, and Filetta. Each time he had returned to Florence feeling refreshed, only to suffer a relapse soon afterward.

Despite the trip to Spedaletto, by January 1492, the pain in his joints had grown so excruciating that it kept him confined to his palace and forced him to cancel all his appointments. Although toward the end of the month he was sufficiently recovered to leave the palace for short periods, two weeks later he was back in bed, "so tormented with pain all over the body" that it was impossible for him to get any rest. By February 16, his condition had improved, only to deteriorate once more at the beginning of March, when for three days "no one was able to speak to him." On March 8, he seemed to be feeling better although there were occasional twinges of pain which one visitor attributed to "the perverse and very cold weather." Despite the weather and the occasional pain, March 9 was a supremely joyful day for him, for on that day his 17-year-old son Giovanni finally received his cardinal's hat.

Giovanni was Lorenzo's second son. As a second son, he had been destined for the priesthood from the moment he emerged from his mother's womb. He was still a toddler when Lorenzo asked the manager of the Medici bank in Lyons to keep an eye out for French benefices. The boy was not yet 7 when Louis XI gave him the abbey of Fonte Dolce, with an income sufficient to meet the needs of most adult churchmen. The king would have also given him the archbishopric of Aix en Provence had it not been for two unforeseen circumstances: the pope, who had been perfectly willing to welcome a 7-year-old abbot into the hierarchy, decided that a 7-year-old archbishop would never do; and the incumbent archbishop, until then presumed to be dead and buried, turned out to be alive and well.

To compensate Giovanni for these disappointments, Louis conferred the abbey of Passignano on him the following year. Thanks to his father's relentless pursuit of benefices, by the time Giovanni entered his teens, he was also abbot of Monte Cassino, Morimondo, Vajano, Monte Piano, Tours, Arezzo, and Fiesole; canon of the cathedrals of Florence, Arezzo, and Fiesole; prior of Monte Varchi; proposto of Prato; and precentor of San Antonio in Florence. The campaign to make him a cardinal began in 1484 when he was 9. That year, Pope Sixtus IV died and was succeeded by the infinitely more pliable Giovanni Battista Cibo, who took the name of Innocent VIII. Sixtus had made four of his nephews cardinals, one of them when he was only 17. Among the articles of concession the new pope signed was a solemn promise to appoint no new cardinals under the age of

30. To be in the best possible position to induce the pope to break this promise, Lorenzo arranged a match between his 16-year-old daughter Maddalena and the pontiff's illegitimate 40-year-old son Franceshetto. When Innocent still appeared reluctant to make Giovanni a cardinal, Lorenzo enlisted the aid of the king of France and two of the cardinals. He also instructed the Florentine ambassador in Rome to approach the other members of the College of Cardinals, and he himself barraged the Holy Father with letters until in March 1489, when Giovanni was not yet 14, the pope yielded. The appointment, however, was *in petto*, which meant that it had to be kept secret for three years.

Fearful that neither he nor the pope would last that long, Lorenzo at first sought to add two years to his son's age, then ordered the Florentine ambassador in Rome to do everything he could to have Giovanni's period of probation shortened. The prospective cardinal was a tall, nearsighted, perspiring youth with an unusually large head, a short, beefy neck, an even beefier frame, and legs which appeared far too slender to support so much weight. Although his appointment to the sacred college was supposed to be a secret, it became known immediately. Hence, it could have been to Giovanni that Savonarola was alluding when in one of his Lenten sermons for 1491, he attacked fathers who urged their sons to enter the ecclesiastical life in order to obtain benefices and stipends, "so that ye hear it said, 'Blessed be the house that owns a fat curate.' "

Nevertheless, there was much to be said for having this particular fat curate in the College of Cardinals, where, it seemed to the Florentines, he could be counted on to look out not only for the interests of his family, but for the interests of his native city as well. The Sunday Giovanni received the great broad-brimmed scarlet hat with the hanging cords and tassels that made his appointment official, all Florence went wild with excitement. Impatient to see the new cardinal, a huge multitude streamed out the San Gallo gate in the direction of the Badia Fiesolana, the ancient cathedral of Fiesole where the investiture had taken place. Within the city itself, banners fluttered from every other window, and every doorway and rooftop along the route the cardinal would take on his way to the Medici palace was thronged with well-wishers. Although it was then the first Sunday in Lent, the atmosphere was reminiscent of a carnival, with lighted torches, bonfires, firecrackers, bands of wandering musicians, and singing, dancing, and feasting that lasted far into the night. When the cardinal attended mass in Santa Maria dei Fiore the following morning, the cathedral was so packed that he and his party had to elbow their way to the doors.

Although Lorenzo was in too much pain to attend the mass or to head his table at the great banquet in his palace that afternoon, he insisted on being carried into the banquet hall to greet the guests. Despite his pain, he had begun to ride again, but no permanent improvement in his condition seemed likely until the weather improved, which in Florence seldom occurred before the end of April or the beginning of May. And that was more time than Lorenzo had. A few days after the banquet, he began running a low but persistent fever which attacked his nerves and intestines and appeared to be destroying "the very principle of life." In the hope that a change of air would bring down the fever, his doctor, Pier Leone, suggested that he leave Florence.

Of the numerous villas owned by the Medici, Lorenzo's favorite was at Poggio a Caiano on the road to Pistoia, perhaps because he had bought it himself and had it remodeled to his taste. Over and over in his poetry, he had celebrated the beauty of the surrounding countryside: "the clamorous cranes…each with outstretched neck"; the leaves of the olive trees in winter, now green, now white, according to the direction of the wind; the return of spring when "the shepherd from the fold brings forth his flock." With what one visitor called "that magnificence which characterizes all his undertakings," Lorenzo had arranged for water for the fields to be transported many miles by aqueduct; planted groves of mulberry trees where, said Poliziano, the silkworm spun "his lustrous thread"; and filled the woods with pheasants and peacocks imported from Sicily.

But Poggio a Caiano is almost 12 miles from Florence. As much as Lorenzo wished to be carried to his beloved villa, he lacked the stamina for the journey, so he was carried instead to the villa at Careggi, where his father and grandfather had died.

With him went his sister Nannina, his eldest daughter, Lucrezia, his son Piero, and Angelo Poliziano, Piero's former tutor and Lorenzo's friend and protégé. The Medici villa at Careggi is set amidst pines and cypresses on the hill of Montughi, 2 miles northwest of Florence. From his first-floor bedroom adjoining the great hall where guests were welcomed, Lorenzo could see the terraced gardens below, and beyond them the green hills of Tuscany. In those peaceful surroundings he seemed to improve, but as usual the improvement was short-lived. On April 5, when Duke Ercole of Ferrara asked to see him, he was told that Lorenzo was too ill to see anyone. Ercole's son-in-law Ludovico Sforza had offered to send his personal physician, Lazarus of Pavia, to Careggi. Now everyone was awaiting the doctor's arrival.

April 5 was the Thursday after the fourth Sunday of Lent. Since the beginning of Lent, Savonarola had been preaching in the basilica of San Lorenzo. In that vast colonnaded gray-and-white church, with the tomb of Cosimo dei Medici under the main altar and the tombs of Cosimo's father, Giovanni de Bicci, and Lorenzo's father, Piero, in the sacristy, he scoffed at "those great men" who, "as though they did not know they were men like others, wanted to be honored and blessed by all." And he spoke also of the coming scourge. Once he had said he was *nearly* sure of these things; then he said that he was sure of them. Now he told his audience he was more than sure. No longer would he relate things that were past. Instead, he would tell of the calamities to come, "just as one would speak of things that have already passed." Nor was he the only one to speak of these things. Both the Lenten preacher at Santa Maria Novella and Fra Domenico da Ponzo, whose sermons in the cathedral attracted 15,000 people each morning, were also predicting unheard-of disasters unless the Florentines put an end to their vices, especially the vice of sodomy. But it was Savonarola whose sermons attracted the most attention.

As he had been doing ever since his return to Florence, he built each sermon around a verse from the Scriptures. For his sermon on Friday, April 6, he had chosen a verse from the story of Lazarus. But try as he would, he could not seem to develop this to his satisfaction. As so often happened when he was dissatisfied with what he planned to say, he was too overwrought to sleep. And so he remained at his desk long after everyone else was in bed. He was sitting there with the story of Lazarus spread out before him, hoping for an inspiration, when suddenly there burst from his lips the words *"Ecco gladius Domine super terram cito et velociter.* Behold the sword of the Lord, swift and sure over the peoples of the earth." The day had been exceptionally clear for April, but at eleven that night, there was a sudden gust of wind followed by hail and lightning and a huge crashing sound that seemed to make the whole earth tremble. Although like everyone else in Florence, Savonarola must have been startled by this sound, no place in his writing does he indicate whether he heard it before or after the words concerning the sword of the Lord issued from his lips. In either case, the sound could only have bolstered his conviction that God had placed the words on his tongue and that the Almighty wished him to build his sermon around them.

By the time he entered the pulpit to deliver the sermon the next morning, all Florence knew that the sound heard the previous night had been the sound of lightning striking the cupola of Santa Maria dei Fiore. The lightning had split the lantern and sent two niches and several other pieces of marble plummeting earthward. One of the niches had split the roof of the church before coming to rest in the brick floor. The other had split the roof of one of the houses opposite and then buried itself in the ground under the cellar. Several pieces of marble had struck the roofs of other nearby houses, but without causing as much damage.

Those in the houses thought that the end of the world had come, and they considered it a sign of God's grace that no one had been injured. Noting that the day had been clear and that there had been no sign of fire or smell of sulfur when the lightning struck, many in Florence were convinced that this had been no ordinary thunderbolt but "a great marvel...significative of some extraordinary event." And they listened in awe as Savonarola repeated the words God had placed in his mouth. God's anger was stirred, he told them, and the sword was being made ready to strike.

Speaking in the damaged cathedral, with the split roof and the cracked pavement there for all to see, Fra Domenico da Ponzo also told his audience that this had been no ordinary thunderbolt but a sign from heaven. Savonarola had repeatedly warned of the coming scourge, said Fra Domenico, but the Florentines had refused to believe him. Now they ought to believe him because he was a holy man. Furthermore, Fra Domenico continued, God had given this sign because he wished the Florentines to repent. If they did not repent by the following August, the streets would run with blood. And he invited them to cut off his head if this did not come to pass.

"Everyone is terrified," wrote Francesco Guicciardini's uncle, Niccolò. "Most of all myself." To allay God's wrath, the preacher at Santa Maria Novella suggested organizing a religious procession that included many boys dressed in white, but there was some doubt as to whether the Signoria would permit it.

Meanwhile, at Careggi, Lorenzo's condition grew steadily worse. By the morning of April 7 it was clear that there was no longer any hope. Toward midnight he received that last communion known as the viaticum, then asked to be left alone with his son Piero. He had just finished speaking with Piero when Lazarus of Pavia, the doctor sent by Ludovico Sforza, entered the sickroom.

Like many physicians of the time, Lazarus of Pavia put great faith in the therapeutic power of gems, but he believed they ought to be ingested, not worn. Although it seemed clear to Poliziano that Lazarus had been summoned "too late to be of any use, yet to do something, he ordered various precious stones to be pounded together in a mortar," so that Lorenzo might swallow them. Seeing this, Lorenzo asked what the doctor was preparing. He was preparing a remedy to comfort the intestines, said Poliziano. "O Angiolo, art thou here!" Lorenzo cried on hearing his friend's voice. And he took both Poliziano's hands in his and pressed them tightly. Unable to stifle his sobs, Poliziano turned his face away, but Lorenzo, showing no emotion, continued to press his hands. Seeing that Poliziano was too overwrought to speak, he released his hold, and Poliziano ran into the adjoining room where he could give free vent to his grief.

When Poliziano returned to the sickroom, Lorenzo asked him what his friend Pico was doing. Poliziano replied that Pico had remained in town for fear of molesting Lorenzo with his presence. "And I," said Lorenzo, "but for the fear that the journey here might be irksome for him would be most glad to see him and speak to him for the last time before I leave you all."

Although it was past midnight, Pico was immediately sent for. On his arrival, he sat beside the sickbed while Poliziano, "in order to hear Lorenzo's languid voice for the last time," leaned against Pico's knees. He would die more willingly after having seen so dear a friend, Lorenzo told Pico. Pico had no sooner left the sickroom than Savonarola entered. According to Fra Placido Cinozzi and some of Savonarola's other sixteenth-century biographers, he had been summoned to Careggi by Lorenzo. "Go for the father, Fra Girolamo," Lorenzo is supposed to have said, "for I have never found one save him who was an honest friar." However, it seems more likely that Savonarola had accompanied Pico to Careggi and that it was Pico who persuaded Lorenzo to see him.

During their only meeting, Savonarola behaved as any priest would behave with a dying man. He exhorted Lorenzo to remain firm in his faith and if God granted him life, to live free from crime, or, if God willed, to receive death willingly. To which Lorenzo replied that he was firm in his religion, that his life would always be guided by it, and that nothing could be sweeter than death if such were the divine will. Seeing that Savonarola was preparing to leave, he asked the friar for his blessing. Ignoring the grief openly shown by those at his bedside, Lorenzo bowed his head and, "immersed in piety and religion," repeated Savonarola's words and prayers. Contrasting his calm with the agitation of the others, it seemed to Poliziano that "all save Lorenzo were going to die."

He had already swallowed the pulverized gems, a medicine which could have only brought the end that much closer. Not wishing to appear idle, his doctors kept urging still other remedies on him. He in turn "submitted to everything they suggested not because he thought it would save him, but in order not to offend anyone even in death." Asked how well he liked some food he had been given, he replied, "As well as a dying man can like anything." After tenderly embracing everyone and asking pardon for whatever inconvenience he had caused, he prepared to receive extreme unction. The gospel describing the passion of Christ was then read to him, and he indicated that he understood it by moving his lips, raising his tired eyes, or occasionally moving his fingers. "Gazing upon a silver crucifix inlaid with precious stones and kissing it from time to time, he expired." He was only 43, but so great had been his suffering during those last weeks that in his death mask he looks like a very old man. He was buried next to his brother Giuliano under the great marble and porphyry sarcophagus which Verrocchio had fashioned for their father Piero and his brother Giovanni in the sacristy of San Lorenzo. He had lived "long enough for his own glory," said King Ferrante of Naples, but "too short a time for Italy."

Because the people did not know what to expect from his son Piero, and because Savonarola and the other preachers had convinced them of God's desire to punish them for their sins, they felt certain that the Almighty had intended the destruction of the cupola as a sign that ruin would follow Lorenzo's death. Nor, when they reflected on it, had this been the only sign. As Lorenzo lay dying, a comet had spread its fiery tail over Careggi. Marsilio Ficino had seen ghostly giants fighting one another in the garden of his villa. One of the two lions kept in a cage behind the Palazzo della Signoria as emblems of the republic's power had killed the other. During the Lenten sermon at Santa Maria Novella the previous Wednesday, a fanatical *pinzochera*, or lay sister of Saint Francis, had begun shrieking that a bull with flaming red horns was destroying the church. At the precise moment the thunderbolt struck the cupola of Santa Maria dei Fiore, one of the seven golden balls in the Medici coat of arms was also shattered. For three nights before Lorenzo's death, strange lights had appeared in the sky. Just as he drew his last breath, a life-size waxen votive image modeled after a sketch of Lorenzo made by Verrocchio at the time of the Pazzi conspiracy fell from its niche in the church of Santa Annunziata. Two days later, Lorenzo's physician, Pier Leone, disconsolate at not having been able to save him, threw himself into a well and drowned.

To the uneasy mind of Savonarola, forever in quest of reassurance that he was indeed God's chosen prophet, these signs were a vindication of all he had predicted and a powerful spur. So great was his fervor, so vehemently did he express himself, he would later recall, that many in his audience expected the vein in his neck to burst. All men would feel the scourge of God, he warned. Wherever they went—whether to a villa in the country or to Rome or France or anyplace else—when God passed judgment, He would find them. And then on the morning of April 13, Savonarola announced that God had passed judgment. Now there was nothing left to do but to await the scourge. Nevertheless, he continued to hope that "prayer and contrite hearts and humility would ward it off."

In this atmosphere of universal foreboding, Piero dei Medici began his reign as unofficial master of Florence. The evening before Savonarola announced that God has passed judgment, the Council of Seventy voted to waive the age restrictions that would have kept the 20-year-old Piero from assuming all the offices his father had held or might have held.

III

PIERO'S TIME

'Tis seldom human wisdom descends from sire to son
Such is the will of him who gave it
That at His hands we may implore the boon.
> Dante (quoted in Machiavelli's
> *Discorsi*, Book I, Chapter 11)

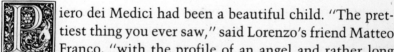iero dei Medici had been a beautiful child. "The pret-
tiest thing you ever saw," said Lorenzo's friend Matteo
Franco, "with the profile of an angel and rather long
hair which stands out a little and is charming to see." Lorenzo
feared his adorable child's impetuous nature, but Poliziano, who
became Piero's tutor when the little boy was only 3, seemed
confident that with the proper training he would fulfill their expectations. By the time Piero was 7, he was writing to his father in Latin, in order, as he put it, "to give a more literary tone
to his letters." He was also studying Greek, although, he confessed in one letter, he did not seem to be making much pro-
gress. He must have persisted, however, for in the Laurentian
library there is a copy of the works of Hesiod presented to him
by Lorenzo "as a reward for his good behavior and love of study."

Piero had learned very early that to be well-behaved, to show
a love of study, and to work hard were the ways to please his
magnificent father. And pleasing his father was all-important
to Piero. When Lorenzo sent him a much-longed-for pony, he
was quick to write how much the pony's arrival had incited him
to work. "I owe you and I send you many thanks for such a fine
gift," he continued, "and I shall try to repay you by becoming
what you wish. Of this be sure."

Because as the eldest son he was destined one day to succeed his father, everyone tried to make Piero shine. Not only

were the humanists in the household forever calling attention
to his precocity by thinking up questions for him to answer,
but also, said Franco, "the poor lad could not go outside without all Florence running after him." This excessive adulation
so annoyed Lorenzo that more than once he declared that he
would not have his son bothered this way. On the other hand,
Lorenzo himself did not hesitate to impose far heavier burdens
on his winsome boy.

Piero was only 12 when Lorenzo sent him to Rome to congratulate Pope Innocent VIII on his election. While in Rome,
Piero was instructed to pay his respects to numerous foreign envoys and cardinals and to take special pains to ingratiate himself
with his mother's relatives, the Orsini. "They," said Lorenzo,
"having deigned to become our relatives," by which Piero was
the chief gainer "as being of higher birth" (than his Medici forebears who, like all Florentines, were looked down upon as mere
shopkeepers and usurers). Although grateful for his higher birth,
Piero must never flaunt it. On the contrary, he must be careful
not to take precedence over his elders in the Florentine delegation. For, said his father, "although thou art my son, thou art
but a citizen of Florence."

To be noble with the nobles and democratic with the dem-
ocrats was not an easy task under any circumstances, and it became harder after Lorenzo married his son to Alfonsina Orsini,
the 13-year-old daughter of the deceased constable of Naples.
The marriage, which, like Lorenzo's own, had been arranged for
diplomatic reasons, was celebrated by proxy in the Neapolitan
royal palace; and it was not until three months later that the
17-year-old bridegroom went to Rome to claim his bride. By then
the angelic-looking boy upon whom all Florence had doted had
grown into a tall, broad-shouldered youth with a barrel chest
and an enigmatic, withdrawn expression. Although he retained
the love of humanist studies instilled in him by Poliziano, his
principal interests appeared to be women and sports. So skilled
was he in boxing and soccer that athletes from all over Italy
came to Florence to compete with him and to learn from him.
Nor did he have any equal in riding and jousting. And it may
have been his pride in his athletic prowess coupled with his

newfound success with women and the exhilaration of having brought home a semiroyal bride that accounted for a certain insolence in Piero's bearing at this time. The Florentines, however, were quick to blame the change in their erstwhile darling upon his Orsini heritage. Because of his foreign mother, the Florentine blood in him was bastardized, they declared, so that he lacked the "good nature and the sweetness" ordinary in their nation. He was "too haughty and insolent" for their way of life.

Even Lorenzo seemed troubled by Piero's arrogance. It was about this time that he supposedly told a friend that of his three sons, one was good, one wise, and one foolish; the good one being the youngest, Giuliano; the wise one, Cardinal Giovanni; and the foolish one, Piero "of the swell head." If we believe Guicciardini, Lorenzo also "frequently lamented to his most intimate friends that his son's recklessness and arrogance would be the ruin of the house of Medici." But fathers of adolescent sons are prone to outbursts of irritation with their offspring. Despite his irritation, Lorenzo continued to groom Piero to succeed him. In 1490, Piero represented his father at the wedding of Gian Galeazzo Sforza, duke of Milan, to Isabella of Aragon, a granddaughter of the king of Naples. As Lorenzo's health continued to deteriorate, he often talked of spending the rest of his life with his humanist friends "away from the city and its noise," leaving Piero to govern Florence in his stead.

In governing the city, Lorenzo had always depended on the goodwill and cooperation of the so-called *cittadini principali*— the wealthy and influential principal citizens whose fathers and grandfathers had composed the oligarchy. Without their support, he knew his regime could not long remain in power. Like their forebears at the time of the oligarchy, these citizens were in the habit of meeting at one another's homes to discuss the affairs of the city and make recommendations about how it ought to be run. In the summer of 1489, Lorenzo secretly began pressing them to include Piero in their deliberations, "he being now a man and soon to have children of his own" and also "of singular talent." Soon afterward, Lorenzo's secretary, Ser Piero Dovizi, informed him that the *cittadini principali* had voted to include Piero in all their secret meetings and to accord him "all possible authority and esteem." Although this involved taking Piero "away from his pleasures," the citizens felt certain it would benefit both him and Florence. But either because Piero was reluctant to give up his pleasures or, perhaps, because he did not feel comfortable with these august gentlemen, all of them his seniors by many years, he managed to find excuses not to attend their meetings.

One of the most influential and vocal of the citizens who attended these meetings was Piero's uncle by marriage, Bernardo Rucellai. Rucellai had carried out all sorts of delicate assignments for Lorenzo. Early in his regime, when there were problems with King Ferrante of Naples, it was Rucellai who was sent to negotiate with the king. When Milan began causing problems, it was Rucellai who was sent there. And when Lorenzo needed someone to act as Piero's proxy at his marriage to Alfonsina Orsini, it was once again Rucellai who was chosen. By then, however, Rucellai had grown alarmed at what he considered Lorenzo's high-handedness. And because Rucellai was both outspoken and irascible, he did not hesitate to let Lorenzo know how he felt. Had he not been married to Lorenzo's sister Nannina, Lorenzo might have taken steps to silence him. As it was, he did nothing.

Among the *cittadini principali* who shared Rucellai's resentment of Lorenzo's peremptory manner was Lorenzo's first cousin Paolantonio Soderini. After Lorenzo's death, Rucellai and Soderini both urged Piero "to use his authority moderately," and move toward a more genuinely republican order rather than continue doing "those things that smacked of tyranny and had caused hostility toward Lorenzo." Rather than detract from his power, they told Piero, such a course would heighten it. Piero was too young and inexperienced to know what would heighten his power. Moreover, he wasn't at all sure he could trust either Rucellai or Soderini. When he asked Ser Piero Dovizi, who was then acting as his chancellor, what he thought, Dovizi told him that the suggestions "had not been proffered in his interest" and that those who gave them "wanted him to lose power." Whereupon Piero not only ignored the suggestions, but took it on himself to slight the men who had proffered them.

Soon afterward, Bernardo Rucellai decided to marry one of his daughters to a son of Filippo Strozzi, and Paolantonio Soderini decided to marry his son Tommaso to Strozzi's daughter Fiametta. Next to the Medici, the Strozzi were the wealthiest family in Florence, and the Rucellai and the Soderini were not far behind. Lorenzo had always been wary of alliances between such wealthy families. Because he preferred "to pair people off in a way that would not cause him worry," he had insisted that none but the most unimportant marriages take place without his consent. Eager to emulate his father in everything, Piero continued the practice. He had no clear idea, though, of what constituted a dangerous union and what an innocuous one. Once again, it fell to Dovizi to enlighten him. When Dovizi heard that Piero had given his consent to the proposed marriages, he immediately let him know that Lorenzo would never have permitted them. Surely Piero must remember that his great-grandfather Cosimo had exiled Filippo Strozzi's father Matteo. Filippo himself had also spent much of his youth in exile. Although he had later been allowed to return to Florence and had lent money to Lorenzo, not only had Filippo used trickery to induce him to approve the plans for the Strozzi palace, but he had boasted of his trickery to others. To allow such a man to unite his family with the families of two other men who were unfriendly to the regime was to encourage sedition. And Dovizi urged Piero to withdraw his consent immediately.

Ser Piero Dovizi had been trained as a notary. Except for the Medici, he had no ties to any of the great Florentine families. Technically, he wasn't even a Florentine. He had been born in the hamlet of Bibbiena, one of the many Tuscan villages under Florentine hegemony. To aristocrats like Soderini and Rucellai, he seemed a country bumpkin, a mere *contadino*, or peasant. Lorenzo had made a practice of training such men and giving them responsible posts because unlike the *cittadini principali*, they had no power without him and hence no alternative but to be loyal to him. Although it was too late for Piero to act on Dovizi's suggestion about the marriages, the very fact that this "haughty and overbearing peasant" had dared to make it enraged Soderini. The next time he saw the presumptuous fellow, he

walked up to him and gave him a resounding box on the ear.
The gesture tickled Dovizi's enemies, of whom there were many.
It also led Piero to exclude both Soderini and Rucellai from the
government. Pleading regret for what he had done, Soderini tried
to regain favor. But Rucellai, "whose nature [said Guicciardini]
was such that he would rather break than bend," grew ever more
outspoken in his criticism of the regime.

Nor was Rucellai the only one whom Piero managed to antagonize during his first year in power. A potentially more dangerous foe was Ludovico Sforza, regent of Milan. Shortly after
the conspiracy of the Pazzi, Milan, Florence, and Naples had
joined together in a so-called Triple Alliance intended to keep
peace among the numerous Italian states. Eight days before
Lorenzo's death, Cosimo Sassetti, the Medici agent in Paris, informed him of the arrival of an embassy from Ludovico. Ostensibly, the embassy had come to thank Charles VIII for renewing
the ancient alliance between France and Milan and to congratulate him on his marriage to Anne of Brittany. Actually, Ludovico sought the king's assurance that in the event of a conflict
between Milan and Naples, Charles would side with him against
King Ferrante and his allies, Pope Innocent VIII and Lorenzo dei
Medici. A few months earlier, Ludovico had sought the king's
promise to maintain him as regent indefinitely.

Ludovico Sforza was the fourth son of the famed condottiere
Francesco Sforza, and the first to be born after his father became
duke of Milan. At the time Ludovico began his negotiations with
King Charles, he was 41 years old and had been regent of Milan
for a little over a decade. In an altarpiece painted a few years
later, he appears silky, sensual, and treacherous, all of which he
was. This broad-faced man with the bulging eyes and the soft,
pudgy hands loved power, luxury, learning, and women; seldom
if ever expressed his true feelings to anyone except his younger
brother Ascanio; and never lost his temper no matter what the
provocation. To the French writer and diplomat Philippe de
Comines, who, like many people who knew Ludovico well, eventually came to hate him, he seemed a very shrewd man but a
very timid one. "And," said Comines, "he is unusually slippery

when he is afraid....He is a man without faith if he sees profit in breaking it."

After the assassination of Ludovico's eldest brother, Galeazzo Maria, who had succeeded their father as duke of Milan, Galeazzo's widow, Bona of Savoy, was named regent for the couple's 7-year-old son, Gian Galeazzo. To Comines, Bona seemed "a woman of little sense." Consequently, it was not difficult for Ludovico to insinuate himself into her good graces and to then seize control of both the regency and the treasury, a treasury reputed to be the greatest in Christendom. Although Ludovico allowed his nephew to be crowned duke of Milan, he had no intention of ever surrendering either the treasury or the government to him. Since, like his mother, Gian Galeazzo was unusually dull, there was nothing to fear from him. Once he reached puberty, he was easily kept quiet with a succession of male and female lovers and a plentiful supply of liquor. But Gian Galeazzo's father had betrothed him to Isabella of Aragon, a granddaughter of the king of Naples. And Isabella was not so easily shunted aside. After her marriage to Gian Galeazzo, she wished to be duchess in fact as well as in name. Her frequent complaints to her father and grandfather and their action on her behalf terrified Ludovico. As he later confided to Ascanio, he sought an alliance with King Charles not because he wanted the French to invade Italy but because the threat of an invasion "would compel King Ferrante to attend to his own affairs instead of meddling in the affairs of others."

As early as 1486, Charles and his counselors had begun making plans to invade Italy with a view to conquering Naples. Because the king's Angevin ancestors had once ruled there, Charles considered the kingdom lawfully his. Moreover, his chief spiritual adviser, the Calabrian monk Francesco di Paola, had convinced him that the conquest of Naples was a necessary preliminary to a crusade against Islam, a crusade that would end with Constantinople once more in Christian hands and Charles the arbiter of Europe. By 1492, Italian merchants, scholars, and diplomats who visited France reported seeing preparations for "the Neapolitan expedition," as it was called. Shortly before Lorenzo's death that April, the manager of the Medici bank in Lyons informed him that the invasion was "a distinct possibility." That an alliance with Milan would encourage Charles to go ahead with his plans did not trouble Ludovico. In those first days of their association, he had no doubts about his ability to manage the king, whom he considered almost as inept and inexperienced as Gian Galeazzo. Managing Lorenzo dei Medici was another matter. Not only was Lorenzo allied to King Ferrante, but he considered the Triple Alliance "the common league which assured the equilibrium of Italy." And he did not trust Ludovico, whom he had once described as being "all puffed up" and wanting "to see Italian affairs go to the bad."

Lorenzo's death just as the negotiations with France were drawing to a close left another inexperienced young ruler for Ludovico to manipulate. In the letter of condolence he sent to Piero, Ludovico assured him that he looked on him and Cardinal Giovanni as sons, or brothers, and that he would do whatever he could to help them. That May, the Florentine ambassador in Milan reported finding Ludovico warmer and more affectionate toward Florence and toward Piero in particular than he had ever been. He bore Piero a singular love, Ludovico told the ambassador. Because of this love, he had resolved to be completely open with him and to confer with him about everything. If Piero would be as open with him, Ludovico would cherish his communications and use them for a worthy purpose.

But Ludovico's treaty with Charles VIII made Piero uneasy. Mindful of his father's devotion to the Triple Alliance, he urged his ambassador to do everything he could to reconcile Naples and Milan. The ambassador was still trying to effect a reconciliation when Pope Innocent VIII died. Ludovico immediately instructed his brother Ascanio, one of the most influential cardinals in Rome, to spare no expense to guarantee the election of a pro-Milanese pope. King Ferrante put aside 200,000 ducats to ensure the election of a pope favorable to Naples. After what appeared to be a hopeless deadlock in the College of Cardinals, Ascanio succeeded in mustering enough votes to elect a compromise candidate: Cardinal Rodrigo Borgia, who took the name of Alexander VI.

As was customary whenever there was a papal election, all the nations of Christendom prepared to send ambassadors to Rome to congratulate the new pope. To take the edge off Ascanio's machinations and show King Ferrante that the Triple Alliance was not yet dead, Ludovico suggested that rather than deliver separate messages of congratulation, the ambassadors of Florence, Naples, and Milan allow Ferrante's ambassador to speak for all three.

Piero was planning to head the Florentine delegation himself. So that he and the other delegates might appear to the best advantage, an army of tailors, coatmakers, and embroiderers had been put to work on the clothing and other finery they would take with them. Piero's necklace alone was rumored to be worth 200,000 florins. Besides priding himself on his ability to wear such expensive stuff superlatively well, Piero prided himself on his voice, which unlike his father's was pleasing and mellifluous. Although Lorenzo's former tutor Gentile Becchi, bishop of Arezzo, would deliver the principal address, Piero, who had a reputation for speaking well on almost anything, was undoubtedly looking forward to adding a few words of his own. Were he to accept Ludovico's suggestion, he and Bishop Becchi would have to renounce their share of the limelight. Because Piero did not find the suggestion at all to his liking, it was easy for Becchi, who liked it even less, to persuade him to turn it down. Rather than inform Ludovico of his decision himself, Piero asked King Ferrante to do it for him. To a man as fearful and suspicious as Ludovico, this could only mean that Florence and Naples were conspiring against him, and he immediately ordered his astrologer to determine if Piero dei Medici brought bad luck. The astrologer must have decided that he did, for not long afterward Ludovico began treating Piero like an enemy to be watched rather than a young man to be guided.

The growing antagonism between them proved an unexpected piece of good luck for Savonarola.

*   *   *

As a young novice in the convent of San Domenico in Bologna, Savonarola had repeatedly criticized the *tiepidezza*—the luke-warm commitment to a life of voluntary poverty—of so many of his fellow monks. Nor, he was fond of recalling, was he the only one to find them wanting. Once when the friars were pray-ing to Saint Dominic, addressing him as *Babbo*, or Father, as was their wont, a disembodied but angry voice snapped back: "I am not your father, and you are not my children."

To be a true son of Saint Dominic, to have his friars live in a manner that would be pleasing to the founder of their order— a manner that would make him proud to call them his chil-dren—these were the first tasks Savonarola set himself after be-ing elected prior of San Marco. The world was all depraved darkness, and it was time to regenerate God's children, he would later write. "It was time, it was time, it was indeed time to adopt a singular way of life."

One great obstacle to such a way of life, however, was the convent itself. San Marco, with its high vaulted ceilings and slen-der ionic columns, its sumptuous library filled with illuminated manuscripts donated by Cosimo, its great brass bell fashioned by Donatello, its frescoed walls and shaded flower beds, was far too grand for monks who had taken Dame Poverty as their spouse. What was needed, Savonarola told his friars, was a new convent more in keeping with their vows. This new convent would be in a remote and lonely place where they could live "as in a sepulcher," dead to all worldly ties and pleasures. Rather than being of marble or sandstone or any other material the world found precious, it would be a simple, low-slung building with small cells divided by partitions made of board or wattle screens. Neither in the cloister nor in the church would there be any arches; the columns would be of undecorated wood or baked brick. The door frames too would be of wood, and in place of iron bolts or keys, there would be wooden latches, so that any thief might enter. The friar's clothing would be coarse and crude, their diet abstemious, their minds free of all carnal long-ing as a result of constant laceration of the flesh. And when men came to the door wanting to speak to a friar, the porter would ask, "Are you simple people? If you are simple, enter; if not, depart, for none enter here but the simple."

Prelates and preachers were chained to earth by love of earthly things, Savonarola thundered. Only a return to the simplicity of the early fathers could save the church! But despite his election as prior, he lacked the power to make his vision of the simple life a reality for his friars. A little over a quarter of a century earlier, the rule under which they lived had been relaxed in order to permit them to own property. Soon afterward, both San Marco and the convent of San Domenico in Fiesole had joined the Lombard congregation. Any change in the rule first had to be approved by the head of that congregation. And even if it were approved, there was no guarantee that Savonarola would be able to effect the desired reforms, for as long as San Marco was affiliated with the Lombard congregation, he could be transferred to another convent of that congregation at any time. If, on the other hand, San Marco were to separate from the Lombards and be reconstituted as an autonomous Tuscan congregation, he would have free rein.

Although the idea of separating first came to him during the weeks following Lorenzo's death, he was too uncertain of how it would be received to speak of it to anyone. Those were weeks of great agitation for him, weeks filled with strange predictions and even stranger visions: a great wind like that described by Elijah, which would strike the mountains; a black cross rising from the midst of Rome and bearing the inscription *Crux Irae Dei* (the "Cross of God's Wrath"); a tempest of wind, lightning, thunderbolts, hail, fire, and hurtling swords, during which an immense multitude was slain. By the time he was ready to discuss the separation the following autumn, constant prayer had convinced him that, like those dreadful visions, the idea of separating San Marco from the Lombard congregation had come to him from God. "*In te Domini confido*, in God is my faith," he told his friars, and he urged them never to cease praying for the new city of the spirit he had begun to build.

But to Ludovico Sforza, who as regent of Milan controlled the Lombard congregation, the proposed separation had noth-

ing whatsoever to do with God's will or the building of a new
city of the spirit. Instead, Ludovico saw it as a pure and simple
bid for power, an insidious attempt to divest the Lombards of
one of their most flourishing convents, thus reducing the importance of the congregation and depriving him of a much-
needed foothold in Florence. The prospect of depriving Ludovico
of a foothold in Florence would have been agreeable to Piero
under any circumstances. Had he been on good terms with Ludovico, however, he might have thought twice before crossing him.
Since by then relations between them were quite strained indeed, Piero did not hesitate to offer Savonarola his assistance.

That December, Savonarola was asked to preach the Advent
sermons in the cathedral. On the night before he was to deliver
his last sermon, he beheld a hand in the heavens grasping a
sword inscribed with the same words that had burst from his
lips the previous Lent: *Ecco gladius Domine super terram cito
et velociter.* The arm to which this hand was attached seemed
to emanate from three faces, which he immediately took to signify the Holy Trinity.

> "The wickedness of my sanctuary cries out to me from
> earth," said one face.

> "Therefore I will visit their iniquities with a rod and their
> sins with stripes," the second replied.

> "My mercy I will not remove from him, nor by my truth
> will I hurt him!" the third exclaimed. "And I will have
> mercy on the needy."

All three voices then joined in a terrible threat of vengeance
unless men repented in time, after which clouds of angels dressed
in white and bearing red crosses came down to earth to offer every
mortal a white robe and a cross. Some accepted; others, whom
Savonarola immediately recognized as "the half-hearted and wicked priests," neither accepted nor allowed others to accept. Whereupon that heavenly hand turned the sword toward earth, and
immediately the air was darkened and swords and hail rained down
and fire and lightning struck the earth, which was at once assailed
by plague, war, famine, and dreadful tribulation. Although the vi-

sion ended with a command to make these things known, Savonarola could not bring himself to describe what he had seen for fear of being ridiculed. In his sermon the following morning, he did what he had done so many times in the past when unsure of how one of his visions would be received: he repeated the words of the Lord without identifying them as such.

Neither in this sermon nor in the others he preached that Advent did he include any attacks on Piero and his government similar to the attacks he had directed at Lorenzo. Not that Piero was any less tyrannical than his father had been. Like Lorenzo, he always appeared in public surrounded by a guard of young toughs who, said the chronicler Piero Parenti, "made the entire city want to throw up." There were also rumors that, like his father, Piero was helping himself to government funds. But Piero had indicated a willingness to press for the separation of San Marco. Since the separation was God's will, he became an instrument of God. And one did not attack God's instruments.

That winter, Savonarola and one of his friars were sent to Bologna to preach the Lenten sermons. In a letter to the brethren of San Marco, Savonarola described the two of them as "very lonely, like two turtledoves who await the coming of spring in order to return to warmer climes." He also made guarded references to the work he had in hand, which was, of course, the separation of San Marco. By the time he returned to San Marco at the end of April, he had decided to send two of his friars to Rome to enlist the support of the protector of their order, Cardinal Oliviero Caraffa.

Fra Alessandro Rinuccini belonged to an old Florentine family. After a lifetime as a businessman, he had elected to replace self-interest with self-transcendence by becoming a brother of San Marco. Fra Domenico da Pescia and Savonarola had been novices together in the convent of San Domenico in Bologna. Although Fra Domenico was a few years older than Savonarola, Domenico had always allowed himself to be guided by his strong-willed friend; never for an instant did he doubt that God spoke through him.

Fra Alessandro and Fra Domenico set out for Rome armed with letters of recommendation from Piero, from his brother the cardinal, and from the Signoria. By the time they arrived at Cardinal Caraffa's palace behind Piazza Navona, the cardinal had also received a letter from Giacchino Torriano, the director general of the Dominican order. Since removing San Marco from the Lombard congregation would increase Torriano's power over this large and flourishing convent, he found the idea very much to his liking. His letter, coupled with Caraffa's long-standing friendship with the Medici, induced the cardinal to present the case for separation to the pope.

The case against separation would be presented by Cardinal Ascanio Sforza. The four friars whom the Lombard congregation had sent to Rome also had the support of many Italian princes, including the Sforza's archenemies King Ferrante of Naples and his heir, Alfonso of Calabria. Because, like Ludovico, every one of these petty tyrants controlled a number of prosperous convents, it had been an easy matter for him to convince them that the separation would be a dangerous precedent. At his urging, they wrote letters to the pope protesting the move.

Overwhelmed by the extent of the opposition, Fra Domenico thought it might be a good idea to demonstrate that God was on the side of San Marco by throwing himself at the feet of the Holy Father and offering to resuscitate a corpse. Where Domenico proposed to find his Lazarus and how he proposed to bring him back to life we will never know. The day before he was to see the pope, the matter was settled.

By then, Alexander VI had grown thoroughly bored with the squabble over separation. Because he was so bored, he found it difficult to concentrate on the arguments of the opposing parties and to decide the merits of their respective briefs. When Cardinal Caraffa arrived at the papal consistory carrying the brief for separation, he was greeted with the announcement that the pope would sign no briefs that day. Rather than accept the pope's decision as final, Caraffa resolved to speak to him again when the consistory was over. As the cardinal had half suspected he would, Alexander reiterated his decision not to sign any briefs. Whereupon the cardinal playfully removed the pope's signet ring from his finger and affixed the papal seal to the brief. Although Alexander protested the cardinal's action, he did nothing to stop him. Probably he was relieved to have the matter settled so effortlessly.

On June 28, Savonarola and Fra Domenico were both permanently affiliated to the convent of San Marco. On November 15, Savonarola was given the powers of a provincial over the newly formed Tuscan congregation. He had won a formidable victory, but in the process he had gained a formidable enemy. Perfidious himself, Ludovico Sforza was constantly on guard against the perfidy of others. Savonarola had gotten the better of him this time; Ludovico intended to make sure that the wily friar did not get the better of him again.

But Savonarola did not know this. To him, his victory was the will of God, a heaven-sent mandate to proceed with the reform of San Marco. Not long after the separation became official, he had a vision in which Saint Augustine, Saint Thomas, and Saint Catherine of Siena revealed to him that of twenty-eight friars who had died at San Marco, twenty-five had been damned, the majority for being unduly attached to their belongings. The vision so terrified his friars that they gave him their gold and silver crucifixes, their illuminated Bibles, and other cherished possessions to sell. The sale brought in 300 florins, which Savonarola promptly donated to the poor. Spurred by his assurance that they were an elite whose ascetic lives would "stupefy" the world and eventually lead to the reform of the entire church, his friars slept on straw mattresses covered with a single sheet, ate the coarsest and crudest of food, wore rough, patched habits, and fasted frequently. One of them, Fra Piero Lotti, until then reputed to be the most sensual friar in the convent, went for three days without eating anything except bread and raw grass.

But this Spartan regime did not suit everyone. Because so many of the friars became ill, their rations had to be increased and their fast days decreased. And there were other difficulties as well. Even before the separation became official, a wealthy Florentine had donated land for a new convent beside a chestnut grove on Monte Cavo above Careggi, and another wealthy citizen had agreed to pay for the erection of the necessary buildings. The younger friars and the novices were enthusiastic, but when their families learned of the plan, they protested that this new convent would be a "slaughterhouse of friars." Though in May 1494 the pope gave verbal permission for the new convent, it was never built.

If parental disapproval could thwart the transfer to Monte Cavo, it could not thwart the rush to enter San Marco at this time. There was a harsh and terrible beauty in Savonarola's vision of an uncompromising asceticism in the service of God that attracted young men uncomfortable with the prospect of a life in the countinghouse, older men who, like Fra Alessandro Rinuccini, had grown weary of that life, and humanists seeking to resolve the conflict between their predilection for Greek philosophy and their desire for Christian salvation. Angelo Poliziano, who had once sung of Orpheus and Eurydice and maidens in May, began attending the weekly discussions of philosophical subjects in the library of San Marco and eventually became a lay brother of the convent. The Jewish scholar Blemet, whom Pico had converted to Christianity, became a friar. More than once, Pico too "came halfway to taking holy orders," but by then he had a concubine. Despite Savonarola's warnings that he was inviting eternal damnation by resisting his vocation, Pico could not bring himself to substitute the pleasures of the scourge for the pleasures of the bed.

Many other scholars and artists who, like Pico, were not prepared to take holy orders were drawn to Savonarola by the resemblance between the humanist conviction that some great upheaval was at hand and his apocalyptic warnings. To the end of Michelangelo's life, it seemed to him that he could hear the friar's voice. Under the spell of that voice, all of Botticelli's latent religiosity surfaced. In *Calumny*, painted in 1494, only the pale green sea in the background recalls *The Birth of Venus*. Fraud and Treachery, who twine roses in Calumny's hair; Calumny herself, who drags a half-dressed young Innocence by the hairs of his head; Remorse, who is pictured as a black-clad old crone; and the golden-haired but curiously unseductive Naked Truth, who raises her arm heavenward in a gesture of faith—all reveal the influence of the friar's sermons.

In 1492, those sermons had warned of the coming scourge—

the sword of the Lord swift and sure over the peoples of the earth. By 1493, Savonarola had persuaded himself that the only hope remaining to the righteous was that the sword would soon strike the earth. "O Lord!" he cried that Advent, "Thou hast dealt with us as a wrathful father. Thou hast cast us out from Thy presence. Hasten then the chastisement and the scourge, that it may quickly be granted us to return to Thee!"

By the beginning of 1494, it seemed as if God were preparing to oblige him.

Although Ludovico Sforza had entered into his alliance with Charles VIII under the impression that he could manage the king, it had not taken him long to realize that it was Charles who would manage him. The first hint of what lay ahead came in September 1491, when the king's special envoy, Jean Cloppet, spoke of the Neapolitan expedition as if it were a foregone conclusion. Taken aback, Ludovico "had nothing particular to propose." But the conversation made him uneasy. It was, after all, one thing to use the threat of a French invasion of Naples to keep King Ferrante in his place and quite another to have to deal with an actual invasion. That winter, Ludovico fluctuated between his fear of France and his fear of Naples, alternately encouraging Charles and seeking to dissuade him.

Meanwhile, Charles went ahead with his plans. Because Naples was a fief of the papacy, only the pope could invest its rulers. Although Innocent VIII had promised the investiture to Ferrante's son Alfonso, Charles announced that he would seek it for himself. So that he would be free to send his soldiers to Naples, he decided to placate his enemies. In January 1493, he signed a treaty with Ferdinand of Spain. On May 21, he signed a treaty with Maximilian, the heir-elect to what was left of the Holy Roman Empire.

Having wangled a promise of nonintervention from Maximilian, the king announced plans to invade Italy as soon as possible. He also set up a five-member commission to handle Italian affairs and sent his special envoy, Perron de Baschi, to Milan to ask Ludovico to serve as the Italian director and chief of the expedition. After speaking to Ludovico, de Baschi would visit the other Italian rulers in order to demand free passage for French troops, as well as arms and money. The ambassador would then go to Rome, where he would demand the investiture of Naples for his king.

As Ludovico saw it, there was only one possible reply he could give de Baschi. With unctuous enthusiasm, he declared himself ready to provide arms and equipment for the expedition that very day if such was the king's wish. Soon he was reveling in the power his new role gave him. "The time has come," he told the Florentine ambassador, "when from all over Italy men will look to me to remedy the evils now being prepared."

King Ferrante tried to make him understand the dangers to which a French invasion would expose Lombardy and begged him not to allow matters to reach the point at which it would be impossible to stop the French. Piero decided to send a special ambassador to King Charles.

Francesco della Casa had his first audience with the king on June 28. The 24-year-old second Charlemagne, whose plans had set all Italy on its ear, was a tiny, almost dwarflike figure with an ugly face, large, lusterless eyes which saw badly, an enormous hooked nose, and thick lips which were always open. He stuttered and had a convulsive twitching in his hands which were never still. Because he had been a delicate and sickly child, much effort had gone into developing his frail and unprepossessing body, and almost none into developing his mind.

The king understood so little of what was going on, della Casa told Piero, that the ambassador felt ashamed for him. He seemed to be pulled now this way, now that, and he was in the habit of listening to the first person who came along. As a result, his court was in a state of total confusion. The two men who exerted the greatest influence on the king were Etienne de Vesc, seneschal of Beaucaire, and Guillaume Briçonnet, bishop of Saint Malo. Both were men of low estate, disliked by the other members of the court, and both were eager to use their connection with the king to make their fortunes. Della Casa had thought to bribe them, but Ludovico had bought them off months before. Hence, the only thing left to do was either to agree to the king's demand for free passage through Florentine territory or to refuse it. In either case, there was nothing to worry about. Since there wasn't a man of sense at court who supported the expedition, it had very little chance of ever materializing.

Gentile Becchi and Piero Soderini, the two ambassadors Piero sent to join della Casa that September, were also convinced that the expedition was an impractical and foolish fancy. Aside from a taste for glory and a few young women, the king's only interests were hunting, dogs, birds, and horses, said Becchi. So devoted was Charles to these pleasures that some thought he wanted Naples in order to hunt there, and the ambassador was inclined to agree with them. Nevertheless, he urged Piero to consent to the king's demands without delay, meanwhile assuring King Ferrante that Florence had no intention of ever making good on its commitments. But the normally slippery Ferrante refused to be a party to this particular deception, and without Ferrante's approval, Piero would do nothing.

Neither Piero's *si* (that is, his consent to the demands of King Charles) nor his *no* would move or remove the Neapolitan expedition, Bishop Becchi told him that November. But his *si* would help Florentine merchants who were dependent on trade with France for a livelihood. And the bishop reminded Piero that his enemies had more money, more soldiers, and more arms than he did. By then, all three ambassadors had decided that in labeling the expedition a chimera, they had reckoned without the strange little king's indomitable will.

Charles had already put aside between 500,000 and 600,000 ducats to pay the Italian mercenaries he planned to hire. That Christmas, he announced plans to go to Lyons to prepare his infantry for its march across the Alps. At about the same time, Duke Ercole of Ferrara entered into an alliance with the king, and the Venetians promised not to assist the enemies of France. But still Piero could not bring himself to take a stand. One reason for his indecision was his distrust of Ludovico, whom he quite rightly suspected of having designs on Pisa. Another was his conviction that Lorenzo would have wished to keep the French out of Italy. A third was his tie to the Orsini. Since childhood, he had been taught to place great store on his connection with them. Because, as his wife and mother-in-law were constantly reminding him, Virginio Orsini, the head of the clan, was King Ferrante's chief condottiere, it would be unseemly for one who was part Orsini himself and also married to an Orsini to support the French. On the other hand, as Bishop Becchi was constantly reminding him, every Florentine Signoria took an oath never to oppose the French, and Florentine commercial interests depended on good relations with France.

To take his mind off his problems, Piero decided to organize a great tournament, one which would rival the tournaments his father and his uncle Giuliano had given in their youth. While he was organizing this tournament, Florence had the severest snowstorm within anyone's memory. From the singing of the *Ave Maria* on the morning of San Sebastian's Day to the singing of the *Ave Maria* the following morning, the snow and the wind did not abate; the streets were impassable in many places, and "there was not the slightest crack or hole, however small, that did not let a heap of snow into the houses."

Feeling the need for further diversion, Piero summoned Michelangelo and ordered him to carve a statue from the snow in the courtyard of the Medici palace. Although Piero was delighted with the sculptor's handiwork, neither Michelangelo's elegant snowman nor the preparations for the tournament could long drive the specter of the French invasion from his mind. On January 29, Ferrante of Naples died and was succeeded by his son, Alfonso of Calabria. On February 2, a letter signed by all three ambassadors arrived from Amboise. Charles had ordered Florence to declare itself without delay, they told Piero, and he had demanded that the Florentines send him 300 lances, 1000 foot soldiers, and 6 galleys—all to be maintained at their expense. A six-hour conference with Briçonnet had produced no results. The king was adamant.

By then, a mood of grim foreboding had settled over Italy. In the Piazza del Castello in Milan, a blind Augustinian preacher went so far as to warn Ludovico from the pulpit: "My Lord, beware of showing the French the way, else you will repent it."

In many places, men found images of the saints covered with sweat. Near Arezzo, armed phantoms were reported riding through the sky astride giant steeds. On the outskirts of Siena,

a lone pilgrim shouldering a heavy cross through the silent countryside suddenly turned and shook his fist at the city. In Puglia
one night during a thunderstorm, a flash of lightning revealed
three suns surrounded by clouds.

Although the disaster that menaced the peninsula could easily have been predicted without the aid of heaven, to most people it appeared as the fulfillment of Savonarola's prophecies—
flagellum Dei, the scourge of God, with which he had been
threatening them these many years. In the warm glow of their
credulity, whatever doubts of his prophetic calling Savonarola
still had were soon forgotten. Like some celestial newscaster,
he ascended the pulpit of San Lorenzo that Lent, prepared to
deliver further bulletins from on high.

A new Cyrus was even then preparing to cross the Alps, he
told the people. God would be his guide and his leader, and he
would pass over the rocks and the mountains, and the fortresses
would fall before him, and no arm would be capable of resisting
him. At the news of his approach, said Savonarola, the leader of
Florence would behave like a drunken man doing the opposite
of what ought to be done. But Savonarola did not blame him for
behaving thus. "O Church, because of you this storm has aris-
en!" he cried the first Friday of Lent. Using passages from the
story of Noah, he devoted part of each sermon to the building
of a mystical ark in which the righteous might take refuge from
the approaching flood of foreign invaders. Its length would be
faith, its width charity, and its height hope; and each plank and
nail had its own meaning. On the Monday after Passion Sunday, he ended his sermon with a cry of *Cito! Cito!* ("Quickly!
Quickly!") to indicate that the scourge would soon be upon
them, and they dared not tarry.

"Let all hasten to enter the Lord's ark," he declared on Easter Sunday. "Noah invites you all today; the door stands open;
but a time will come when the ark will be closed, and many
will repent not having entered therein."

A few days before Easter, Piero dei Medici had mounted his horse
and headed for the Pisan countryside. He no longer wanted to

think about the salvation of the state or the city or the peace of Italy, he told Ser Piero Dovizi. On March 6, Charles VIII had entered Lyons. The king's court was in as great a state of confusion in Lyons as it had been in Paris, della Casa told Piero. But in all this confusion, one thing was certain: before the year was over, Charles would be in Italy. And della Casa warned Piero that Ludovico's agents were poisoning the king's mind against the Florentines.

Meanwhile, Alexander VI issued a papal bull granting the investiture of Naples to Alfonso of Calabria. There would be no benefices for Cardinal Giovanni unless Florence continued to support Alfonso, the pope warned Piero. Unwilling to desert Naples for other reasons besides the benefices for his brother, but convinced that he must do something to appease the French, Piero recalled Becchi and Soderini and sent two new ambassadors to Lyons in their stead. The new ambassadors were Guidantonio Vespucci and Piero Capponi.

Of Vespucci's integrity, there was never any doubt. Capponi's integrity was another matter. Piero Capponi came from a family whose bank in Lyons had always been a rival of the Medici bank. Like Bernardo Rucellai and Paolantonio Soderini, he had had his differences with Lorenzo. Like them, he was even more unhappy with Piero. As a merchant and banker who depended on good relations with France for his livelihood, he considered Piero's pro-Neapolitan policy a disaster. But Capponi was an expert dissembler who, said Guicciardini, "sometimes wavered and sometimes shammed." Consequently, Piero had no inkling of his true feelings. Because Capponi was a gifted speaker, Piero sent him to Lyons with instructions to tell King Charles that the king's father, Louis XI, had commanded the Florentines to abandon their alliance with France in favor of a league with Naples. Since the league was still valid, Florence could not in good conscience renounce it.

However, says Comines, Capponi did not stop there. Instead he "underhandedly informed the French of what needed to be done in order to have the city of Florence turn against Piero. And he made his allegations more bitter than was the case." Every day, della Casa told Piero, there were reports that rather than seeking to improve relations between the king and the Florentines, Capponi and his son were making them worse. But when Briçonnet offered Capponi money and equipment if he would lead an uprising, Capponi discussed the offer with his fellow ambassadors and immediately sent word of what had happened to Piero. Soon afterward, however, he undercut this act of seeming uprightness by telling the French that the one way to undermine Piero's regime was to expel all Florentine merchants from France.

That April, Lorenzo and Giovanni dei Medici, Piero's third cousins, were also involved in a plot to overthrow him. The cousins had quarreled with Lorenzo over money and with Piero over women. Both were openly and unashamedly pro-French. To keep them that way, Charles VIII had made one his chamberlain and the other his steward and given them each a sizable pension. Using Bernardo Rucellai's son Cosimo as an intermediary, the two began negotiations with Ludovico Sforza. When, soon afterward, they entertained Briçonnet's son at their villa, Piero became suspicious and ordered them arrested. Following a trial before the Council of Seventy, they were condemned to life imprisonment and the confiscation of all their goods. On reflection, however, Piero decided that it did not look right for him to be so harsh to his own flesh and blood. At his insistence, they were released from prison and banished to their villas outside the city with the proviso that they remain there indefinitely. To make sure they did, Lorenzo's two small children were taken as hostages.

To the French, Piero's treatment of his cousins seemed further proof of his pro-Neapolitan bias. That June, Charles dismissed all three Florentine ambassadors at his court and expelled the agents of the Medici bank in Lyons. The French planned to send their heavy artillery to Genoa by boat, the ambassadors warned Piero before leaving. As soon as the fleet arrived, he must be sure to remove all beasts of burden from the shore, or they would be used to transport the artillery inland.

Charles had planned to be in Italy by the end of June. But the little king had brought a gaggle of mistresses with him to Lyons, and he kept finding new ones to replace those he discarded. As a result, it was not until September 3 that he and his army forded the Graviere, the little Alpine brook that separated the kingdom of France from the duchy of Savoy. The king's white silk standard announced that he had come *voluntas a Deo* ("by the will of God") and *missus a Deo* ("as a messenger of God"). Waving flags and shouting *Francia! Francia!*, all Savoy turned out to greet him. On September 5 he entered Turin; on the sixth, he was in Cheri; on the ninth, he reached Asti, where Ludovico and his father-in-law, Ercole of Ferrara, were waiting to greet him. Never had Ludovico felt prouder or more important. "It is I who brought him to Italy," he kept repeating, "and it is I who will bring him still further."

To console the king for the loss of the mistresses he had left behind in Lyons, Ludovico sent him a bevy of beautiful and experienced courtesans from Milan. Charles had made his cousin Louis of Orleans admiral of the French fleet. After the fleet arrived in Genoa that summer, there had been a number of skirmishes with the Neapolitan fleet anchored in the nearby Bay of Spezia. The skirmishes ended with the Neapolitans being forced to retreat to Livorno. The day before Charles entered Italy, they returned and landed troops at Rapallo. On learning that the Neapolitans had occupied the town, Louis brought his fleet into position opposite Rapallo. Under cover of the French artillery, he sent ashore a contingent of Swiss and Genoese mercenaries, who drove out the Neapolitans and retook the town. As Italian mercenaries had always done, the Genoese plundered the inhabitants and then let them go. The Swiss sacked Rapallo and slaughtered everyone in their path, including the sick and the injured.

The sack of Rapallo sent a shudder through Italy. Every town within range of Louis's artillery wondered if it would be next. When news of what had happened reached Florence, Piero left for Pisa to prepare the defense of the port. But the Florentines had little faith in his ability to defend either Pisa or them. Savonarola had told them that the king of France was the scourge of God against whom all defense was futile, and it was to Savonarola that they turned for guidance.

He had not spoken to them from the pulpit since Easter. When he heard that the French had come, he announced that he would preach in the cathedral on September 21, the Feast of Saint Matthew. That morning, a rumor that Charles had entered Genoa began circulating in Florence.

Long before Savonarola was scheduled to speak, not an empty seat was to be found in the cathedral. By the time he ascended the pulpit, the crowd had spilled over into the Piazza del Duomo and the surrounding streets. He stood for a moment contemplating that multitude of upturned and frightened faces, the men on the left, the women on the right, with a curtain running the length of the nave to separate them; then he slowly opened his Bible to the point in the story of Noah at which he had left off the previous Easter: "*Ecce ego adducam aquas super terram.* Behold, I bring a flood of waters upon the earth."

As the words resounded through the cathedral and were relayed to the vast throng in the piazza, Pico felt a cold shiver run through the marrow of his bones, and his hair stood on end. All around him, he could hear men and women shrieking and sobbing. Seeing them so overcome, Savonarola too began to sob, and it was a long time before either he or his audience was sufficiently composed for him to continue. When the sermon ended, the crowd filed out of the cathedral in silence and "only half alive."

Michelangelo wondered if he ought not to leave the doomed city while there was still time. Since the snowstorm, he had been living in the Medici palace. Living in the palace with him was a lutist by the name of Andrea Cardiere. Cardiere had been a great favorite of Lorenzo's. While Michelangelo was trying to make up his mind about leaving Florence, Cardiere had a dream in which Lorenzo appeared to him wearing a tattered black cloak, and he asked Cardiere to go in search of Piero and to warn him that he would soon be driven out of his house, never to return. But Cardiere, who knew how little it took to arouse Piero's violent temper, could not bring himself to be the bearer of such dreadful tidings. A few nights later, Lorenzo once again appeared to him wearing the same threadbare black cloak, and he gave Cardiere "a mighty blow" for not having done as he was bidden. Prodded by Michelangelo, Cardiere then went in search of Piero, but Piero refused to take the dream seriously. To Michelangelo, his refusal was the last straw. Without a word to Piero, he left the Medici palace and headed for Venice.

At the time Charles was supposed to be entering Genoa, he was still in Asti recuperating from an attack of smallpox. It was not until October 6 that he felt well enough to leave. Two days before he left, another of his envoys arrived in Florence. Like Perron de Baschi and all the other envoys who had preceded him, he demanded that the Florentines grant Charles free passage through their territory and that they break with Naples. He also warned the Signoria that this was the last time his king intended to make these requests. The Signoria, which did nothing without Piero's consent, kept postponing its reply until the envoy left in disgust. "Everyone thought it had been a piece of folly and rashness not to give the safe conduct readily," said Luca Landucci.

Charles retaliated by banning all Florentine merchants from his kingdom. Competition from British textiles had already left a sizable number of artisans and *sottoposti* without steady work. Deprived of their most lucrative market for gold thread, cloth of gold, and silk, many of the workshops in the neighborhood of the Porta Santa Maria and along the Via Maggiore shut down, which in turn caused the shops dependent on them for orders and material to shut down. As the rate of unemployment grew, so did criticism of Piero. The people cursed him "body and soul," said the Venetian ambassador. Had he been the Grand Turk himself, they could not have hated him more. If things went on this way, it was only a matter of time before there would be riots in Florence.

To protect himself against an uprising, Piero doubled the troops around the Bargello and instituted a night watch. But he continued to fear the worst, especially after his cousins Lorenzo and Giovanni slipped out of the villas in which they had been under house arrest and headed for Piacenza, where the French were expected momentarily. In a futile effort to take his mind off his problems, Piero began spending "whole days in the street publicly playing football." And this only reinforced the by then almost universal conviction that he was a mere "pumpkinhead," a "pod without seeds," who "lacked the gravity required for a person in his position."

The city was on the verge of revolution, Piero's cousins told Charles when they arrived in Piacenza. If the king came to Florence, the people would hail him as their liberator for they bore "as much good will toward the house of France as hatred toward Piero." The two brothers could not have chosen a more opportune moment to speak to the king. For days, Charles had been trying to decide whether to proceed to Naples via the Romagna or via Tuscany. After speaking to them, he decided to go via Tuscany. On October 20, the first French troops crossed into Florentine territory at Pontremoli on the river Magra. From there, the road to Florence ran through a desolate section of the northern Apennines known as the Lunigiana. It was protected by a number of fortresses which had been taken from Genoa during Lorenzo's time. Of these, the most impregnable were the fortress of Sarzana, with its neighboring citadel of Sarzanella, and the fortress of Pietrasanta. On October 22, the French arrived at the gates of Sarzana. Charles, who wished to direct the siege of the fortress himself, left Piacenza the following morning. Ignoring the advice of his physicians, who feared that his meager frame would not be able to support the load, Charles insisted on wearing a full suit of armor.

When Piero heard that the French had invaded Tuscany and were headed for Florence, his first thought was to resist. But when he asked for money for troops and provisions, he found no one willing to give it to him. To resist the power of France was to invite ruin, said one of the twelve procurators in charge of the city's finances. Piero's brother-in-law Paolo Orsini was a paid condottiere of the republic. Not knowing what else to do, Piero sent Orsini to the defense of Sarzana. But Orsini had only 300 foot soldiers and fewer than 100 horsemen. Without reinforcements and provisions, they couldn't be expected to make much of a difference.

After the conspiracy of the Pazzi, when Lorenzo was being blamed for an expensive and unpopular war with Pope Sixtus IV and his ally King Ferrante, he had decided to go to Naples alone to negotiate with the king. His courage had impressed both his countrymen and Ferrante, and he had returned to Florence in triumph bringing "public peace and private security." With the impetuosity Lorenzo had always feared, Piero decided to emulate his father by going to King Charles. Taking only his cousin Lorenzo Tornabuoni and a few close friends with him, he set out for the French camp. In a letter to the Signoria, he pictured himself as a voluntary sacrifice upon the altar of peaceful relations with France, prepared either to exculpate himself or to receive due punishment in his own person rather than in the body of the republic. And he entreated the priors "by the fidelity and affection" which they owed to the ashes of his late father—their Lorenzo—to remember him in their prayers.

After being admitted to the French camp at Sarzana on October 30, he told Comines he considered himself lost in Florence unless he did everything the king wanted. In his eagerness to please, he readily agreed to turn the fortresses of Sarzana, Sarzanella, and Pietrasanta over to the French for the duration of the Neapolitan expedition. He also agreed to give them the fortresses at Pisa and Livorno, as well as an indemnity of 200,000 ducats.

The French, who had asked for all these things as a first step toward negotiating a more equitable settlement, were flabbergasted and made fun of Piero behind his back "for granting such great things which they had never expected." Ludovico Sforza, who showed up at the French camp at this time, was equally flabbergasted. Ludovico's nephew Gian Galeazzo had died a few weeks earlier—of immoderate coitus, according to Guicciardini; of a slow poison administered by his uncle, according to a physician who had seen the corpse. With Gian Galeazzo out of the way, Ludovico had lost no time having himself proclaimed duke of Milan. Had French troops not been in the city at the time, he would never have gotten away with it, for Gian Galeazzo had left a son. But Ludovico was not one to feel obligated to his benefactors. Now that he had what he wanted, he would have liked nothing better than to see Charles and his troops return to France. The part of the Lunigiana between Sarzana and Pisa was a marshy and unhealthy place in which it was impossible to provision an invading army. Because the road was so narrow in many places that a wagon with two pieces of artillery thrown across it could effectively bar the way, Ludovico had expected the Florentines to hold off the French at least until the following spring, by which time he hoped they would decide to abandon the Neapolitan expedition and go home. Now that the way through Tuscany lay open to them, he decided to make the best of a bad bargain by asking Charles to turn the fortresses and the city of Pisa over to him. When Charles refused, he left in a huff, resolved to make common cause with his old enemy Alfonso of Calabria.

The death of Gian Galeazzo had made the French so distrustful of Ludovico that they probably wouldn't have given him the fortresses under any circumstances. At the time he showed up at the French camp, however, there was also another reason for refusing to oblige him. Because Piero had no official title in Florence, they had been calling him *Il Gran Lombardo*, "the Great Money Changer." Not at all sure this *Gran Lombardo* had the right to cede the fortresses to them, they insisted that he send Lorenzo Tornabuoni back to Florence to have the agreement ratified by the Signoria.

Even before Piero ceded the fortresses to the French, Charles had announced that he would be in Florence by the middle of November. On Wednesday, October 29, when Piero was still awaiting a safe conduct to the French camp, the city learned that the French had sacked the town of Fivizzano some twenty miles inland from Sarzana and defeated the fortress.

"O Florence, the time for singing and dancing is at an end; now is the time to shed floods of tears for thy sins!" Savonarola cried in his sermon that Saturday. He also reminded his terror-stricken audience that not two full years had elapsed since he had said to them: "*Ecco gladius Domine super terram cito et velociter.* Not I but God was responsible for bringing this prediction to you," he told them. "And behold it has come, and it is coming!"

God had sent him to them in this their hour of affliction

that he might show them the way to atone for their sins, he continued. "O sinners, O obstinate ones, see how merciful God is, see how even now he wishes to lead you into the ark.... Repent, repent without delay. Repent, for only repentance can save you. Believe this friar when he tells you that all else is in vain."

That Sunday the cathedral once again echoed with the cry of repentance, and he repeated it so often and so vehemently that once again, as had happened two years earlier, it seemed that the vein in his neck must surely burst. On Monday, November 2, with French quartermasters already in the city marking the doors of the houses in which they wanted their officers lodged, he continued to preach repentance and the life of spiritual perfection represented by the ark as the only bulwarks against the deluge soon to engulf them. Although nowhere in any of these sermons did he mention Piero dei Medici by name, he did remind the people of the many times he had told them that "these governments were not pleasing to God." And his need to present himself as all of a piece made him forget that in those first days after the separation of San Marco, he had announced his intention to do all that Piero might desire.

After Piero left for the French camp, criticism of his regime grew more open and more intense. Although he had boasted that the new Signoria which took office on November 1 was more to his liking than any previous one, it immediately became evident that two of the priors were opposed to him. At their insistence, the Signoria decided to send seven ambassadors to overtake Piero and keep an eye on him. With him or without him, they were to inform King Charles of the "incredible happiness" their countrymen derived from the news that His Majesty intended to come to Florence. Like most Florentine ambassadors, the seven were all members of the *cittadini principali*. One of them, Francesco Valori, had twice been gonfalonier and had recently become a disciple of Savonarola. The ambassadors left Florence on November 2. On November 3, Lorenzo Tornabuoni reached the city with the agreement concerning the fortresses and the 200,000 ducat indemnity.

Even before the Signoria had finished discussing the matter, all Florence seemed to know the terms of the agreement. The general opinion was that by surrendering the fortresses, Piero had delivered the city into the hands of a foreign power. Some excused him on account of his youth and blamed Piero Dovizi and his other advisers for misleading him, but the majority blamed Piero himself. All that Florence had conquered in 100 years had been ceded in a day by this thoughtless and stubborn young man. What galled them most was that, with the arrogance so typical of him, he had made the agreement without consulting the Signoria. Neither his father nor his grandfather nor his great-grandfather had ever shown such disregard for the city's institutions.

As was customary in times of great danger, the Signoria decided to convoke a *pratica*, an ad hoc committee of leading citizens whose function was to advise the priors. Although almost everyone summoned to the *pratica* had once been a supporter of the Medici, by then the great majority were disgruntled. A few, like Bernardo Rucellai and Piero Capponi, had been opposed to Piero for years. Normally, when a *pratica* was convened, no one spoke until invited to do so by one of the priors and then only in support of a measure the Signoria had proposed. Since these were not normal times, Luca Corsini, one of the two priors hostile to Piero, decided to ignore this unwritten rule. Things were going from bad to worse; the city was in a state of anarchy; some strong measure was required, he declared. Taken aback by his presumption, some of his more conventional colleagues began to murmur and cough until he grew so flustered he could not continue. No sooner had he sat down than Jacopo dei Nerli, a member of the sixteen gonfaloniers of the companies, a body second in importance only to the Signoria, rose to endorse what Corsini had said. But dei Nerli too quailed under the coughs and stares of his colleagues, and his embarrassed father asked the assembly to excuse his son because he was "young and foolish."

During this exchange, Piero Capponi grew increasingly restive. Immediately after Tanai dei Nerli had finished apologizing for his son, Capponi rose to address the assembly. "Piero dei Medici is no longer fit to rule the state!" he shouted. "The republic must provide for itself. Let us have an end to this government of boys!" And he urged the Signoria to send new ambassadors to King Charles to explain that Piero had caused all the evil and that the city was well disposed toward the French.

"Let honorable men be chosen to give a fitting welcome to the king," he continued, "but at the same time let all the captains and soldiery be hidden away in the cloisters. And besides the soldiery, let all men be prepared to fight in case of need, so that when we shall have done our best to act honestly toward this most Christian monarch, we may be ready to face him and show our teeth if he should try us beyond our patience."

Since his return from France, Capponi had become a frequent visitor at San Marco. Either because he admired Savonarola or because he thought that the mention of the friar's name would lend authority to what had been said, he concluded with a plea to "send Father Girolamo Savonarola as one of the ambassadors, for he has gained the entire love of the people."

Like a torch hurled into a pile of dry tinder, Capponi's speech set the members of the inert and directionless *pratica* ablaze. Soon everyone was speaking out against Piero. As Capponi was walking home from the meeting that evening, his friend Piero Vettori told him that he had spoken so well and so forcefully that should Piero dei Medici return to Florence, he might be in danger of losing his life.

"Do you really think that?" Capponi asked him.

"Yes, I do," Vettori replied.

"In that case," said Capponi, "it is to be hoped that he will not return."

IV

THE REVOLUTION BEGINS

Despite Capponi's eloquence, three of the priors remained loyal to Piero. But these three could not keep the *pratica* which convened the following morning from choosing five ambassadors to negotiate a more favorable settlement with the king. As was to be expected, Piero Capponi was one of the ambassadors. Like him, three of the others were *cittadini principali* dissatisfied with the rule of the Medici. As Capponi had urged, the fifth ambassador and the one named to head the delegation was Savonarola.

Popes and cardinals might involve themselves in politics; indeed, they had to if the church was to survive. As soldiers of God, members of the religious orders were expected to remain aloof from all worldly business. Hence, Savonarola's first impulse was to refuse the appointment. But everyone he spoke to, including his friars, urged him to accept. Had he been sure of his own mind, nothing they said could have influenced him. Since he wasn't, he allowed himself to be persuaded; and he sought to play down the political implications of what he was doing by insisting that he was going to the king "for reasons of charity." Rather than discuss the status of private persons, by whom he obviously meant Piero dei Medici, he would confine himself to imploring the king to guarantee the safety of the city. But if the self-deception so characteristic of him was at work here, it played no part in his assessment of what had happened in Florence.

"The Lord has heard your prayers and caused a great revolution to end peaceably," he told the Florentines before setting out. His fellow ambassadors were to leave for the French camp the following morning with all the pomp and circumstance obligatory on these occasions. Rather than be a party to such frippery, he left on foot that evening in the company of his alter ego Fra Domenico da Pescia and two other friars. The Signoria, which could not bear to see one of its ambassadors travel with so little panache, sent richly caparisoned mules after him. Savonarola, of course, sent the mules back to Florence.

When he left the city, French quartermasters were still marking the houses in which they wanted their troops lodged, and French men-at-arms and infantrymen were going through the streets saying, "Open there," not caring whether the owners of the houses they commandeered were rich or poor. Inevitably, the presence of so many Frenchmen exacerbated "the commotion and the suspense" in which the city had been living since Charles had begun his march through Tuscany. "Everyone was excited and distrustful, continually expecting great events," said Luca Landucci. The news that a falcon had died after hurling itself against the side of the Palazzo della Signoria was immediately taken to presage the imminent fall of the city's chief governing body. The disappearance of two fingers from the statue of Saint John the Baptist was also considered portentous, as was a lightning storm a few days earlier. Even more unsettling were the rumors that the French "had come with the idea of sacking the city," and that Piero had offered Charles 100,000 ducats if the king would keep him in power. Among the *cittadini principali*, there was talk of deposing Piero forthwith and replacing him with his cousin Lorenzo.

That evening, Luca Corsini and Chimenti Cerpellone, the two priors most hostile to Piero, urged the Signoria to recall Lorenzo and his brother Giovanni to the city. The gonfalonier, an easygoing man, "inclined to let matters take their course," raised no objection, but the three priors still loyal to Piero immediately sought to table the motion. Realizing that he would get nowhere with them, Corsini rushed off to ring the great bell which would summon the people to a *parlamento*. His opponents rushed after him. Before they could restrain him, however, he had managed to ring the bell several times. Since it was not yet ten o'clock, the long, drawn-out "mooing" of the bell sent people streaming into the piazza from every quarter of the city. Most assumed they had been called to a *parlamento*, but hearing nothing more and seeing no movement inside or outside the palazzo, "they returned home wondering what had happened."

Matters in Florence were getting out of hand, Piero's friends told him. They urged him to return to the city as soon as possible. Before setting out, he ordered Paolo Orsini to mobilize his troops and follow him to Florence. To the contemporary historian Jacopo Nardi, it seemed clear that Piero wanted Orsini's troops in the vicinity because he intended to take over the Palazzo della Signoria, make himself an absolute ruler, and exile or put to death all who opposed him. Piero was so demoralized by then, however, that he may very well have wanted the troops nearby because he had no idea of what sort of welcome to expect when he reached Florence and wished to be prepared for the worst.

He arrived at his palace on the Via Larga toward evening on November 8. Whatever his private misgivings, he put up a brave front in public. To Luca Landucci, who was in the crowd before the Medici palace, he seemed "in the best of humors." Another chronicler, Botticelli's brother Simone Filipepi, thought him "as happy as could be." He had settled everything satisfactorily with the king, he told the crowd. As his father had done after reaching an agreement with King Ferrante, he sought to heighten the impression of victory by throwing sweetmeats to the people and ordering wine distributed. But the coolness of their response disheartened him and may have made him wonder how he would be received at the Palazzo della Signoria.

During their two months in office, the priors and the gonfalonier ate and slept in the palazzo. When Piero arrived there later that evening and asked to speak to them, he was told that they were at dinner and could not be disturbed. Had he been more certain of his hold on the city, he might have taken umbrage at this rebuff. As it was, he agreed to return at a more convenient time. Piero Parenti, who, like Jacopo Nardi, was an ardent foe of the Medici, believed that Piero had originally intended to set fires in various corners of the city that night and to use the resulting commotion as a pretext for seizing control of the state. But, said Parenti, his brusque treatment at the hands of the Signoria and the coolness of the people's reception made him realize how little support there would be for such a move. Consequently, he decided to begin storing arms in the garden of his palace. He also sent word to Paolo Orsini to move his troops to the San Gallo gate. That the presence of 500 horsemen and a large number of foot soldiers would give rise to all sorts of rumors and intensify the suspicion that he was up to no good does not seem to have occurred to him. Orsini's troops were already ensconced at the gate, and the church bells were summoning the faithful to vespers when, at five o'clock the next day, Piero once again set out for the Palazzo della Signoria with an entourage that included members of his family, his chief adviser, Ser Piero Dovizi, his footmen, and a number of armed infantrymen.

By then, the opposition had managed to win over two more priors, so that the only one still loyal to him was Antonio Loreno. Fortunately for Piero, that Sunday it was Loreno's turn to be *proposto*. As such, he had custody of the keys to the campanile and the exclusive right to propose measures for discussion. Hence, he had been able to block consideration of measures hostile to Piero and to prevent any of the priors from circumventing discussion by summoning the people to a *parlamento*. But he had not been able to prevent Jacopo dei Nerli and a few other equally headstrong young men from coming to the palazzo armed, locking the doors, and standing guard behind them. When Piero arrived and asked to be admitted, dei Nerli opened the wicket and told him to dismiss his entourage and enter alone through the postern gate. Rather than accept such humiliating terms, Piero raised his finger in a gesture of contempt and turned to leave. He and his party had taken only a few steps when they were summoned back by *Il Buschetta*, the priors' mace bearer.

He had been sent after them by Antonio Loreno, who was determined to admit the entire party. But Loreno had reckoned
without Luca Corsini. No sooner did Corsini realize what Loreno
was up to than he bounded down the stairs. With his help, dei
Nerli and his colleagues were able to drive Piero away once
again, not, says Nardi, before Jacopo dei Nerli had used "hurt-
ful words" to him.

Since it was a Sunday and not yet dark, the piazza was filled
with late afternoon strollers. Seeing Piero refused entrance to
the palazzo a second time, some of them called out to him to
take himself off and not defy the will of the Signoria. Others
wagged the tips of their hoods at him, and a few street urchins
and ne'er-do-wells started to hiss and throw stones. For whatever reason—perhaps because he had never been exposed to
street violence before and did not know how to handle it, perhaps because he sensed that this was the beginning of the uprising he had been dreading for so long—the normally bold and
stalwart Piero became so unnerved by the stones and the catcalls that he tried to lose himself in the midst of his followers,
and the entire company slunk off without ever turning to face
their tormentors. As they were leaving the piazza with the mob
at their heels, they ran into the sheriff. Seeing what was happening, he ordered his soldiers to come to Piero's aid. This so
enraged the crowd that they seized the sheriff, and, after dis-
arming and robbing his men, led him to his palace, where they
compelled him to release the prisoners in his custody.

Encouraged by the fracas in the piazza, the seven priors opposed to Piero forced Antonio Loreno to surrender the keys to
the campanile. While a few of the priors took turns ringing the
great bell, the rest stood at the windows of the palazzo crying,
Popolo e libertà! At the sound of the bell, men and women all
over the city snatched whatever weapons they could find, including billhooks, spits, and stakes, and rushed off in the direction of the palazzo. Very few had any clear idea of what the
tumult was about. However, the cries of *Popolo e libertà!* led
them to believe that whatever was going on was directed at Piero
dei Medici, and they wished to be part of it.

The bell had only just begun to sound the alarm and the peo-

ple were still streaming out of their houses when Francesco
Valori, one of the seven ambassadors sent to King Charles on
November 2, came riding into the city on his mule. Valori's long
white hair and ascetic countenance belied his impulsive and fiery temperament. Without pausing to determine the reason for
the uproar, he galloped off in the direction of the Piazza della
Signoria shouting, *Popolo e libertà!* Because, says Guicciardini,
"he was an honest man and loved justice and because he was
known to have opposed Piero, the entire population received him
with great rejoicing."

Still astride his mule, he launched into a tirade against Piero
and his "disgraceful" agreement with King Charles. Having inflamed both his audience and himself, with a cry of *Abbaso le
Palle!* ("Down with the balls!"), he galloped off in the direction
of the Medici palace, followed by an ever-growing multitude.
By then, the Tornabuoni and some of Piero's other relatives had
armed themselves, and with cries of *Palle! Palle!* had also rid-
den off in the direction of the Via Larga. Seeing them, Piero
mounted his horse to come into the piazza with his men, start-
ing several times and then stopping. Both Nardi and Guicciardini
said that shortly before this, Cardinal Giovanni had left the palace with a contingent of armed men shouting, *Palle!* Ignoring
the jeers and catcalls that greeted them on every side, he and
his men rode in the direction of the Piazza della Signoria until,
at the Church of San Bartolomeo, they collided with Valori and
his followers and were driven back. However, Luca Landucci
tells us that rather than coming to Piero's aid, Giovanni "rode
down the Corso as far as Orto San Michele, crying *Popolo e
libertà!* like all the rest and declaring that he had separated from
his brother." "The only consequence," said Landucci, "was that
the Piazza turned against him, menacing him with the points
of their weapons and shouting 'traitor!'"

In either case, by the time Giovanni escaped from the mob
and made his way back to the Medici palace, Piero was gone.
On learning that a proclamation had been issued forbidding anyone to aid or abet him on pain of death, he had mounted his
horse. Taking his 16-year-old brother Giuliano with him, he
headed for the San Gallo gate, where Paolo Orsini and his sol-

diers were awaiting him. The proliferation of palaces in the center of the city had forced many of the poorer artisans and *sotto-posti* into the ramshackle neighborhoods on the outskirts of town. When Piero reached the neighborhood around San Gallo, he decided to make one last effort to gain a constituency by reminding the humble working men he met of their traditional loyalty to his house and offering them gold in exchange for their support. In the excitement of the moment, he seems to have forgotten that the chief victims of the unemployment resulting from his anti-French policy and the rise in prices resulting from his father's hated "white money" had been those same workingmen. Rather than follow him, they countered his cries of *Palle!* with cries of *Popolo e libertà!* until he realized that the only thing to do was to ride through the San Gallo gate and head for Bologna.

At the time he left the city, his brother Giovanni was kneeling at a window of the Medici palace "with joined hands praying heaven to have mercy." Luca Landucci, who caught sight of him there, was touched, considering him to be "a good lad and of upright character," neither of which he really was. After being denied asylum by the monks of San Marco, he managed to lay hands on a Franciscan habit ample enough to encompass his bulk. In this disguise, he too fled in the direction of Bologna.

And thus ended the sixty-year rule of the Medici.

With Piero and his brothers gone and their followers in hiding, the thoughts of the people turned to looting and burning. Led by Jacopo dei Nerli, a group of soldiers pillaged the house of Piero's legislative notary, Ser Giovanni della Riformazione. Joined by an eager crowd, they then rushed off to the house of Antonio di Bernardo, the official in charge of the public debt. Next they stripped the palace of the sheriff. Since the booty was immense, the number of soldiers and civilians bent on plunder began increasing geometrically, until finally concern for their own residences led the priors to issue a proclamation forbidding any more houses to be pillaged on pain of death. So that there would be no mistaking the priors' intent, the sixteen gonfaloniers of the companies patrolled the city, carrying lighted torches and crying *Popolo e libertà!* Except for the wounding of one of the

Tornabuoni who announced that he was changing sides by shouting *Popolo e libertà!* and the death of a poor demented servant of the sheriff whom the mob attacked when he came into the piazza shouting *Palle!* there was no further violence that night. Soon afterward, the Signoria recalled all those who had been exiled by the Medici for political reasons, including Piero's cousins, Lorenzo and Giovanni. So that none might question their devotion to the popular cause, the cousins replaced the Medici balls on their palace with the arms of the people and changed their name to Popolani.

The day Piero was driven out of Florence was also the day King Charles reached Pisa, and it was there that he met with Savonarola and the other four ambassadors sent to negotiate with him. Rather than speak in Italian from notes as he usually did, Savonarola had prepared a set speech in Latin for the occasion. In the speech, he assured Charles that although in obedience to God's will he had never mentioned the king by name, it was to him that he had been alluding when for the past three years he had warned the people of God's intention to reform His church with a great scourge. "At last you have come, O King," he told Charles. "You have come as God's minister, the minister of His justice. With joyful heart and cheerful countenance we welcome you."

Charles could barely sign his name, and he had, of course, never learned Latin. But he liked the sound of the preacher's words, and when they were translated into French for him, he liked them even better. Rather than allow Savonarola to leave with the others, he asked to have a private audience with him.

Like every ambassador who had dealt with Charles, it could not have taken Savonarola long to recognize the pitiful inadequacy of the slavering little monarch whom he had hailed as God's scourge. Fortunately, there was an easy way out for use on such occasions, namely, that God can and does employ unworthy instruments for the working out of His own higher designs. If, as seems likely, Savonarola chose this way, he would have no need to confront the disconcerting possibility that he

had been mistaken in calling Charles the minister of God's justice or the even more disconcerting possibility that, if he was
mistaken about Charles, he might also be mistaken about other
messages he had supposedly received from God. Instead, he
could continue to believe in the king's divine mission, continue
to believe that this dim-witted and misshapen little prince was
both the new Cyrus destined to scourge Italy for its sins and
the second Charlemagne who would cleanse the church, conquer the infidel, and unite the world in one flock under one pastor.

The house in which Savonarola and the king met that Sunday
was one of the many houses in Pisa belonging to Piero dei
Medici. Like the armed citadel which stood on the site of what
is now the public gardens, the ornately carved Florentine lion,
or *Marzocco*, on a marble pillar at the end of one of the bridges
spanning the Arno, and the red lily of Florence on the facades
of so many of the public buildings, it reminded the Pisans that
theirs was not a free city. That afternoon, when Charles was on
his way to mass, he and his courtiers were followed by a huge
crowd of men and women, many with tears in their eyes and
all crying *Libertà! Libertà!* While the king was at dinner in the
Opera of the cathedral that evening, a delegation of Pisan citizens presented him with a petition for *Libertà*. Sensing the king's
bewilderment, one of his councillors, either, says Comines, "because he had promised to do so, or because he did not understand what they were requesting," urged the king to grant the
petition. The good-natured little king, who had no clear understanding of the implications of the word *Libertà*, replied that
he was content. No sooner was this reply relayed to the vast
crowd gathered under the windows than a great cry of "Bravo!"
went up, and everyone rushed off in the direction of the Arno.
After knocking that proud symbol of Florentine power the *Marzocco* off its pedestal and dragging it in the mud for a while, the
crowd flung it into the river. All the rest of that night they
roamed through the city, effacing the Florentine lilies on the
buildings and sacking the houses of the Florentine officials who

had so recently been their masters. Hearing the mob approach, Piero Capponi and his friends sought refuge in the Capponi bank. They were saved from what Guicciardini was pleased to call the "malice and perfidy of the Pisans" by the arrival of the king's guards.

Although the rebellion of the Pisans appeared to be spontaneous, it wasn't. When Piero dei Medici had agreed to turn the fortresses over to King Charles, Ludovico Sforza, it will be remembered, had urged the king to turn Pisa over to him. Angered by the king's refusal to do so, he resolved to find some other way to lay hands on the city. After thinking about it, he decided that the best way would be to encourage the Pisans to ask Charles for their liberty. Once free of Florentine domination, they would be so weak that they would have no alternative but to turn to Ludovico for assistance. It would then be only a matter of time before he made himself their ruler.

Ludovico's son-in-law, Galeazzo di San Severino, represented him at the court of King Charles. The king had no sooner arrived in Pisa than, at Ludovico's instigation, San Severino invited a number of the town's leading citizens to his quarters. They must rebel against the Florentines and ask Charles for their liberty, he told them. Seeing themselves advised by such a powerful man as the son-in-law of the duke of Milan, the Pisans lost no time convening a council and going en masse to petition the king.

The loss of Pisa deprived the Florentines of their principal access to the sea. It was of such great and inestimable harm to Florence, said Guicciardini, that many citizens wondered if it wasn't more important than the expulsion of the Medici which occurred the same day. Human nature being what it is, only a handful of Florentines were willing to concede that the Pisans had as much right to expel them as they had to expel the Medici. The elation that had followed Piero's ouster gave way to an angry, suspicious mood. Once again, there were rumors that Charles planned to sack the city, to which were added rumors that the king intended "to restore Piero and perhaps even become master of Florence himself."

That Tuesday, someone reported passing men-at-arms and

infantrymen belonging to Piero on the road to the Porta alla Croce. In less than half an hour, the news had spread to the farthest corners of the city; everyone was in arms and "men of all classes rushed to the Piazza...with deafening cries of *Popolo e libertà!* Although the story was later found to be untrue, Luca Landucci, who recorded it in his diary, thought that the Lord had permitted such a demonstration to take place in order to show the French the sort of people they were dealing with.

Even before the demonstration occurred, Charles had decided to put off his triumphal entry into Florence until the city had quieted down. The Signoria took advantage of the interim to learn more about the king's intentions. But all Charles would tell the various delegations sent to question him was that everything would be settled *dentro la gran villa* ("within the great city").

On Monday afternoon, November 17, he entered Florence through the San Frediano gate. As early as the previous Tuesday, the Signoria had directed all the citizens "to do him honor on the day of his arrival by going toward the Porta San Frediano in the finest array they could muster." Resplendent in the ermine-collared crimson coats that were the badge of their office, the eight priors and the gonfalonier awaited him on a special platform just inside the gate. Eight drummers pounding on four barrel-sized drums joined two fifers to produce the ear-splitting racket that heralded the approach of his infantrymen. His Swiss guards carried steel halberds, and their officers wore helmets surmounted by thick plumes. In their gold-embroidered vests, his archers of the royal bodyguard gave the impression of being "all counts or at the very least seigniors." Many of his other archers were so tall they seemed "more like wild beasts than men." His cavalry wore engraved armor and carried gold-embroidered velvet banners. His trumpeters were all in violet and gold livery; his foot lackeys wore cloth of gold and velvet.

When the entire company had passed through the Porta San Frediano, the tolling of the city's myriad bells announced the approach of the king. He rode into view astride an immense black charger with one medium-sized eye, and he held his lance at rest on his hip as a sign that he had come as a conqueror in triumph. Over his jewel-studded armor, he wore a jacket of gold brocade topped by a purple velvet cloak. Four of his knights supported the silken baldachin over his head. "A beautiful sight," said Guicciardini, "but little appreciated because our people were full of fear and terror."

The sun was beginning to set when, after crossing the Ponte Vecchio and stopping at the Piazza della Signoria where masked men on stilts who kept themselves aloft with the aid of poles made to look like walking sticks vied with elaborately bedecked triumphal cars for his attention, Charles finally reached the steps of the cathedral and was helped from his horse. Astride that splendid black charger, with the baldachin held above his head, the king had seemed a truly majestic figure—the very image of a conquering hero. When he dismounted, the people realized to their surprise that "he was in fact a very small man." "The tiniest man you ever saw," said the chronicler Bartolomeo Cerretani, "with a white complexion, hair midway between red and platinum, an immense head, blue eyes, a huge nose, and black velvet slippers cut in a way that made his feet resemble those of an ox or a horse."

It was rumored that Charles wore these hoof-shaped slippers because he had a sixth toe. Wishing to flatter him, his courtiers wore slippers cut in the same fashion. Although the Florentines could not help snickering at this outlandish footwear, it did not keep them from shouting *Francia! Francia!* as the king and his velvet-shod barons padded down the aisle which had been cleared for them between the double row of torches leading to the main altar. "All Florence was there," wrote Luca Landucci, "either in the church or outside." Whether all Florence included Cristoforo Casale and his brother Martino, there is, of course, no way of knowing. Given the brothers' circumstances, it seems unlikely that it did.

Cristoforo Casale was Pico's secretary; Martino Casale managed Pico's household. On September 1 of the previous year, Pico had lent Cristoforo a large sum of money. Soon afterward, when Pico revised his will, he divided this sum into two equal parts. One part he bequeathed to Cristoforo, the other to Martino. He also left any domestic animals on his estates at the time of his death to Martino. As Pico's secretary, Cristoforo knew of these bequests, and it wasn't long before he and his brother began thinking of how best to hasten the day they received them. The simplest way, they decided, was to poison their employer. Rather than give him one lethal dose, which would be likely to arouse suspicion, it seemed safer to poison him gradually. The important thing was to pick a time when most people were too preoccupied with other matters to pay much attention to what happened to Pico. That November, when everyone's thoughts were on the French invasion, seemed unusually propitious. Soon after the brothers slipped the first minuscule dose of poison into Pico's food, he began running a fever which attacked his viscera. Since none of the doctors called to his bedside suspected foul play, the brothers grew bolder. By November 13, Pico had ingested so much poison, his physicians could not find his pulse for almost four hours. On November 16, he asked Savonarola to witness a codicil he wished to add to his will.

Although Pico was only 32 and had taken it for granted that he had many years ahead of him, like his doctors, he assumed that his illness was the result of natural causes. Since this made it the will of God, he felt obliged to accept it "with the joyous assurance of one directing his steps toward a celestial homeland." Whereas in the past, he had always ignored Savonarola's demand that he accept his divine vocation by taking holy orders, now that the end was near, he asked the friar to receive his vows and permit him to be buried in the Dominican habit.

Among the many women who had become Savonarola's ardent followers was Camilla Rucellai, a middle-aged and somewhat foolish patrician matron noted for her incomprehensible prophecies. Two years earlier, Camilla had predicted that Pico would take the habit "at the time of the lilies." In those days, everyone had assumed that she meant in the spring, when the lilies were in bloom. Now it seemed clear that even if she hadn't realized it herself, she had meant the time when every house in the city would welcome the French with blue banners embroidered with the gold lily of France.

Pico died just as the first French troops prepared to march through the San Frediano gate. The Queen of Heaven herself had come to him during the night, he told those at his bedside when he died, and she had assured him of salvation. The assurance of salvation which meant so much to him was small comfort to his friend Girolamo Benivieni. So utterly desolate was Benivieni, so incapable of accepting a world without Pico, that he could think of no reason to go on living.

To Savonarola, such inordinate grief, or in fact any grief, was a repudiation of God's will. While Pico was alive, Savonarola had sometimes threatened him with divine retribution and had sometimes even prayed to God to punish him a little (though not, Savonarola would later insist, as much as He had done, depriving him of the great glory he would have known had he lived). Now that Pico was dead, the friar asked himself if one who had resisted his vocation until the edge of the grave and had moreover been guilty of innumerable sins of the flesh could expect salvation. Nor is it difficult to see why this should have concerned him. As prior of San Marco, he was, after all, constantly seeking new recruits. If Pico could be saved without ever having to expiate his sins, might not other potential recruits feel free to resist their divine vocation and take concubines? If, on the other hand, Pico were consigned to the fires of hell despite his numerous good deeds—the alms he had distributed during his lifetime, the bequests to hospitals and convents in his will— would this not discourage other sinners from doing good? Only God could provide a satisfactory answer, but during those first hectic days after Charles entered Florence, His chosen prophet was too busy with other matters to consult Him.

The enthusiasm with which the people had hailed the king as their liberator and shouted *Francia! Francia!* quickly dispelled. For one thing, there was the strain of playing host to all those Frenchmen. "You may think what it is like to have all this crowd in our houses," said Luca Landucci, "with everything left as usual and with the women about and having to serve them with whatever they need at the greatest inconvenience." Then, too, said Guicciardini, "the citizens were very frightened, for they were unaccustomed to arms and had a very powerful army in their midst."

The army would not leave until a satisfactory treaty had been negotiated with the king. But negotiating such a treaty was no simple matter. Because Charles had entered Florence with his lance on his hip, he insisted that, according to the laws of France, the city belonged to him. Not only did he wish to leave a representative in Florence, but he demanded the return of Piero dei Medici.

After Piero's ouster, Ludovico Sforza had hastened to congratulate the city and had promised to side with the Florentines against whosoever threatened to deprive them of their newly found liberty. As usual, Ludovico had ulterior motives, but the priors were too in need of help to care. On the evening of November 20, they sent Bernardo Rucellai to Milan to ask Ludovico to do what he could to prevent Piero's return. On November 21, they convened a *pratica* to draft a suitable reply to the king. While this *pratica* was in session, two Frenchmen asked to be admitted to the palazzo. Since they refused to believe that no outsiders could be admitted during a *pratica*, what Landucci calls "a little disturbance" arose in the piazza. Immediately the rumor spread that the men had been sent by M. de Bresse, one of the king's councillors known to favor Piero, and that they had orders to break up the meeting. This in turn revived the old fear that the French were planning to sack the city. Without a word being said, all the shops closed, and everyone went home, "one sending his silk goods, another his woolen goods away to his house or some place of security."

Seeing all this activity and suspecting "they knew not what," the French took up arms. While the cavalry seized the Porta San Frediano and the bridges so as to be able to escape in the event of an uprising, the infantry mobilized before the king's quarters in the Medici palace. When the members of the *pratica* heard that the shops had closed and the French were mobilizing, they decided that further discussion was pointless. A delegation must be sent to the king to inform him of the city's determination to fight to the last man rather than accept Piero. Before this dele-

gation went to the king, however, it might be a good idea for
Savonarola to have a word with him.

After his return from Pisa, Savonarola had likened the government of the Medici to a government of robbers and devils
holding captive the Florentine spirit. The cause of the revolutionaries was the cause of God, he had told the people. Hence it
was surely God's will that he warn the king of the consequences
of reinstating Piero. He would say later that when he asked to
see Charles, the soldiers at first refused to admit him. But without his knowing exactly how it happened, God took him by the
hand and in an instant brought him into the royal presence. During his first meeting with the king, Savonarola had warned him
of the terrible scourges which would be his lot should he ever
forget the task for which the Lord had sent him to Italy. Now
that he knew how the king's mind worked, he evidently decided
that further blackmail would not be amiss. When the king stood
up to pay him respect, as was the custom of the kings of France
in the presence of a holy man, Savonarola took a small brass
crucifix from his bosom. Holding this crucifix aloft and pointing to it as he spoke, he bade the king respect instead "Him
who is king of kings and lord of lords and will ruin you and your
army if you do not desist from your cruel intent regarding this
city."

The king, who had asked for Piero's return only because M.
de Bresse and some of his other councillors had urged him to do
so, could see no reason to invite God's wrath for the sake of
someone he scarcely knew. If the Florentines did not want Piero,
that was that, he declared. In his eagerness to remain on the
good side of the Lord, he also reviewed the terms of the proposed treaty and was in general so agreeable that Savonarola left
the palace under the impression that everything had been settled.

Soon afterward, he had a revelation concerning Pico, and he
was so delighted with this revelation that he decided to share it
with as many people as possible. "I have a secret to reveal to
you," he told the vast crowd gathered in the cathedral that Sunday, "a secret which I had not wanted to tell you before because
I was not as certain of it as I have been for the past ten hours."

Each of you, I believe, knew Count Giovanni Pico della Mirandola who lived in Florence and died a few days ago. I tell you that his soul through the prayers of the *frate* and others and because of the good works which he performed in his lifetime is in purgatory. *Orate pro eo* ["pray for him"]. He was late in coming to religion in his lifetime, although it was hoped that he would and therefore he is in purgatory.

A dispassionate observer might have been wary of the close correspondence between what God had revealed to the preacher and the preacher's own hopes and interests. But if there were any dispassionate observers in the cathedral that Sunday, history has lost track of them.

Pico's murderers would not be apprehended for another four years, and then only as the result of an investigation into a very different matter. Nor were they the only malefactors to benefit from the French occupation. Never had there been so many robberies, murders, and assaults. Although Savonarola had come away from his meeting with the king under the impression that the king would soon leave, Charles continued to put off signing a treaty. The longer he procrastinated, the shorter grew the temper of the people. That Monday there was a riot in the Borgo Ognissanti, one of the working-class districts on the outskirts of town.

The riot began when some boys came upon a French soldier leading an Italian prisoner of war through the streets, forcing him to beg for his ransom by tugging at the knotted end of a rope fastened around his neck and body. Goaded by the indignant crowd which had gathered around the pair, the boys swooped down on them and cut the rope. The prisoner, of course, immediately fled, followed by a veritable army of Frenchmen. But their hoof-shaped slippers were not equal to the chase, and it wasn't long before they lost sight of him. In the ensuing free-for-all, pots and pans, sticks and stones, ashes and tiles, and boiling water rained down on the king's men from every rooftop and window, and as a result, says Piero Parenti, "the greater part of them, armed soldiers though they were, gathered together trembling like women."

The next day the king announced that he would sign the treaty. Before doing so, however, he asked to have the terms read aloud to him once more. All went well until it came to the indemnity. Although a few days earlier Charles had said he would accept 120,000 florins, 50,000 to be paid at once and the remainder before the end of July, he suddenly decided that he wanted 150,000 florins. When Domenico Bonsi, Guidantonio Vespucci, Francesco Valori, and Piero Capponi, the four syndics sent to negotiate with him, told him that this was more than the republic could pay, the king threatened to sound his trumpets, which was another way of saying he would mobilize his troops and sack the city. "If you sound your trumpets, we will ring our bells," Piero Capponi replied. Snatching a copy of the treaty from one of the secretaries, he waved it in the king's face, tore it in half, and stalked out of the room followed by the other three syndics. To everyone's surprise, Charles called all four syndics back. After chiding Capponi for being a bad *ciappon* ("capon"), the monarch, who only a few minutes before had insisted that he would yield no more on any point, accepted the lower indemnity and signed the treaty. The next day on the altar of Santa Maria dei Fiore, before Jesus Christ, on the word of a king, he swore to observe all the articles he had signed. But still he made no move to leave. On November 27 the Signoria, in desperation, asked Savonarola to have another talk with him.

Once again, Charles was delighted to see him. Once again Savonarola seems to have decided that the only way to deal with the featherbrained fellow was to threaten him with divine vengeance. "Most Christian king," he told Charles, "hearken now to the voice of God's servant. Pursue thy journey without delay. Seek not to bring ruin on this city and thereby arouse the anger of the Lord against thee."

Although some said that Charles left the next day because one of his captains insisted that he leave, to most Florentines the king's departure was yet another proof of their friar's ability to work miracles. Surely the fasts and the good works he had imposed on them had caused them to find grace in the eyes of the Lord! "God has loved you, Florence, wherefore he has acted compassionately toward you," he told them. They must show themselves worthy of God's love by opening the shops, gathering alms for the poor, and living together in peace and harmony. But the only time they ever lived together in peace and harmony was when they were facing some great external danger. With Charles gone and a new government needed to replace that of Piero, the goddess of discord was busier than ever.

The impetus for the revolution that unseated Piero had come from the *cittadini principali* led by Piero Capponi, Bernardo Rucellai, Paolantonio Soderini, the dei Nerli, and Piero's two cousins Lorenzo and Giovanni dei Medici. They were all wealthy, ambitious men who loved power, and it was their intention to control the new government. Two days after the French left, when the Signoria convened a *pratica* to advise it on the people's wishes concerning a new constitution, it was these citizens, not the people, who dominated the proceedings. Since all important offices, including the Signoria, were chosen by lot from leather bags containing the names of all eligible citizens, everyone agreed that the lists would have to be purged of Medici supporters who, if elected, might vote to reinstate Piero. A resolution introduced by the *cittadini principali* proposed that twenty *accoppiatori*, or commissioners, be chosen to draw up the new lists. During the twelve months it would take to do this, the *accoppiatori* would act as an interim government, selecting the eight priors and the gonfalonier every two months, as well as the members of the two most important government commissions: the Ten of *Balia*, entrusted with waging a war for the recovery of Pisa, and the Eight of the Ward, responsible for all measures necessary to prevent Piero's return. So that the people would not feel left out, the resolution also proposed that the hated "white money" be abolished and that all these new measures be submitted to a *parlamento* for its approval.

"Whoever said *parlamento* said ruination" was an old Florentine proverb. Like the *ekklesia* of ancient Athens, the *parlamento* was an assembly of all the citizens. Unlike the *ekklesia*, which met regularly, it was convened only when there was a crisis. Invariably, the citizens were asked to grant extraordinary powers to a commission set up to deal with the emergency. Since approval was given by shouting Yea! and there was no discussion from the floor, it was easy for a few loudmouths scattered through the crowd to drown out the nays if the group in power wanted them drowned out. As a result, every new group that came to power, including the *ciompi*, the oligarchy, and the Medici, had begun its reign by convening a *parlamento*. The *parlamento* summoned to the Piazza della Signoria on December 2, 1494, was as easily manipulated as these others had been. "We know how things are done on such occasions," wrote Piero Parenti, who was in the piazza that Tuesday. "Some people shouted yea, and this was considered enough."

The next day, the twenty *accoppiatori* were chosen, and they in turn chose the Ten of *Balia* and the Eight of the Ward. As far as the *cittadini principali* were concerned, the revolution was over.

The people, on the other hand, felt betrayed. They had thought they were fighting for their liberty; they realized to their chagrin that they had fought "not for the liberty of the people, but for preserving in power the same men who had ruled before." The only difference was that instead of having one tyrant to contend with, they now had twenty! Nor did it help matters to see the Eight of the Ward spend so much money to celebrate their entry into office that they were dubbed the "Eight of Enjoyment."

The city's precarious economic situation aggravated the discontent. Although Savonarola had urged the reopening of the shops, the loss of Pisa and the uncertain business outlook kept many shops closed. As if this were not frustrating enough, there was the question of the so-called *Bigi*—the men who had supported Piero to the very end and were now seeking his reinstatement. Like the many citizens who had been exiled by the Medici and were then returning to Florence, the people, said Guicciardini, "thirsted for revenge." Piero Capponi, Francesco Valori, and the other leaders of the *cittadini principali*, however, would not hear of it for the simple reason that they too had collaborated with the Medici for many years—fifteen of the twenty *accoppiatori* had served on Medici commissions at one time or another as had any number of other *cittadini principali* in the new government. Once the *Bigi* were eliminated, what was to prevent the people and the returning exiles from banding together to drive them out?

On the other hand, the people might very well drive them out for refusing to act. Obviously, something had to be done to contain popular unrest. But agreeing on what ought to be done was another matter. To a small faction headed by Paolantonio Soderini, it seemed clear that the only way to avoid a popular uprising was to grant the people more of a say in the government. As a punishment for giving Ser Piero Dovizi a box on the ear, Soderini had been excluded from government office until the summer of 1494, when he had been named ambassador to Venice. Immediately after the revolution, he had been recalled to Florence. Since he and Bernardo Rucellai had opposed Piero from the start, Soderini had assumed that, like Rucellai, he would be one of the twenty *accoppiatori*. But Piero Capponi and Francesco Valori did not trust him, and they joined together to block his appointment. Hence, Soderini had a score of his own to settle with those in power.

While in Venice, he had had a chance to study the Venetian form of government. Like many aristocrats, he considered it superior to the Florentine, if only because it had lasted for over 200 years without any of the revolutions and coups d'état so common in Florence. Of the many excellent features of the Venetian system, the one Soderini thought most applicable to his native city was the *Consiglio Grande*, or Great Council. Although Florence had never had such a council, it did have two smaller councils: the 250-member Council of the Commune and the 300-member Council of the People. Soderini proposed a change in the constitution that would replace these councils with a much larger Great Council, which, like its Venetian counterpart, would pass on legislation, elect magistrates, and levy taxes. And he wished to give shopkeepers and artisans far greater representation in this new council than they had in either of the existing councils.

Although by then Piero Capponi, Francesco Valori, and the other *cittadini principali* recognized the need to make some concessions to avoid a popular uprising, sharing power with shopkeepers and artisans was not one of the concessions they had in mind. Because Soderini realized that he would never overcome their opposition to a *governo popolare* by himself, he decided to seek the help of Savonarola, who, said Piero Parenti, "had such authority with the people that whatever he said had to be approved." If Savonarola could be induced to present the case for a Great Council from the pulpit, the *cittadini principali* would be forced to accept it, and Soderini would increase his power at the expense of those who had blocked his appointment to the *accoppiatori*.

Savonarola too wished to increase his power, not for reasons of personal advantage or revenge, but in order to continue the work of spiritual renewal, for which, he was convinced, God had sent him to Florence. As a result of one of those sudden intuitions which were responsible for so many of his pronouncements, and which he seldom bothered to examine closely, he decided that a popular government would be more apt to devote itself to spiritual purification than would the existing oligarchy. The first time he linked spiritual renewal and popular government in one of his sermons was on December 6, when he assured his congregation that God would give them the grace to find a good form for their new government, either as the Venetians had done or in some better way to which He would inspire them. Still in the grip of this new revelation, which seemed to "consume his bones and compel him to speak," the following day he urged them to pass a law making it impossible for anyone to establish himself as their head, "in such manner that the others would have to bow down before him and acknowledge him as their superior."

Later that same week, a large sum of money was found hidden under coal and heaps of nails in the customs office. Under torture, Antonio di Bernardo, the official in charge of the public debt during Piero's reign, and Ser Giovanni della Riformazione, who had been Piero's legislative notary, admitted that the money found in the customs office was government money which they had hidden there when the revolution began. Meanwhile, more government money was found hidden in a convent in Pistoia. In response to the public outcry, Antonio di Bernardo was hanged at the windows of the *Casa del Capitano* on Friday morning before dawn and remained hanging there until eight that evening. The people were eager to see Ser Giovanni hanged too, but Savonarola rescued him by calling for a universal peace to wipe out past offenses. "I tell you this and I command you in the name of God," he declared. "Pardon everyone."

That was on December 14, in the course of what came to be known as his great political sermon, a sermon to which all the officers of the government were invited. Women and children, on the other hand, were instructed to stay at home. Given the intense public interest in the friar's sermons, says Jacopo Nardi, it would have been unfair to have them occupy places which could be occupied to better advantage by the more intelligent (that is, the adult male) members of society. But even without the women and children, who normally constituted from one-third to one-half of his audience, the great cathedral was filled to overflowing when Savonarola entered the pulpit that Sunday.

Although his call for a universal peace was pleasing to the *cittadini principali*, there were other parts of his sermon which must have made those among them who had turned to him for help wonder if it had been wise to place themselves under obligation to a friar. There was, for instance, his appeal to the Signoria to pass a law against sodomy, "that accursed vice for which Florence was infamous throughout Italy." Although he conceded that gossip could have exaggerated the extent of the perversion, he insisted that the law be merciless, in such manner that every last offender be stoned and burned. In the interests of spiritual purification, which was, after all, the sine qua non of his program, he also asked the Signoria to pass laws against poetry, gaming, drinking, indecent dress in women, and "all those things which are pernicious to the soul's health."

On the other hand, his support for the Great Council could not have been more unequivocal. There was no better form of government than that of the Venetians, he declared. Florence ought to follow the example of Venice, leaving out those things which were not suitable to its way of life, such as the Doge, and being sure that artisans were in some way made eligible for office.

God had inspired him to speak thus, he told the 13,000 men in the cathedral. If they heeded his words and acted in good faith, he could promise them, on God's behalf, remission of all their sins and great glory in paradise. He did not wish, however, to impose his ideas on them. They had in their city sixteen gonfaloniers of the companies, each responsible for a different section of the city. Let every citizen meet under the standard of his particular company. Then let each company present the form of government that its citizens decided upon. Thus, there would be sixteen plans. From these sixteen let the gonfaloniers choose the four that seemed best and most stable and bring these before the magnificent Signoria. "There, after the Mass of the Holy Spirit has been sung, they will choose one of the four, and know that without a doubt, that one will be from God."

Such popular participation in government was a far cry from what the *cittadini principali* had had in mind when they had conspired to overthrow Piero. On the other hand, there was so much support for the friar's recommendations that they dared not oppose them openly. What they did instead was to solicit plans for constitutional reform not from the citizens at large, as he had suggested, but from the members of the various government commissions, including the *accoppiatori*, the Ten of *Balia*, and the Eight of the Ward. By then, all of these worthies knew they would have to accept the Great Council. What men like Piero Capponi and the dei Nerli hoped to do was to limit its functions and power. But just as Savonarola had outwitted Lorenzo dei Medici and Ludovico Sforza, so now he outwitted them. While they debated the makeup of the Great Council at the palazzo, he continued to preach in the cathedral.

He began by disposing of the rumor that he was Soderini's mouthpiece. "What I told you yesterday in my sermon, don't think anyone persuaded me to do so," he declared on December 15. He went on once again to picture the riches and the glory that would accrue to Florence if the citizens followed his advice. If, on the other hand, they ignored him: "I tell you, city of Florence, that I see a great evil hanging over you and your ultimate inundation."

The message was loud and clear, and it reverberated in the palazzo. On December 19, members of the various government commissions adopted the plan for government reform proposed by the Ten of *Balia*, whose most influential member was Paolantonio Soderini. Before submitting the plan to the Council of the People and the Council of the Commune for final approval, the commissioners had it read aloud to Savonarola in the presence of the Signoria. In one of the rejected plans, Piero Capponi had suggested that the method of electing the Signoria be postponed, for in the course of one or two years, some flaws in the constitution might emerge.

In a speech which seemed to echo Capponi, Savonarola assured the Signoria that it was enough to fix on a plan that was good in general. Its shortcomings in particular cases would be recognized in due time and corrected and eliminated at leisure. If this was intended to placate those who, like Capponi, had doubts about the new government, it didn't. As Luca Landucci put it in his diary: "One wished it boiled, another roasted. One agreed with the friar; another was against him."

Those who agreed with Savonarola believed that his every word came from God; those who opposed him thought that a friar had no business mixing in politics. Although the question of clerical intervention in politics was a sore point with him, he realized that he would have to answer their objections. Like Jesus, on whom he was beginning consciously to model himself, he began his Sunday sermon with a parable, the parable of a young man who leaves his home to go to sea. At a port he begins to fish. When his skill increases, he is given a boat so that he may go out to sea to catch bigger fish. Before he knows it, he is on the high seas. Realizing that he can no longer see the shore, he begins to complain to the master of the boat. And then Savonarola paused, and, as he had done so many times before, looked out over the vast throng in that stark, gray cathedral.

"O Florence," he cried,

...the young man who went out on the high seas and complained that he was out of sight of the haven stands here
before you....The Lord has driven my barque into the open
sea....The wind drives me forward and the Lord forbids my
return....Last night I communed with the Lord and said:
"Pity me, O Lord, and lead me back to my haven....I will
preach if I must, but why must I meddle with the government of Florence?"

"If thou wouldst make Florence a holy city, thou must establish her on firm foundations and give her a government
which favors virtue."

"But, Lord, I am not sufficient for these things."

"Knowest thou not that God chooseth the weak of this
world to confound the mighty? Thou art the instrument, I
am the doer."

Then was I convinced and cried, "Lord, I will do thy will;
but tell me, what shall be my reward?"

"Eye hath not seen nor ear heard?"

"But in this life, Lord?"

"My son, the servant is not above his master. The Jews made
me die on the cross, a like fate awaits thee."

"Yea, Lord, let me die as Thou didst for me."

Then He said: "Wait yet awhile; let that be done which must
be done, then arm thyself with courage."

There were times when he was so overcome by the import
of what he was saying that he had to ask permission of his audience "to rest awhile in this storm."

How much of this was art and how much artless, he scarcely
knew himself. In either case, there was no denying its effective-
ness. That Monday the Council of the People passed the reform
bill. On Tuesday it was passed by the Council of the Commune.
In place of the two councils, Florence would now have a 3100-
member Council of the Commune and the People, or Great
Council. As a concession to Piero Capponi, who had pleaded

for a senate modeled on the Venetian *Pregadi*, the Great Council would appoint a Council of Eighty to advise the Signoria and choose ambassadors and commissaries. The Eighty would discuss and pass upon all provisions approved by the Signoria before they were submitted to the Great Council for final approval. Since the Great Council could do nothing without a quorum of 1000 men and there was no place in the palazzo large enough to accommodate such a crowd, plans were made to build a Great Hall modeled on the Sala del Gran Consiglio in Venice.

Besides making it impossible for one man to seize control of the state, the Great Council gave shopkeepers and artisans far more of a share in governing the city than they had had before. On the other hand the *sottoposti*, the so-called People of God because they belonged only to the celestial body politic, continued to be denied all earthly power. However, their exclusion from government, which Savonarola, like most members of the upper and middle classes, defended as necessary to prevent disorder, did not keep them from being among his most fervent supporters. He might not want them in the Great Council, but he had, after all, opposed Lorenzo's "white money"; he was constantly demanding alms and other assistance for the poor, and in addition his uncanny ability to foretell the future was well-known.

Because he was so unquestionably the real ruler of Florence, the same day the Council of the Commune passed the reform bill, it also passed all the other laws he had demanded, including a law against sodomy. The first time an offender was arrested, he would be exposed on the outer wall of the Palace of the Bargello for one hour with his hands bound behind him to one of the iron rings and a placard on which his crime was written placed on his breast. The second time, he would be fastened to a pillar. The third time, he would be burned. Nor did Savonarola see any contradiction between this law which he had demanded and his announcement that Sunday that God desired to give Florence a head and a king for its government. "And this new head is Jesus Christ, He wishes to be your king."

With Christ as king of Florence and Savonarola as His prime minister, the ship of state would surely move toward the port—

that is, toward the peace that Florence would enjoy after its tribulation. But even as the friar exulted in the prospect of peace under the rule of Christ, Ludovico Sforza was doing his utmost to make sure there would be no peace.

Ever since Charles VIII had refused to give him either the fortresses ceded by Piero or the city of Pisa, Ludovico, like Janus, had been facing in two directions. While one face continued to give the king the impression that Milan was his loyal ally, the other feverishly sought to persuade Emperor Maximilian and the Italians to form a coalition that would drive the French out of Italy. Pope Alexander VI and the Neapolitans had always wanted such a coalition. Since by then Ferdinand of Spain also wished to see the French out of Italy and even the once-neutral Venetians were beginning to feel threatened, a Holy League against the French seemed a distinct possibility. There was, however, one stumbling block. Florence, which was in the very center of Italy and hence an invaluable ally, refused even to consider becoming a member.

Since the overthrow of Piero, Ludovico had been following the same Janus-like policy toward Florence that he was following toward France. While his agents in the city assured the Florentines of his intention to befriend and protect them at all costs, his agents in Pisa encouraged the Pisans to stand firm against their former masters. Although Ludovico was sufficiently adroit to keep his machinations in Pisa a secret from the Florentines and his machinations in Florence a secret from the Pisans, it did not take him long to realize that no amount of maneuvering was going to persuade the Florentines to join a league against France as long as Savonarola continued to assure them that God had sent Charles to Italy. That being the case, Ludovico began searching for ways to discredit the friar. One way that immediately came to mind was to incite the pope against him. Toward the end of December, the friar received a papal order to preach the Lenten sermons at Lucca. The order had ostensibly been sent at the request of the elders of the town. But many of Savonarola's contemporaries were convinced that Ludovico and his brother Ascanio had persuaded the Holy Father to grant the request. Even if the Sforzas were not responsible for the order, there can be no question that they were doing their best to inflame the pope.

Stirring up the pope was not enough. Everyone in Florence who either overtly or covertly opposed the friar must also be aroused. On January 1, a new Signoria entered office and, said Luca Landucci, "it was a great joy to see the piazza filled with citizens...thanking God who had given this impartial government to Florence...and all at the instigation of the *Frate*." Behind this peaceful facade, however, the spirit of factionalism was already at work. The twenty *accoppiatori* had, after all, voted for the Great Council only because they feared a popular uprising. Except for Francesco Valori, who was beginning to think that championing the cause of the people might be to his advantage, the *accoppiatori* felt uneasy with the prospect of *governo popolare*. Under pressure from Jacopo dei Nerli's father, Tanai, they had chosen as gonfalonier Filippo Corbizzi, "a man of little quality, authority, or talent, but one who could be counted on to oppose the popular government." Since a sizable number of *cittadini principali* also opposed popular government, Ludovico instructed the Milanese envoy in Florence, Paolo Somenzi, to make common cause with these men and to do whatever else he could to turn the people against the friar.

To inflame the populace further, Ludovico arranged for the Signoria to recall Fra Domenico da Ponzo to the city. Fra Domenico was a great bull of a preacher with a booming voice, an aggressive manner, and no scruples to speak of. When Ludovico had been pro-French, Fra Domenico had called Savonarola a holy man and had urged the Florentines to heed his warnings of the coming scourge. Now that Ludovico was anti-French, Fra Domenico was prepared to take exception to Savonarola's every word.

After announcing that God had chosen Jesus Christ to be king of Florence, Savonarola had retired to his cell to rest, leaving his subordinates to preach in his place. But his overpowering need to be in control made rest impossible. On Saint Sylvester's Day he hurried to the palazzo to press for a universal amnesty, the *pace universale* which he considered indispensable to the success of the popular government. On January 6 he was back in the pulpit urging Florence "to forgive and make peace and cry not again: 'Flesh and more flesh, blood and more blood!'" It was then that he brought up the matter of the six beans. In Florence, all voting was done with black and white beans. By the six beans he meant the plurality of six with which the priors passed judgment on political and criminal offenders. It was not right for six men to have the power of life and death over an entire city, he told the people. Political offenders ought to have the right to appeal the verdict of the six beans before the Council of Eighty.

The campaign against him began that afternoon when Ser Giovanni della Reformazione confessed—or was said to have confessed—that at the time of the revolution, he had deposited all his money and jewels and gold bars in San Marco for safe-keeping. Obviously, the friar was supporting a general amnesty because he had reached an agreement with Piero dei Medici, some said. He had hidden the Medici treasure in the convent and was preventing the government from confiscating it, others said. And there were even rumors that he planned to enrich himself with the hidden treasure. The very preposterousness of the rumors made them all the more painful to deal with. "You may know in your sorrows how fleeting are the things of this world," Savonarola told his congregation that Sunday. "Take the example of myself, who a few days ago was being called the father of this city and now suddenly am called its robber." The rumors were untrue, he insisted. He was entirely for the people and the common weal. To show that "these foxes," as he called his calumniators, could not intimidate him, he reiterated his plea for a general amnesty as well as a small stick in the form of a council of appeal for the law of the six beans to rest on.

More than ever he was a man living "on the dangerous edge of things," as eager to keep his constituency as any secular politician and as calculating, but subject to fits of reckless verbal extravagance, which he interpreted as the working of God's will within him. In a sermon delivered two days later, he reminded his audience of how much of what he had foretold had come to pass; then he offered ten reasons for believing that a renovation of the church was imminent. First and foremost was the pollution of the priesthood. As to the cause of this pollution: "When you see a head which is healthy, you can say that the body is healthy. But when the head is bad, look out for the body!... When therefore you see that God allows the head of the church to wallow in crime and simony, I say that the scourge of the people approaches."

Then realizing that he was treading on dangerous ground, he suddenly backtracked. He was not saying that all this was true of the church, he declared, but merely *when* it happened. However, the references to the wickedness and simony of Rome which kept recurring like a leitmotif through the rest of his sermon belied his disclaimer. Because there was no love left in the Holy City but only the devil, God would give Rome to others to cultivate, he told his audience. He also reminded them of his numerous visions: the sword of the Lord swift and sure over the peoples of the earth; the black cross over the Babylon that was Rome, and the golden one over Jerusalem. What prompted him to turn from the concrete and pressing problem of the six beans to these apparitions at this particular time, he could not say.

"I know that I sound crazy this morning," he declared more than once, "but God wishes me to speak thus."

> O Italy, O princes, O prelates of the church, the wrath of God is upon ye, neither is there any hope for ye unless ye be converted to the Lord....Repent ye therefore before the sword be unsheathed...otherwise neither wisdom, power, nor force will avail.

By then Fra Domenico da Ponzo was already in Florence. There were no longer any prophets, nor could there ever be any, said Fra Domenico in his first sermon in Santa Croce. And he proceeded to attack the reform of the six beans as well as the very idea of a friar involving himself in politics. That Saturday, when Savonarola again spoke of the need for a general amnesty and a reform of the six beans, many in the audience grew angry with him, saying he would bring them hard luck.

On Sunday, he was suddenly and unexpectedly called upon

to defend his intervention in politics before the Signoria. The case for nonintervention would be presented by Fra Domenico da Ponzo, assisted by Fra Tommaso Rieti, the prior of Santa Maria Novella, a wisp of a man whose sharp tongue had earned him the nickname of *Il Garofanino*—the "spicy little clove."

Although Savonarola had no way of knowing that it was Fra Domenico who had persuaded the gonfalonier to organize this debate, it was obvious that both Ponzo and Rieti had been informed of the meeting beforehand and that they hoped to trick him into saying something he would regret. Rather than reply to the attack then and there, he announced that he would answer it from the pulpit.

He spent the next two days gathering instances of Dominican intervention in politics: Saint Catherine of Siena, who had made peace in Florence at the time of Pope Gregory; Cardinal Messer Latino, who had reconciled the Guelphs and the Ghibellines; Archbishop Antoninus, who used to go to the palazzo to prevent the passage of iniquitous laws; and last but not least Saint Dominic himself. But like the master showman he was, he knew instinctively that something more was needed: some great flamboyant gesture which would rally the people behind him and make it impossible for his opponents to continue their attacks.

He would no longer preach about the six beans, he declared in his sermon on the feast of Saint Sebastian. Like Jesus, who, when he saw that many were angry with him, gave that anger room by leaving the city, he would leave Florence for Lucca, where he had been ordered to preach the Lenten sermons. "I will go away to my cell," he told his congregation on January 25.

> And do not send again for me. For if the King of France comes, or the Emperor, I shall not come. You in your councils do as God inspires you, and do not draw me in in any way, for now I must cede to anger. I shall go to Lucca and then perhaps farther afield. Pray God to give me grace to go and preach to the infidels, for I greatly desire to do so.

Had he gone away and stayed away, this would be the end of the story. But not only was he committed body and soul to the spiritual renovation of Florence; he also hoped to induce King Charles to undertake the renovation of the church. And though he was too intent on emulating Christ to admit it to himself, he enjoyed dealing with kings and politicians and bending them to his will.

As long as the Corbizzi-led Signoria remained in office, he remained in his cell. On March 1, when a Signoria more hospitable to the idea of popular government took office, he returned to the pulpit. Since by then Soderini and his Ten of *Balia* had persuaded the pope to rescind the order to preach in Lucca, he was free to deliver the Lenten sermons in Florence. No sooner did he begin preaching in Santa Maria dei Fiore than Fra Domenico da Ponzo begin preaching in Santa Croce.

The time was at hand when they would lack nothing, Savonarola told the people. But evil times would precede the good, and they must be prepared for them. Moreover, their sins were so great that they could not expect to regain Pisa until they purged themselves of internecine hate and presented a united front to the world.

The times were good and getting better, said Fra Domenico. Never had the state of Florence found itself in such a prosperous situation.

If they wished their new government to endure, said Savonarola, they must pass a law granting amnesty to all who had supported Piero before November 9, and they must reform the law of the six beans.

They must be careful lest they be tricked into pardoning their enemies, said Fra Domenico.

If he wanted to, he could turn the key on the coffer from which a thousand misfortunes would burst forth, said Savonarola.

Only his love for the people and the city kept him from lifting the lid on the kettle from which sulfur and brimstone would rise up to the very heavens, said Fra Domenico with tears in his eyes.

During those raw, windy days of mid-March, the crowds alternated between Santa Croce and the cathedral, unwilling to miss any part of the great debate. However, much though they relished Fra Domenico's verbal high jinks, they did not trust him. On March 19, the Great Council approved the reform of the six beans by a vote of 543 to 163. Soon afterward, Fra Domenico went to preach in Arezzo.

On April 1, a triumphant Savonarola announced that he had twice spoken to the Virgin Mary. Addressing him in Tuscan with a propriety and elegance which astonished him, she had assured him that Florence would become more glorious, more powerful, and more wealthy than ever before. The city's lesser lilies would mingle with the greater ones of France, bringing immense joy to both parties. Pisa would be restored, and just as Savonarola had predicted four years earlier, its rebellious subjects would be severely punished for their temerity.

"All these things he spoke as a prophet," said Luca Landucci, "and the greater part of the people believed him, especially quiet people without political passions."

"The friar's words gave comfort to their agitated minds," said Piero Parenti. "Since all his other prophecies had been fulfilled, they assumed that these too would be fulfilled."

Why God should be so solicitous of the welfare of Florence and so indifferent to that of Pisa was a question that did not concern him any more than it concerned his audience. Just as he was God's chosen prophet, so Florence was God's chosen city. Since God's will was inscrutable, there was nothing more to be said about the matter. Of far greater importance was the indisputable fact that although the great majority in Florence believed in him, there remained a small but hostile minority which didn't.

Even before Fra Domenico da Ponzo had begun preaching in Santa Croce, Savonarola had warned of the lukewarm priests, or *tiepidi*, as he called them, who, because they lacked both spirit and devotion, would seek to discredit him. His bout with Fra Domenico made him more wary of them than ever. Because by then he had also gotten wind of Ludovico Sforza's machinations, that April he alternated impassioned pleas for moral reform and aid to the destitute with equally impassioned attacks upon the *tiepidi*.

The *tiepidi* had gathered together to conspire against him, he declared on April 4. And they had agreed to do many things to harm him, not only in the city but outside as well. Although he would later make it clear that "they" included laymen as well as priests, he never said which laymen and priests. Nor did he ever say where "they" had gathered, perhaps because he knew of no specific gathering, but with his flair for the dramatic, had managed to convince himself that one had taken place.

The war which the *tiepidi* would wage against him would be more intense than the war of the tyrants against the martyrs or the heretics against the faithful, he told his congregation. However, since the *tiepidi* wished to appear good in the eyes of the people, they would not oppose him openly. Instead, they would resort to secret and surreptitious attempts to obtain writs of excommunication, precepts, and similar injunctions. And just as the unacknowledged fear that his visions did not really come from God led him to constantly justify them, so the fear that his more reckless attacks upon the corruption of the church might induce the pope to excommunicate him made him insist that any writ of excommunication directed at him must necessarily be erroneous. But despite persistent rumors that Alexander was planning to excommunicate him, Lent passed without any word from Rome. Soon afterward, the imminent return of Charles VIII made all other problems seem insignificant by comparison.

Charles and his army had encountered so little resistance on their march down the Italian boot that it had seemed to the pope as if they were conquering the country with chalk, by which he meant that in most towns they had nothing to do but mark the houses in which they wanted their troops billeted. Terrified by their easy victories, King Alfonso of Naples had nightmares in which he heard "all the trees and rocks calling France." By the time the French arrived at the gates of his city, Alfonso had abdicated, and the son to whom he had left his kingdom had set sail for Ischia.

To the tired French soldiers Naples, with its glorious harbor, its mild climate, and its thousands of courtesans, seemed an earthly paradise. Beguiled by the pleasures of this newfound Eden, Charles and his men forgot that the ostensible purpose of their expedition was a crusade against the Turks and devoted themselves to Venus and Bacchus. Bacchus provided his customary delights, but Venus had a surprise in store for them: the

French called it the sickness of Naples; the Neapolitans called it the French disease. "Syphilis, the sinister shepherd," the Italian doctor Girolamo Fracastoro would call it in his famous poem.

"Not only did the evil befoul the human race with pimples and ulcers," said one chronicler, "it also attacked the joints of the body, eating into the marrow. The pains...were so intense that the sick screamed endlessly....Many remained marked, some on the arms, others on the legs, and many died a horrible death." The disease is thought to have existed in Europe before the return of Columbus from the New World, but not in the same virulent form. Camp followers and deserters would soon spread it to every part of Europe. Six years later, the first cases appeared in China—the final bitter fruit of the king's mission to scourge Italy.

Although there were rumors that Charles himself had been stricken, he did not make up his mind to return to France until he learned that a treaty establishing the Holy League had been signed in Venice. Before he left, he had himself crowned king of Naples. Since his new kingdom was a fief of the papacy, the coronation was meaningless without an investiture from the pope. However, Alexander was a member of the Holy League and had no intention of granting the investiture. No sooner did the pope hear that Charles and his army were approaching Rome than he moved his court to Orvieto. When the king sought to meet him there, Alexander moved on to Perugia, and Charles decided to head for Tuscany.

Long before the king set foot on Tuscan soil, the news that he might once again wish to quarter his army in Florence threw the city into a panic. As they had done in every other crisis since the death of Lorenzo, the people turned to their preacher for guidance. In a letter written on May 25, Guglielmina della Stufa, the wife of the Florentine commissioner in Arezzo, told her husband that Fra Girolamo had assured them of the happy times when they would lack nothing but had also warned that evil times would precede the good. "And in order that the evil may be less, he has bidden us fast and pray from now to Pentecost. And we must not doubt that God is merciful and will lighten the troubles that shall fall upon us."

Because devoted followers like Guglielmina frequently burst into tears at his sermons, as did Savonarola himself, the friar's enemies called them *Piagnoni*, or weepers. Not content with this one pejorative, they also called them *Frateschi*, or followers of the friar; *Mastecapaternosti*, or prayer mumblers; *Stroppiconi*, or toadies; and *Collitori*, or wrynecks. The *Piagnoni* retaliated by calling their detractors *Arrabbiati*, or mad dogs. The *Arrabbiati* wished the Florentines to show they were good Italians by joining the Holy League. The *Piagnoni*, of course were determinedly pro-French. "Make no league except with Christ," Savonarola warned them on May 24. And he assured them that they would have Pisa back if only the butcher shops remained closed until Pentecost. Since by then the butchers were beginning to fear that this business of fasting to regain Pisa would end by bankrupting them, it could have been a few disgruntled members of their guild who sought to attack the friar in the Via Cocomero after the sermon. On the other hand, it could have been some of the *Arrabbiati*, incensed by his remarks about the league, or perhaps some thugs hired by Ludovico Sforza.

Whoever was responsible, Savonarola had no intention of allowing the attack to deflect him from what he saw as his God-given mission to keep Florence loyal to France. Charles was then approaching Rome. Because the friar believed that the king was the second Charlemagne, destined to cleanse the church, he had high hopes that, as he told his audience on May 25, they would see the Holy City "confounded." Since he also knew how forgetful of his divine mission this scatterbrained second Charlemagne could be, he thought it best to send the king a letter reminding him that among all other Christian princes, God had made choice of him "for the carrying out of this mystery of the renovation of the church."

At the same time, Savonarola decided it would not be amiss to warn the king of the tribulations God had in store for him if he did not treat Florence well and abide by his promise to return to Pisa. To make the warning more palatable, he insisted that he was delivering it not for the sake of the Florentines—as a foreigner, their welfare was of no concern to him—but for the king's own good and the honor of God. And with the ingenuousness that so often walked hand in hand with his guile, it did not occur to him that the Florentines might find what he had written objectionable.

Despite the letter, Charles passed through Rome without lifting a finger to reform the church. Soon afterward, the Signoria sent new ambassadors to him to determine his intentions toward Florence. So that the Florentines "should have grace in the midst of the trouble afflicting them," the priors also had the tabernacle of our Lady of Santa Maria dell'Impruneta brought into the city. On June 12, Charles and his army reached Siena. Since Siena's northern border was only 50 kilometers from Florence, the Florentine ambassadors asked the king what route he planned to take through their territory. "They should prepare for him the whole dominion," Charles replied.

On June 14, the vanguard of his army crossed the border and entered Poggibonsi, where the soldiers did "every kind of damage." Hearing the news, peasants began streaming into Florence from all the surrounding countryside, and the Florentines placed wood at every corner so as to be able to barricade the streets should the need arise.

As early as June 9, Savonarola had hinted that he would be willing to speak to the king. Since all other attempts to deal with Charles had failed, the Signoria sent the friar to Poggibonsi on June 15 as "procurator and advocate of the Florentine people." As usual, Charles treated him with the greatest respect, asking Savonarola to hear his confession and wishing to receive communion from his hands. Since by then the king had received word that the armies of the Holy League were mobilizing in the vicinity of Parma and he knew that he dared not tarry, he was ceding nothing when, in response to the friar's demand, he agreed to bypass Florence. But to Savonarola's repeated warnings that God would send him "great tribulation" if he did not live up to his commitments to the city, including the return of Pisa, the king's only reply was that he would live up to those commitments "when the time came." Although this led Piero Parenti to write that in going to the French camp, the friar had lost more than he had gained, the majority of Florentines believed that their preacher had once again saved them from certain disaster. Between 13,000 and 14,000 people crowded into the cathedral on June 21 to hear him describe how he had warned the king to do well by Florence or face divine punishment. At this time, it seemed to Luca Landucci, "the *Frate* was held in such esteem that there were many men and women who, if he had said 'Enter the fire' would have actually obeyed him."

Before going to the king, he had persuaded the *accoppiatori* to resign, thus paving the way for the Great Council to elect the Signoria. Immediately after his return, he induced the people to give up the annual horse race, known as the *Palio di San Giovanni,* and to distribute the money usually spent on this festival to the poor. "Nor," said Piero Parenti, "was it deemed unfitting to give up this ancient custom and national feast, so great was his authority with us."

But the Pisan question gave the *Arrabbiati* a lever with which they hoped eventually to tip the balance in their favor. On June 25, when the Florentine ambassadors sent to confer with the king at Lucca returned without any decision as to Pisa, the *Arrabbiati* were quick to tell the people: "There, you see how you can trust the *Frate* who declared that he held Pisa in the hollow of his hand."

Nevertheless, the Signoria had sufficient confidence in him to send two new ambassadors to Charles on July 6. That same day the king and his men clashed with the armies of the Holy League at Fornovo on the river Taro. It was deemed a famous victory, but just whose victory has never been established. Because the Italians were not driven from the battlefield, their commander, the Marchese of Mantua, assumed that the victory was his and commissioned Andrea Mantegna to paint the superb *Madonna della Vittoria,* now in the Louvre. Because the French were able to cross the Taro and continue on to Asti, they assumed the victory was theirs. If it was, it was the last victory they would have in Italy for a long time.

On the same day that they clashed with the Italians, an uprising in Naples restored the deposed King Ferrantino to the throne. He was "received by the multitude with cries of joy, the women showering him with flowers and perfumes from their windows," and some of the most noble dames "running into the streets to embrace him and wipe the sweat from his brow." Soon afterward, the Aragonese recaptured Rapallo "and other places where they had been defeated the year before." Meanwhile, Ludovico and the Venetians made plans to besiege the French-held town of Novara.

Even before that, the pope, perhaps at Ludovico's instigation, perhaps on his own, sent an envoy to Florence to urge the Florentines to join the Holy League. While in the city, the envoy was to find out as much as he could about this friar who kept telling the Florentines to make no league except with Christ.

V

ENTER THE POPE

odrigo Borgia, who had taken the name of Alexander VI upon his election as pope, was everything that Savonarola was not: tall, handsome, sexually uninhibited, pleasure-loving, and not in the least averse to using his high office to enrich both his family and himself. For him, there had been no agonized flight from the world and its wickedness, no sense of vocation, no struggle for self-transcendence, no mystical union with God. As the second son of a minor Spanish nobleman, he had been destined for the church since birth. And he had had the good fortune to have as his maternal uncle a promising canon lawyer. In 1455, when this promising lawyer became pope, he immediately bestowed a cardinal's hat on his 25-year-old nephew. A year later, he gave Rodrigo the vice-chancellorship, next to the papacy the most important post in the hierarchy, with an annual income of 8000 gold ducats. What with the other benefices the new vice-chancellor managed to accumulate both before and after his uncle's death, by 1480 he was accounted the wealthiest cardinal in Rome. To many he also seemed the most capable. Besides being naturally shrewd and "thoroughly versed in money matters," he was intelligent, conscientious, and hardworking; a man who "knew how to make the most of himself and took pains to shine in conversation and be dignified in his manners."

Since the Donation of Pepin given to the popes in the eighth century had added temporal power over the papal states to the spiritual power conferred on Peter and his successors by Jesus, in time Cardinal Borgia's "brilliant skill in conducting affairs" made him one of that select group considered papal material. Nevertheless, he was given little chance of being elected in 1492. Guicciardini would later say that Borgia purchased the votes of his fellow cardinals "partly with money and partly with promises of offices," and that Ascanio Sforza, "corrupted by his boundless appetite for riches," induced them to sell. But like so many of Guicciardini's stories about the Borgias, this one needs to be taken with a grain of salt.

Though it is true that Borgia would never have been elected without the help of Ascanio Sforza, it was not Borgia who approached Ascanio but Ascanio who approached Borgia. And what motivated Ascanio was not so much his "boundless appetite for riches" as the need to find a candidate who could muster enough votes to break the deadlock in the College of Cardinals. That Borgia would agree to give Ascanio the vice-chancellorship in exchange for his support was a foregone conclusion. Borgia was no idealistic reformer eager to change the existing order of things, but a practical politician who knew how elections were won in Rome. As a young cardinal at the conclave of 1458, he had seen the richer and more influential princes of the church summon the rest and, by dint of promises and threats, seek to gain the papacy for themselves. And he had been a party to the behind-the-scenes maneuvering, the deals, and the bribes that had marked every conclave since then.

Portraits of the Borgia pope, of which the best and the most famous is the fresco by Pinturicchio in the Borgia apartments, reveal a stout, impressive-looking man with large fleshy hands, an aquiline nose, and full lips. Although he does not appear handsome by modern standards, there must have been something in his appearance that the portraits do not capture, for even when he was in his sixties, people spoke enthusiastically of his physical beauty. When he was in his twenties, he was considered so good-looking, so lively and amiable and well-spoken that, said his tutor, he had only to look at beautiful women to attract them to him "with greater force than a magnet attracts iron." Since the handsome young cardinal was as susceptible to the charms of the ladies as they were to his, he was already the father of three illegitimate children when, at the age of 43, he grew tired of flitting from woman to woman and took Vanozza dei Cattanei as his mistress. At the time he was elected pope, only one of the three children of the earlier liaisons was still living, and she had been married to a Roman nobleman for ten years, However, the four children the pope had had by Vanozza were still under his care.

Those who had known Alexander before his election described him as *uomo carnalesco*, by which they meant that he was a man of warm and affectionate nature, devotedly attached to his own flesh and blood. Although he had promised to keep his children at a distance and be a father to all, his great love for the children rendered such a course impossible. Soon after his election, he made his 18-year-old son Cesare bishop of Valencia. Since membership in the College of Cardinals was restricted to legitimate offspring and Cesare was a bastard, making him a cardinal proved more difficult. By the fall of 1493, however, Alexander had found a way around the difficulty, and Cesare became a prince of the church.

Earlier that same year, the pope gave the palace of Santa Maria in Portico on the left side of the steps of Saint Peter's to his 13-year-old daughter Lucrezia. Residing in the palace with Lucrezia were Alexander's cousin, Adriana da Mila, and Adriana's beautiful 17-year-old daughter-in-law, Giulia Farnese. The Romans knew why Adriana was there—she had been Lucrezia's guardian ever since the erstwhile Cardinal Borgia had broken with Vanozza. But they found it hard to believe that Giulia was there because her husband had deserted her. Observing their still virile 61-year-old pontiff and the numerous children he had fathered, they decided that Alexander had sent the young man away so that he could have the beautiful Giulia for himself. Although there was no real evidence that this was so, it wasn't long before stories of Giulia's illicit relationship with the pope spread to every corner of Christendom.

Madonna Giulia Farnese, the "Bride of Christ," one Roman wag called her. "Giulia Farnese, the pope's concubine," Alexander's master of ceremonies called her in his diary. To the Ferrarese ambassador, she was "Madonna Giulia Farnese, about whom so much is whispered"; to the correspondent of the Marchese of Mantua, she was "a beautiful thing to see." Travelers returning to Germany spoke of a cypress grove in which the pope entertained "Giulia Farnese and other loose women"; the Florentine correspondent Lorenzo Pucci detected a marked resemblance between Giulia's infant daughter and the pope.

That Lucrezia's marriage to Giovanni Sforza, the 28-year-old Signore of Pesaro, was celebrated in the Vatican, and that Giulia was one of the Roman ladies invited to the reception added to the aura of scandal surrounding the Holy Father. The marriage had been arranged by Ludovico Sforza as a way of ensuring papal support for him and his allies in their conflict with Naples. When Charles VIII announced plans to invade Italy, however, it became evident that despite Lucrezia's marriage to a Sforza, her father had no intention of giving the king either the investiture of Naples or free passage through the states of the church. "Italy ought to be left to the Italians.... The triumph of France involves nothing less than the destruction of the independence of every state in Italy," the pope told the Roman representative of the duke of Ferrara. The representative said, "He spoke with such vehemence of word and gesture that it was obvious he spoke from the heart, and many times tears filled his eyes."

To the pope, Savonarola's oft-repeated assertion that Charles was the scourge of God sent to punish the Italians for their sins seemed ludicrous. Since Fra Domenico da Ponzo was a paid agent of Ludovico Sforza, Alexander may very well have suspected that Savonarola was a paid agent of the king. In the spring of 1495, when Ludovico and the pope found themselves on the same side, Ludovico and his agents did everything they could to confirm the Holy Father's suspicion. Nevertheless, Alexander refused to silence the friar as long as Charles was in a position to retaliate. Only after the battle of Fornovo made the king's position in Italy untenable did the pope send his envoy Alberto of Orvieto to Florence.

Besides using every means at his disposal to ascertain "the wicked and disparaging remarks Fra Girolamo had made and was continuing to make about the Holy Father and the other Italian rulers," Alberto arranged a meeting with the Ten of *Balia*. Since Charles VIII would soon be leaving Italy and since the king had paid no attention to the treaty with Florence so solemnly sworn on the altar of Santa Maria dei Fiore, Alberto expected to have no problem convincing the Ten that their city ought to join the Holy League. He spoke feelingly of the great need for a union of Italian states in order to discourage any thought Charles might have of launching a new invasion. The pope's envoy, however, made no mention of returning Pisa, and without Pisa, the union of Italy was not in the interests of Florence. "In fact," said Guicciardini, "disunion, another invasion by King Charles, or any sort of upheaval would better serve the city's interests."

But Alberto no more appreciated the Florentine obsession with regaining Pisa than he appreciated the widespread fear that entering the Holy League would give Ludovico and the *Arrabbiati* the upper hand and mean the end of *governo popolare*. As Alberto saw it, it was Savonarola and Savonarola alone who was keeping the city loyal to France. He knew how much store they and their countrymen set by the words of Fra Girolamo, Alberto told the Ten. Rather than being to their credit, however, it was to their shame that they allowed their great republic to be governed by a friar. And the envoy warned them that all Italy would look upon Florence as an enemy if the city refused to join the league. When it became evident that the prospect left them unperturbed, Alberto informed the pope that further conversation was pointless. Florence would never join the league so long as Savonarola remained in the city. That being the case, Alexander must find an excuse to summon the friar to Rome.

Upon returning from his meeting with King Charles at Poggibonsi, Savonarola had had an attack of dysentery and had begun running a fever. The combination of these disorders and a perennially nervous stomach so alarmed his doctors that they insisted he stop preaching until he recovered. But preaching was the core of his existence, the pivot on which all else turned. Though still so infirm he could scarcely mount the steps, on July 5, he was back in the pulpit. "I will try to go gently, if I can, so that the doctors may not reproach me," he told his au-

dience. But how go gently when there was so much wickedness
in the world? Before he knew it, he was assailing Rome as fer-
vidly as ever, warning all in that great cathedral that the church
was done for unless God helped her.

Nor was the church his only target. Turning to the Eight of
the Ward, who were seated together in the section reserved for
government officials, he exhorted them to set a beautiful fire,
"or possibly two or three," there in the piazza, "to consume
these sodomites either male or female, because there are also
women guilty of this abominable vice. Therefore I say, make a
sacrifice of them to God!" And he also managed to insert another admonition "to make no league except with Christ" and
to remind mothers not to dress their children in silk and satin.

It took him a week to recover from the strain of delivering
this sermon. When he entered the pulpit again on July 12, he
knew that everything he said would be reported to the pope's
envoy. It was undoubtedly this knowledge that accounted for
the ardor with which he defended his prophetic calling that day.
"I wish to speak to you boldly," he cried, "and to tell you what
God omnipotent has said to me. And why should I keep silent?
I am telling you what God has said. If God is a liar, I am a liar."

Feeling the need to justify himself further, at about this time
he also sent a letter to the pope. In this letter he insisted that
he preached only those things which he knew to be in the service of God, "being always ready to submit them to the correction of the Holy Roman Church." All unknowingly, he had
provided Alexander with the excuse the pope was looking for.
On July 21, the Holy Father drew up a brief summoning him to
Rome.

To our well-beloved son, greeting and the apostolic bene-
diction.

We have heard, that of all the workers in the Lord's vineyard, thou art the most zealous; at which we deeply rejoice,
and give thanks to Almighty God. We have likewise heard
that thou dost assert thy predictions proceed not from thee
but from God. Therefore we desire, as behooves our pasto-
ral office, to have speech with thee considering these things;
so that, being by these means better informed of God's will,

we may be able to fulfill it. Wheretofore, by thy vow of holy
obedience, we enjoin thee to wait on us without delay, and
shall welcome thee with loving kindness.

Alexander had studied jurisprudence in Valencia and canon
law in Bologna. Besides making him exceptionally wary of self-
styled prophets and mystics, his training had made him unusually adept at cross-examining them. While in Perugia in 1495,
he had been taken to see Suor Colomba of Rieti, a renowned
worker of miracles who, said the Perugian chronicler Matarazzo,
"neither ate nor drank save sometimes some jujube fruit and
even then but rarely." Just as adroit questioning had managed
to confound Suor Colomba, so the pope was confident it would
demonstrate that Savonarola's claims to converse with God were
delusory. Once they were shown to be delusory, there was ample precedent for removing him from his post as prior of San
Marco.

Although the cordial tone of the pope's brief sought to conceal its true purpose, it would require no great shrewdness on
Savonarola's part to realize that Alexander was summoning him
to Rome not to hear about his prophecies but to cast doubt on
them. Since in the depths of his soul Savonarola too sometimes
doubted them, he had to find an excuse for not complying with
the pope's command, and his recent illness gave him an excellent excuse. But he could not leave it at that. Instead, he felt
compelled to insist on the very matters about which he was
most dubious.

Since it was the judgment of "all good and wise citizens"
that his departure from Florence would be to the very great det-
riment of the people, he told the pope, he had no doubt that
God had willed that his illness should stand in the way of his
journey. In a word, it was God's will that he should not leave
Florence. But he hoped that it would soon be possible for him
to go to Rome in accordance with the desires of His Holiness.
Meanwhile, since the pope had expressed the desire to be more
fully informed of his predictions regarding the calamities of Italy and the renovation of the church, Alexander could learn all
that was to be known of the matter from a little book the friar

was printing. More than was contained in the *Compendium Revelationum*, Savonarola was not at liberty to utter, for he had set down only those things which he had been commanded to make known. As to those things which the Almighty had confided to him in secrecy, he was not at liberty to reveal them to any mortal. The other predictions he had committed to writing so that if they did not come to pass as they had been foretold, all the world might know that he was a false prophet, and if they did come to pass as foretold, thanks might be given to God.

Although there was much in this reply to bolster Alexander's conviction that he was dealing with an arrogant and wily charlatan, the pope decided to accept Savonarola's excuses at least for the time being. After Alexander had thought things over, he could always change his mind. Savonarola too needed time to think. Since he had used his illness as a pretext for not obeying the pope, he realized that he would have to behave like an invalid. Among other things, that meant giving up preaching. In his farewell sermon on July 28, he touched on all the subjects dear to his heart: the renovation of the church; the urgent necessity of finishing the new hall for the Great Council as quickly as possible; the need to punish sodomites—it was madness to extend *clemency* to them, he declared—and above all, the welfare of the commune.

He had been thinking about the *parlamento*, he told his audience, and about what a ruinous institution it was. Since the people were now masters of Florence, they must realize that whosoever wished to summon a *parlamento* wished to take control of the government out of their hands. That being the case, they must make certain that everyone elected to the Signoria swore never to summon a *parlamento*. And if, despite this oath, one of the priors did express a wish to summon a *parlamento*, the people must cut off his head.

It was the first time he had called for the death penalty for a political offense, and the call was strangely out of tune with the demands for civic peace and harmony he had been making for so long, and which he included in this very sermon. But he seemed unaware of the disjunction. From speaking of civic peace, he went on to speak of his illness and to notify his audience of his intention to quit the pulpit until he felt better. In one of those dramatic monologues which he so frequently slipped into his sermons, he asked himself what reward he wished for having preached so long and labored so hard as to have shortened his life by many years and "fallen very weak." To which he replied that he would have martyrdom. "I am content to endure it; I pray for it each day, O Lord, for love of this city."

That August he remained in his cell, correcting the proofs of the *Compendium* while Fra Domenico replaced him in the pulpit. However, the influence of his last sermon could be seen everywhere. In answer to his plea to hurry along the building of a hall for the Great Council, the vaulting of the roof was completed on August 12. On August 13 he had the satisfaction of seeing the Great Council pass a law depriving anyone who favored calling a *parlamento* of his life and possessions. Piero dei Medici was then preparing to attack Florence, and to many the law seemed directed at his followers in the city. A few days before it was passed, in the palace of Orsanmichele, the commune began auctioning off Piero's household effects: the velvet counterpanes embroidered in gold, the gorgeous clothing, the rugs and paintings and marble busts which many who saw them believed had been paid for, at least in part, with public funds.

Some of the money realized from the auction would help defray the cost of the Pisan campaign. So costly had this campaign become by then, said Guicciardini, that "the Ten in office at the time—the first Ten elected by the people—were commonly called the Ten Spenders." While the Ten continued to dispense money for guns and soldiers' pay, the Signoria sent ambassadors to negotiate with Charles VIII, who was then in Turin making preparations for his return to France. Although Charles had done nothing to implement the treaty with Florence signed the previous December, the ambassadors renewed that treaty, once again promising the king money and support in exchange for the return of Pisa.

To the pope, the renewal of the treaty seemed unspeakably perverse, a stab in the back certain to undermine the peace for which he had labored so long and so diligently. Only a few days before news of the agreement reached him, the Holy Father had received an autographed copy of the *Compendium Revelationum* from Savonarola. The combination of this book in which the friar represented himself as God's chosen prophet and the treaty signed at Turin convinced Alexander that he had been far too lenient. On September 8, the pope dispatched three briefs: one to the Florentines ordering them to cease giving aid to King Charles or face excommunication, another to the king ordering him to leave Italy forthwith or appear before the Holy Father under pain of excommunication, and a third to the brothers of San Marco.

"We are informed," said this brief, "that a certain Fra Hieronymo of Ferrara...has been led by the disturbed condition of affairs in Italy to such a pitch of folly as to declare that he has been sent by God and that he holds converse with him." Alexander had hoped by "patient forebearance" to persuade the friar to acknowledge the folly of his profession of prophecy. Instead, Savonarola had written a book for "uninformed readers," in which he had put on paper the things which he had previously had the temerity to disseminate only by word of mouth. Because the pope was too occupied with the burdensome task of restoring peace to Italy to try the friar's case himself, he was committing it to Fra Sebastiano Maggi, the vicar general of the Dominican order for the province of Lombardy. Pending examination by Maggi, Savonarola was forbidden to preach, the convents of San Marco and San Domenico of Fiesole were reunited with the Lombard congregation, and Savonarola's three closest associates, Fra Domenico da Pescia, Fra Silvestro Maruffi, and Fra Tomasso Busini, were to be assigned to convents outside Florence.

Either because the pope wished to give this brief the widest possible circulation or as the result of a clerical error, it was originally sent to the Franciscan convent of Santa Croce. Consequently, it did not reach San Marco until the end of September. Long before that, however, Savonarola had learned what it contained. In a letter which he wrote to a Dominican brother in Rome on September 15, he called the brief the work of evilminded citizens who would fain reestablish tyranny in Florence. And he went on to accuse "certain princes of Italy," by whom he obviously meant Ludovico Sforza, of being the accomplices of the aforementioned citizens. Since both the one and the other considered him an insurmountable obstacle to their plans, they were prepared to get rid of him at all costs. And Savonarola implored his Roman brother to act in concert with Cardinal Caraffa, the protector of their order, to defend the innocent.

That August, Ludovico's agent Paolo Somenzi had complained that the Holy Father lacked the courage "to make a friar come to Rome against his will." Consequently, there can be little doubt that the Sforzas and their allies, the *Arrabbiati*, had taken advantage of the pope's anger at the renewal of the treaty between King Charles and the Florentines to induce the Holy Father to dispatch this new brief; just as there can be little doubt that the decision to reunite San Marco with the Lombard congregation had been made at the prompting of the Sforzas. What Savonarola failed to realize, however, was that the Sforzas had succeeded only because Alexander blamed him for keeping Florence allied to France. Since he did not realize this, it was easy for him to assume the role of the injured innocent.

In a letter which he sent the pope after the brief finally reached San Marco, he described himself as "deeply grieved that the malice of men should have gone to such lengths that certain people had not scrupled to suggest to His Holiness a brief so full of false statements and perverse interpretations of his conduct and motives." And he used their enmity as yet another excuse for not doing what he had never intended to do in the first place, namely, go to Rome.

Because of the traps these people were continually laying for him, he told the pope, it was impossible for him to emerge from his convent without taking extraordinary precautions. Hence, he trusted that the Holy Father would consider him not disobedient but prudent if he refrained for the moment from complying with the pope's demand that he come to Rome, in the expectation of receiving a full acquittal. If, on the other hand, His Holiness signified to him what out of all he had written he must retract, he would do so, for as he had often said and written, he submitted himself and all his words and writings to the correction of the Holy Roman Church.

Long before this letter reached the pope, Cardinal Caraffa had spoken to him about the friar's case. Although Caraffa's intervention did not change Alexander's opinion of the danger inherent in the friar's sermons, it did change the Holy Father's opinion of the friar's motives. Rather than predicting future things "out of an evil intent," as the pope had believed hitherto, it now seemed clear to Alexander that the friar preached them "out of a certain simplicity and a zeal misguided, though it might be for the vineyard of the Lord." This being the case, the pope agreed to suspend his brief of September 8 on condition that the friar not preach until such time as it was possible for him to come to Rome or the Holy Father made some other provision.

One of the basic tenets of the Catholic Church is that obedience is due the office, not the man. In other words, as Saint Catherine of Siena had once put it: "Allegiance must be rendered every pope, however bad, under all circumstances." Mindful of this, Savonarola had assured his Roman brother that if there were no other way to save his conscience, he was resolved to make submission so as to avoid even a venial sin.

He had been so certain that his letter to the pope would win him a full acquittal, however, that without waiting for the Holy Father's reply, he had returned to the pulpit. One reason for his haste was that Piero dei Medici was then in the vicinity of Siena with 200 men-at-arms and 2000 infantrymen commanded by his kinsman Virginio Orsini. Those who made it their business to find out such things were convinced that the Venetians were secretly giving Piero money and that the pope was also encouraging him, in large part because Alexander believed that the reinstatement of the Medici was the one sure way to bring Florence into the Holy League. But because, as Piero Parenti put it, "this wasn't the time to displease the pope," Savonarola chose to ignore the Holy Father's role. In the friar's sermon on October 11, he concentrated instead on Piero's supporters in Florence.

"What are you doing, Council of the Eight?" he cried. "It is time to take up the sword. Show them no mercy. I tell you that Christ intends to rule here, and any who fight against his government fight against Christ." And as part of his new, more bloodthirsty approach, he called on the people to cut off the heads of these "rebels against Christ."

Soon afterward, he learned that the pope had forbidden him to preach until he came to Rome. Since he had no intention of ever doing so, on October 25 he announced that Fra Domenico would once again preach in his place. As for himself, he asked those present to pray that God would inspire him when next he entered the pulpit. As he must have known, neither the Signoria nor the Ten was prepared to accept the situation. On November 13, the Signoria asked Bartolommeo della Scala, the chancellor of the republic, to write to the pope. "Holy Father, we need this man of God," said Scala. In fact, the chancellor continued, so desperately did the people of Florence need their friar that His Holiness could do them no greater favor than to allow Fra Girolamo to resume his ministry of preaching. Scala also wrote to Cardinal Caraffa, imploring him to seek permission for the friar to preach during the coming Advent. Fearing that there might not be enough time to draw up a brief before then, the Signoria also had Scala inquire as to the possibility of securing verbal permission for the friar to preach. When the first Sunday of Advent passed with no word from Rome, the Ten urged Ricciardo Becchi, their envoy in the Holy City, to speak to Cardinal Caraffa and, if necessary, to the pope himself. But Becchi's intervention had no more effect than Scala's letters.

Meanwhile, Savonarola sought to dispel the rumor that he had been excommunicated by publishing a *Letter to a Friend*, in which he insisted that the pope had found nothing contrary to the church or holy scriptures in his writings. The *Arrabbiati* lost no time publishing a reply to this letter; one of Savonarola's disciples published a reply to the reply, and a pious nun who claimed illumination from the Holy Spirit announced that all the friar's prophecies would be fulfilled. But for him to keep the devotion of the people during his enforced silence, something more was needed.

Carnival was only a few weeks off, and despite all the pleas for a moral renovation, carnival remained what it had always been: a time when Christ was relegated to the sidelines and Eros and Bacchus reigned supreme. To the *fanciulli*, or boys of Florence, carnival was also a time for tormenting everyone else with stiles, stones, and *capannucci*. The stiles were long pieces of wood with which rival gangs of *fanciulli* barred the streets, allowing no one to pass without paying a fee. The money thus extorted went to buy food and drink, which the gangs consumed in the evening by the light of the *capannucci*, great uprooted trees which the boys placed in the piazzas and the wider streets. Before the revelry began, each gang heaped quantities of wood, sticks, old brooms, and other available combustibles around its *capannuccio*, then ignited the entire mass. When the feasting was over and the fires reduced to glowing embers, the sated and half-drunken gangs pelted one another with stones until far into the night, leaving the wounded, and on occasion the dead, to be carted off the next morning.

So inveterate and ancient a custom was "that foolish and bestial game of stones," said Jacopo Nardi, "that even the severe and terrifying edicts of the magistrates had never been able to repress it, much less root it out." Exasperated by the law's impotence, the fourteenth-century poet Francesco Sacchetti had called for the return of cruel Herod: To kill those from four to twelve years old...for they displease everyone alive."

Surely the man who could think of a way to control these uncontrollable brats would be a hero to their elders. Savonarola's way was to use the combativeness that had gone into the stones and the stiles for his own purposes. As with so many of his projects, it did not take him long to convince himself that his "reform of the children" was the will of heaven. Since he could not propose it from the pulpit himself, he asked Fra Domenico to propose it for him. During those weeks before the onset of carnival, Domenico urged all *fanciulli* between the ages of 10 and 18 to register at San Marco. Those who registered were divided into companies according to neighborhood. Because Savonarola believed that young people needed practice in the use of the democratic process if the republic was to survive, each company elected its own officers. Besides a gonfalonier, these included counselors and confessors, as well as an officer charged with keeping peace among the boys of the neighborhood. Since the friar also wished to discourage the homosexual soliciting of young boys, which was as much a part of carnival in Florence as the stiles and the stones, all boys were expected to wear "simple masculine clothing," to have their hair cut above their ears, and to eschew dancing and fencing. In addition, each boy was called upon to serve God in one of three ways.

The cleaners searched for crucifixes and figures of saints in the vicinity of the public urinals and, after cleaning these sacred objects, removed them "so they would not be kept irreverently in similar places." The alms collectors stationed themselves beside little altars erected on street corners and, crucifix in hand, solicited alms for the poor. The inquisitors ferreted out vanities and luxuries and reprimanded gamblers. Since besides making the boys feel virtuous and important, these assignments offered them innumerable opportunities to harass others much as they had done in the past, by the onset of carnival over 5000 *fanciulli* had enrolled at San Marco.

Every street corner had its altar around which a mob of boys gathered to demand alms for those poor who were too ashamed to beg for themselves, Paolo Somenzi told Ludovico. And the boys carried long poles with which they barred the way, making it impossible for anyone, especially any woman, and particularly any young woman, to pass without first dropping a few *quattrini* into their bowls.

On February 7, Luca Landucci reported seeing a group of inquisitors confiscate a girl's veil holder in the Via dei Martegli. The girl's outraged relatives raised a terrible ruckus, but this only added to the pleasure the correctors took in their holy work. So zealous were the boys of the *Frate*, said Landucci, that at the mere mention of their approach, even the boldest gambler fled; women went about decently dressed, and young and old avoided speaking of "the abominable vice" (sodomy).

That December, when Fra Domenico first proposed Savonarola's "reform of the children," another rambunctious *fanciullo*, Donatello's nude and swashbuckling bronze David, was moved from the courtyard of the Medici palace to the courtyard of the Palazzo della Signoria. Soon afterward, the people dragged the sculptor's Judith from the spot in the Medici gardens, where it had stood since 1456, to the platform before the entrance to the palazzo. The David was intended to remind the world that little Florence had always been a killer of giants and jealous of its liberty. The determined young Judith, brandishing a sword over her head as she prepared to decapitate the drugged and sleeping Holofernes, symbolized the republic's victory over tyranny. But that Pisa should wish to shake off the tyranny of Florence as Florence had shaken off the tyranny of the Medici was as unacceptable as ever. A week before the Judith was moved to the platform, a new ambassador from Charles VIII arrived in Florence to discuss the Pisan question. Paolantonio Soderini, who was sent to negotiate with him, announced that Monsignor Gemel had promised that Pisa would be returned to Florence on January 1.

Like so many other people, however, the monsignor had reckoned without Ludovico Sforza. Because Ludovico still dreamed of making Pisa his, he gave the Pisans money with which to bribe the castellan of the fortress built by the Florentines during their hegemony. Instead of returning this fortress to Florence as his king had ordered, at two o'clock on the morning of January 1 the castellan turned it over to the Pisans, and "all the French left for Lucca." Unaware of Ludovico's role in the debacle, the Florentines immediately assumed that Charles had been mocking them. Obviously, he had never intended to let them have Pisa. Rather than direct their rage at that scatterbrained and exasperating monarch, many chose to direct it at Savonarola who had, after all, urged them to have faith in the king. Every night that week, crowds surrounded San Marco shouting: "This wretched pig of a monk, we will burn the house over his head." Convinced that the *Arrabbiati* were behind the demonstrations, the *Piagnoni*-dominated Signoria issued a proclamation forbidding people to argue about the government, the king, or the monks. Nevertheless, criticism of Savonarola and the French grew louder, and disputes over whether Florence ought to join the Holy League became more frequent.

The merchants whose livelihood was contingent on good relations with France and the wealthy men who saw the French alliance as their one hope of recovering their investments in Pisa both relied on Savonarola to keep the people loyal to King Charles. The friar had been forced to be silent during Advent. If the opposition to him were not to grow bolder, it was essential that he be given permission to preach during Lent. At the end of January, the Signoria once again asked Bartolommeo della Scala to write to Cardinal Caraffa, and the Ten asked Ricciardo Becchi to speak to the cardinal and anyone else who would listen. On February 5, Scala wrote a second letter. Rather than wait for a reply to this letter, the Signoria ordered the friar to preach during Lent, or before that if he should so determine "either in the Duomo or elsewhere," under pain of their great displeasure should he refuse.

Since the pope had forbidden him to preach until he came to Rome, to do as the Signoria asked was to defy the Holy Father and risk excommunication. On the other hand, to refuse to do as they asked was to lose the support of the political faction whose spokesman he had become and to jeopardize the moral renovation for which God had sent him to Florence: the reform of the children; the war against sodomy, gambling, poetry, and indecent dress in women; as well as the eventual renovation of the church. Moreover, there was his urgent need to preach, the sense of well-being that only preaching could give him. Inevitably, he chose to obey the Signoria rather than the pope. He was temporarily saved from the consequences of his choice by the arrival of a letter from Ricciardo Becchi informing the Ten that Cardinal Caraffa had received verbal permission for the friar to preach provided that he did not mention Roman affairs in his sermons.

Even before this letter arrived, the Signoria had made arrangements to increase the seating capacity of the Duomo by erecting tiers of wooden benches in front of the choir and to the height of the first windows along the wall opposite the pulpit. The benches were for the boys of the *Frate*. To call attention to the change he had wrought in them, Savonarola decided to organize a great procession of *fanciulli* after vespers on the last day of carnival.

Shouting "Long live Christ and the Virgin Mary, our queen!" and carrying olive branches, over 6000 boys, some of them no more than 5 or 6 years old, marched from the portico of the Ospedale degli Innocenti, with its blue-and-white medallions of abandoned babes, to the Piazza San Marco. Led by drummers and fifers provided by the Signoria, they then followed the traditional route of all Florentine processions, crossing the Arno at the Ponte Santa Trinita and recrossing it at the Ponte Vecchio, from whence they proceeded past the silk shops on the Porta Santa Maria, through the Piazza della Signoria to the cathedral. All along the line of march that cold February evening, men and women wept to see the change in these once ungovernable children. At the Duomo, where the boys circulated through the crowd collecting alms for the poor, it seemed to Luca Landucci that he had never seen "such tears of holy emotion or so much heartfelt giving."

It was in this same state of pious rapture that the people gathered early the next morning for the friar's Ash Wednesday sermon. Among the first to arrive were the boys of the *Frate* who, in their eagerness to hear him, could not be kept in bed but "ran to church before their mothers." While the vast crowd waited for the friar to appear, the boys filled the church with their singing.

The sound of their youthful, high-pitched voices, some coming from the tiers in front of the altar, some from those facing the pulpit, and the rest from the women's section where boys who could not find places in the tiers had been relegated, was so inexpressibly moving that even the men began to weep, saying: "This is a thing of the Lord's."

When at last the friar entered through the carved wooden doors facing the Via Cocomero (now the Via Ricasoli), the boys hailed him as "the light of revelation to the gentiles and the glory of his people Israel," after which the entire congregation sang the *Ave Maris Stella*. Then he was in the pulpit looking out at those thousands of upturned faces as he had done so many times in the past, feeling once again the same wild excitement he always felt when he stood there waiting to address them. For this, his first sermon in almost four months, he had chosen as his text a portion of the thirty-ninth psalm: "I said, I will take heed to my ways, that I sin not with my tongue; I will keep my mouth with a bridle, while the wicked is before me."

Like the psalmist, he pictured himself as surrounded by unscrupulous men bent on misrepresenting everything he did or said. Even were those reprobates to obtain an order for him to leave Florence or an excommunication, he told his audience, neither would be valid. "For always when it is clear that a superior's orders are contrary to God's, especially where charity is involved, no obedience is due." Not that His Holiness had commanded him to do anything contrary to charity, he hastened to assure them, nor did he believe that the pope would ever do such a thing. But were the pope to do so, the friar would tell him: "Thou art not now a good shepherd, thou art not the Roman church; thou art in error." "O you who write so many lies, what will you write now?" he cried. "You will write that I said one should not obey the pope, and I will not obey him. That is not what I said. Write down what I did say, and you will find that it does not suit you."

If the citizens of Florence only knew what kind of people wrote to Rome and what idiocies those people wrote, he continued, what a good joke they would think it all and how surprised they would be to think that anyone could believe them. Nevertheless, the extent of the opposition "against a poor little man not worth three pence" had caused him to wonder if perhaps he was not taking good heed of his ways and if perhaps his tongue had erred. But after examining his ways one by one, he had found them blameless, and so here he was back in the pulpit. However, since the wicked were still bent on traducing him, he had resolved to heed the words of the psalmist and keep his mouth with a bridle: the bridle of prudence.

Although he did not say so, he knew that among other things, being prudent meant not mentioning Roman affairs in his sermons. But how keep away from Roman affairs when all Florence was buzzing with stories of the sexual transgressions of Alexander and his court: stories of priests taking concubines and of prostitutes being smuggled into the Vatican, not to mention the endless gossip about Giulia Farnese and the baby she

had supposedly borne the pope. The friar, who had always recommended the scourge as the best antidote for impure thoughts,
was obsessed with these stories. Despite his resolve to put a bridle on his tongue, he could not refrain from denouncing the li-
centiousness of Rome from the pulpit. Like Saint Jerome and
Saint Bernard and many another *pauvre vertueux,* he seemed to
take a prurient pleasure in making his denunciations as graphic
as possible.

Already in the very sermon in which he had vowed to be
prudent, he had excoriated those prelates who squandered the
patrimony of Christ on pimps and harlots and were filled with
"adultery, incest, and sodomy." On February 24, he accused the
Roman priesthood of corrupting men with lust and women with
indecency and of leading children to sodomy and filth and turning them into prostitutes.

The following day, the Signoria moved into the as yet un-
paved hall of the Great Council. Two epigraphs composed by
the friar and sculpted in marble adorned the otherwise bare
walls. The first, which was in Tuscan, was a stanza of eight lines
warning that "whoever wishes to have a *parlamento* wishes to
take the government away from the people." The second, which
was in Latin, said:

> If this great council and sure government
> O people, of thy city never cease
> To be by thee preserved as by God sent,
> In freedom shalt thou ever stand, and peace.

To bolster the floor of the edifice, Simone Pollaiuolo, the
architect, had placed great octagonal stone pillars in the courtyard below and connected them with vaulted stone arches. Everything had been done in such haste, however, that many feared
the hall would collapse. But Savonarola assured them that were
human means to fail, God himself would strengthen the floor.
"Do you believe God wants it to collapse?" he asked. Having
settled that question to his satisfaction, he felt free to return to
the question of sexual immorality. On February 27 he compared
the pious Florentine carnival with the decidedly unpious carnival in Rome. On February 28 he announced that the greater part

of his sermon that day would be directed against prostitutes. He chose as his text a portion of the Book of Amos: "Hear this word, ye kine of Bashan, that are in the mountains of Samaria."

To him, these fat kine signified the harlots of Italy and Rome, he declared. One thousand, ten thousand, fourteen thousand were few in Rome, for there both men and women were made harlots. "Women," he roared, "make sure your daughters aren't cows; make sure they cover their bosoms and don't go around wagging their tails!"

Like the cows of Samaria, the harlots were pieces of meat with two eyes, and they had no shame, he told the women. "Is it possible that you too have no shame?" he asked them. "Is it possible that you too are concubines and not only concubines, but concubines of priests?" Then, realizing that he had perhaps overstepped himself, he excused the bluntness of his language by saying that the words he used were not his own but those of the prophet who spoke through him. "Come leaders of the church, come friars, come novices!" he cried. "You go at night to your concubines, and the morning after you go to take the sacraments....O Rome, O Italy, you have provoked the anger of God against you and provoke it always!"

Even before news of these sermons reached Rome, the pope had made it clear to Ricciardo Becchi that the members of the Holy League did not want Fra Girolamo to preach, nor did they wish the Holy Father to grant any spiritual favors to Florence until the city had agreed to join the league. Soon afterward, Becchi learned that the pope was so incensed by what he had been told of the friar's sermons that he was thinking of taking action against both Florence and its preacher. Alarmed, Becchi wrote to the Ten. Meanwhile, Savonarola too had grown uneasy about the reports of his sermons being sent to Rome and seemed bent on justifying himself.

"The Lord threatens Rome and threatens the clergy," he declared in his sermon on March 8. "O you who write to Rome, write this and don't write that I have spoken ill of the pope and the cardinals, because I have named no one.... This friar says that he threatens Rome in general, threatens the clergy and the prelates, and it is not he but God who threatens them."

He was there to defend the truth, he continued, and not to preach to Florence alone, but to all Italy. Moreover, Christ had ordered him to remain in Florence as long as he drew breath. "Go write to Rome and say that Rome may do what she wills, she will never put out this flame."

"O my Lord!" he called out, suddenly turning to the great wooden crucifix in the choir. "You know the first truth and wanted to die for Your truth. Behold I am here, Lord. You wanted to die for me, and I am content to die for You."

As he stood facing the crucifix with the tears streaming down his cheeks, shouts of "*Misericordia*, may Christ our king live!" came from every part of the cathedral, growing ever louder until they reverberated like thunder on a mountain. After waiting for some time for the pandemonium to cease so that he might continue his sermon, he made the sign of the cross over that screaming multitude. Surrounded by the armed escort which now accompanied him everywhere, he quickly left the church.

The memory of his sermon was still fresh on March 10 when the Signoria convened a *pratica* to discuss the news from Rome. Although Piero Capponi thought it might be wise to appease the pope, the majority sided with the friar. Fra Girolamo's enemies were spreading false stories about him, the Signoria told Becchi in the reply it sent the envoy on March 12. The friar had never exceeded "the measure which universal custom allowed to preachers." If he had exceeded this measure or attacked the pope, the Signoria would never have countenanced it. Becchi must urge the cardinals and the pope to place more faith in his words than in those of Fra Girolamo's enemies. He must also stress the comfort the Florentines derived from the friar's sermons and do his utmost to secure a plenary indulgence for Santa Maria dei Fiore.

Encouraged by the support of the priors and the gonfalonier, Savonarola continued his attacks on the sexual mores of the papal court. "O you unbelieving ones," he cried in his sermon on March 13, "since you will neither hearken nor be converted, thus saith the Lord:

Inasmuch as Italy is full of iniquities, harlots, and misera-
ble pimps, I will overwhelm her with the scum of the earth.
I will abase her princes and trample the pride of Rome....
They have turned their churches into stalls for prostitutes;
I will turn them into stalls for horses and swine because
these will be less displeasing to God.

Five days later, Becchi once again wrote to the Ten. The pope
had been given to understand by Cardinal Caraffa that Fra Girolamo would not meddle in Roman affairs which did not concern him and his office, said the envoy. His Holiness exhorted
the Ten to speak to the friar about this. Wasn't it enough for
him that he was allowed to go on preaching against the will of
the Holy Father?

By then, the *Arrabbiati* were spreading the rumor that Alexander had already excommunicated the friar and would soon
place the city under an interdict for supporting him. Fra Girolamo had caused so much dissension, Paolo Somenzi told Ludovico, that "it is thought these Florentines will come to blows
among themselves. In that case," Somenzi added ruefully, "I believe the friar's party will have the best of it, inasmuch as two-
thirds of the people are on his side."

To put a dent in the friar's constituency, Ludovico sent Fra
Gregorio da Perugia of the order of Augustinians to preach in
the church of Santo Spirito. Fra Girolamo was deceiving them,
Fra Gregorio told the people. Even if the pope were the most
wicked of men, anyone who preached against the Holy Father's
will was a heretic and an excommunicate. Besides challenging
Savonarola to a debate, Fra Gregorio challenged him to enter a
fire and remain there for one-eighth of an hour. If he emerged
unscathed, Fra Gregorio promised to enter the same fire and remain there for a full hour. The Augustinian asked his audience
to beseech God that if anything the aforementioned Fra Girolamo had said was true, the Lord should send a judgment on
Gregorio and strike him dead.

Fra Girolamo's reform of the children was also a target of
the preacher of Santo Spirito. Not content with encouraging the
boys to dump the baskets of raisin cakes sold during Lent, and

to spy on their elders, Savonarola was demanding that the commune give legal sanction to the political organization of the *fanciulli*. "A time will come," he told the boys, "when you will see many officials come to you to ask your advice on governing. And they will choose to govern as you govern yourselves."

"Woe to the city administered by *fanciulli!*" cried Fra Gregorio. "I am amazed that the Florentines who are considered so expert…have come into such a decline and lowness that the very children emerge with the upper hand and want to govern."

Nor was Gregorio the only one to express amazement. In Rome, it was thought dishonorable that all the world should say Florence was governed by a friar and a group of children, Ricciardo Becchi told the Ten. The complaint now was not of Fra Girolamo but of the government which allowed him to speak ill of the court of Rome "as if he had special charge of them," and "to do away with freedom of discussion in order to give more assurance to the children and the common people."

"In a word," said Becchi, "you are accused of having lost your heads, and these are the things the pope complains of in conversation alike with the envoys of the League and with those who speak in your favor."

The conviction that the governors of Florence had indeed "lost their heads" could only have been reinforced by the Palm Sunday procession to which both the Ten and the Signoria gave their assent. The procession had been organized by Fra Girolamo with the help of Fra Domenico da Pescia and Girolamo Benivieni. It consisted mainly of children, and it honored the newly established public loan bank, the *Monte di Pietà*. Unlike the four Jewish-run banks, which until then had been the principal source of credit for the *popolo minuto*, the *Monte di Pietà* would charge only enough interest to cover administrative costs. The Franciscans had been advocating just such a bank for years. What had given their efforts new impetus was a short passage against usury in the *Tavole delle Salute*, a theological best-seller by the Franciscan friar Beato Marco di Monte Santa Maria in Gallo. According to Marco's calculations, 100 ducats lent at 30 percent compound interest would bring the lender 49,792,556 ducats 7 denari 6 grossi in fifty years, whereas only 50 ducats lent at the same rate of interest for 800 years would amount to more money than there was sand in the sea.

Since Florentine law forbade Jewish moneylenders to charge more than 20 percent interest, and since the net yearly profit of each of the four Jewish banks in the city had never exceeded 1000 florins, Marco's calculations had little if anything to do with the situation there. Nevertheless, his book caused such an uproar in Florence that at the end of 1495 the Great Council passed a law calling for an end to the "pestiferous abyss of usury" and providing for a commission of eight to draw up statutes for the *Monte di Pietà*. As soon as the bank was established, moneylending by Jews would cease, and Jewish moneylenders would have one year to wind up their affairs before leaving the city. By repeatedly endorsing the bank from the pulpit, Savonarola took much of the credit for originating the idea away from the Franciscans. Perhaps under the influence of the Jewish scholar Blemet, who had become a monk of San Marco after converting to Christianity, perhaps on his own, he also reduced the anti-Semitic thrust of the measure and, in the end, made it possible for the Jews to remain in Florence.

Because the bank needed working capital, he urged everyone who had "money, dowries, deposits, and gifts available for charity" to lend to the bank and he announced that at a certain point in the Palm Sunday procession, a collection would be taken. Besides providing money for the bank the collection would, of course, call attention to the friar's ability to mobilize the people and get things done. But in Savonarola's mind these practical and partially self-serving considerations lay hidden beneath a thick mantle of religious significance.

"Because our Lord has said, 'Thou shalt not appear before me empty-handed,' everyone is to give an offering," he told the people, "and folk are not to give farthings but ducats....And let no one murmur against this procession, since although it is made by the children, it is from God that it comes."

"O Lord!" he cried in his sermon on Palm Sunday. "From the mouths of these little ones shall Thy true praise proceed....

Philosophers praise Thee from self-love, and these from simplicity; philosophers praise Thee with their lips and these with their
works."

Over 6000 boys marched in the procession that afternoon
"in the form of beautiful angels dressed in white." Wearing olive wreaths and carrying olive branches and palm-high red crosses, they emerged from the cloister of San Marco in size places,
three by three, singing lauds interspersed with shouts of "Long
live Christ, the King, and the Queen of eternal life!" Behind
them came a tabernacle sheltering a painted image of Christ "as
He rode through the streets of Jerusalem on Palm Sunday." And
behind this tabernacle walked the clergy, followed by a procession of girls also in white and also carrying olive branches and
red crosses. Next came the city officials, and last of all the adult
men and women.

"So great was the fervor of that day," says one chronicler
"that not children and women alone, but also men of station
and position...laying aside all human respect, robed themselves
in white garments and danced and sang before the tabernacle
like David before the ark, crying out loud with the children:
"Long live Jesus Christ, our king!"

In the Piazza della Signoria, Girolamo Benivieni, who had
once thought that he could not live in a world that did not include his beloved Pico, led the children in singing a canzone he
had composed for the occasion:

> Arise O New Jerusalem and see
> your Queen and her beloved son
> In your City of God who now sit and weep.
>
> Such joy and splendor will yet be born
> as to decorate both you and all the world
> In those days of bliss.
>
> You will see all the world come to you
> devoted and faithful folk,
> Drawn by the odor of your holy lily.

Toward evening, when the procession returned to San Marco,
the friars emerged from the convent dressed in white, "each one

wearing a garland on his head, and they formed a great circle around the entire piazza dancing and singing psalms."

That was on March 27. Three days later, Ricciardo Becchi warned the Ten that the pope was planning to take judicial action against the friar. On Easter Sunday, the Holy Father invited fourteen Dominican masters of theology to the Vatican. It was his intention, he told them, to punish Fra Girolamo as a heretic and a schismatic, a man at once disobedient to the Holy See and superstitious. Moreover, the pope continued, he wished to punish not only the friar but all who favored him. An associate of Cardinal Caraffa named Master Nicholas immediately protested, but with the exception of one young cleric who also took the friar's part, everyone else agreed with the pope. The meeting ended with each of those present being asked to think of suitable measures to take against Fra Girolamo.

Two days later, however, at the insistence of cardinals Lopez and Martino, acting in concert with the pope's secretary, Ludovico Podocatharo, Alexander decided to postpone all hostile measures. At the same time, said Ricciardo Becchi in a letter to the Ten, the pope had asked his secretary to have Becchi inform their excellencies "that His Paternity [Savonarola] ought to speak more modestly of His Holiness and the most reverend cardinals and other prelates, and that he ought not to transgress the methods of other excellent and admirable preachers; nor open his mouth on things which do not pertain to him and his office. And in truth," added Becchi, "His Holiness has put up with no small amount of provocation."

Although Becchi took credit for persuading Podocatharo and the cardinals to speak to the pope, their intervention probably had less to do with Alexander's change of heart than the envoy supposed. Because the pope was an excitable man who frequently lost his temper, it was not unusual for him to make threats which, on reflection, he chose not to carry out. The friar had provoked him beyond endurance not so much by what he had said about Rome as by the spiritual pride that allowed him to go on saying it after being told to keep away from Roman affairs in his sermons. Added to this was Alexander's conviction that Savonarola and Savonarola alone was keeping Florence from joining the Holy League. Although the pope would have liked nothing better than to impose ecclesiastical sanctions on the exasperating fellow, it did not take him long to realize that he had chosen the wrong time to do so. For one thing, the friar had the support of the Signoria and the majority of the people. Besides antagonizing them, imposing sanctions could incite them to open rebellion against the Holy See. For another thing, it would certainly antagonize King Charles, who had just then announced plans to come to the aid of the garrison he had left behind in Naples.

After being assured by the Signoria that Fra Girolamo had spoken "with the greatest respect" of His Holiness, Alexander pronounced himself "well-satisfied" with the affairs of the friar. That May, the pope sent one of his masters of theology, Ludovico of Valenza, on a secret mission to Fra Girolamo. Since Alexander's son Cesare was the cardinal of Valenza, it was only natural for the gossips to confuse the two and to assume that the pope had sent his son to San Marco. Nor was the reason for Cesare's supposed visit a mystery to them.

At the close of 1493, when Alexander had made it clear that he would oppose the French invasion of Italy, Charles had threatened to summon a general council to depose him. Such councils were nothing new. In 1415, the Council of Constance had deposed the antipope John XXIII, who was forced to seek refuge with Cosimo dei Medici. To discourage the summoning of further councils, Pius II had issued the bull *Exacrabilis*, which condemned and forbade any attempt to convene a general council without papal initiative. Although the penalty for disobeying the bull was anathema, this did not keep disgruntled kings and cardinals from continuing to use the threat of a council every time they had a disagreement with the pope. True, Charles had as yet made no move to summon a council, but the pope's enemies, of whom there were many, were constantly urging the king to do so. What could be more logical than for the pope to send his son to San Marco to offer Fra Girolamo some great promotion, possibly a cardinal's hat, if he persuaded the king to forget about a council?

Logical, but as it turned out not so, for according to Savonarola's sworn testimony, the papal envoy, who was, of course, not Cesare but Ludovico of Valenza, told him in strictest confidence that Alexander would like the Florentines either to send him an ambassador or to write him a conciliatory letter. And the envoy sought to have the friar explain the pope's intentions to the people. Since doing so would confirm the oft-repeated charge that the friar was the true ruler of Florence, he suggested that the envoy see either Francesco Valori or Paolantonio Soderini.

If the Holy Father was angered by the rebuff, he was careful not to show it. Nor did he express any anger at the seventeen sermons Fra Girolamo preached between May 8 and July 3, although they were as filled with attacks on Rome and other matters "which did not pertain to the friar and his office" as the sermons he had delivered during Lent.

Toward the end of May, there were rumors that the pope was planning to come to an agreement with King Charles and leave the Holy League. On June 8, however, Ricciardo Becchi reported that the pope was sending his second son, the duke of Gandia, to Siena with Piero dei Medici and a company of men-at-arms who would help the Pisans. As if this were not bad news enough, on June 12, the Florentines learned that the Venetians were also sending soldiers to Pisa. Obviously, said Luca Landucci, the root of the problem with the Pisans was that they were supported by others who were able to pay the cost. Florence, on the other hand, could expect no help from anyone and was fast running out of cash with which to pay for soldiers and supplies.

One reason for the lack of cash was the thousands of florins in tribute and the expensive gifts, including "two lions in wooden cages," the city had bestowed upon King Charles in exchange for his promise to return Pisa. Another reason was the endless rain—during the past eleven months, there hadn't been one full week of sunshine. On May 18, a great flood washed away the young corn in the fields along the Arno and crumbled the walls on the roadside near Rovizzano. At the beginning of June, the Rifredi River overflowed its banks, destroying yet more crops, so that the price of corn rose to 34 soldi a bushel. As usual, the floods brought malaria in their wake, and there was also an epidemic of what Landucci called "French boils"—syphilis.

Toward the end of July, when Piero Capponi replaced Paolantonio Soderini as general commissary for the Pisan campaign, the money he received for arms and other supplies came from the *Monte di Pietà* because, said Ludovico's agent in Bologna, the only available cash the Florentines had was the 20,000 ducats in the *Monte* and the 7000 the Jews had paid the Signoria for the privilege of remaining in Florence. To increase the flow of cash into the treasury and to reduce the flow out, the Great Council approved a forced loan of 50,000 florins from the priests and voted to reduce the salaries of municipal officials in the city by one-half and of those outside the city by one-third. Soon afterward, the council voted that all taxes, including that on salt, be paid in silver coin. Although the government insisted that the increased revenue would be used to keep the cost of corn down in Florence and the surrounding countryside, by August 10 the price had risen to 40 soldi a bushel.

The *Arrabbiati* blamed the city's misery on the friar and his pro-French policy, and, as usual, they were encouraged by the machinations of Ludovico Sforza. To make King Charles think twice about a new invasion, Ludovico persuaded the Holy League to offer Emperor Maximilian 40,000 ducats—20 percent to be supplied by the pope and the remaining 80 percent by Venice and Milan—if Maximilian would come to Italy to arbitrate the Pisan affair. Maximilian, who despite his grandiose title was so impoverished that in the opinion of one writer, "he would almost sell his own teeth for money," immediately sent ambassadors to Florence. The Florentines must show they were good Italians by leaving the king of France and joining the Holy League, the ambassadors told the Signoria. To bolster their cause, Ludovico released letters from Savonarola, purportedly intercepted on their way to France, in which the friar threatened King Charles with dire calamity if he did not obey God's will and come to Italy. But Savonarola insisted the letters were forgeries, and the Signoria, like the majority of the people it represented, continued to believe that joining the League would mean the end of popular government in Florence.

As long as Charles was expected momentarily, there was little risk in putting off the emperor with vague assurances that, despite the absence of a formal commitment, he could count on the Florentines for anything he might desire. At the beginning of October, however, grief over the death of the 3-week-old dauphin led the king to postpone a new invasion indefinitely. Freed of the specter of the French, the Venetians promptly blockaded Livorno, the one outlet to the sea left to Florence.

By then the shortage of food in the city and the surrounding countryside had grown acute. Plague was also spreading, in part, said the friar's critics, because of Savonarola's insistence that no starving beggar or peasant who sought refuge in Florence be turned away. Every hospital was full, and the courtyards of many private homes and palaces had been turned into shelters for the sick and the needy. Lacking the wherewithal to resist a blockade indefinitely, the Florentines appealed to their merchants in France for help. The merchants responded by outfitting a number of vessels and filling them with grain, but a ferocious gale compelled most of the ships to return to Marseilles.

Meanwhile, Maximilian arrived in Pisa. The Pisans were so overjoyed to see him that they tossed the statue of King Charles they had placed on a bridge over the Arno into the river and replaced it with one of the emperor. As they had hoped he would, their new champion immediately set out for Livorno with his army.

"Do you see how the friar has deceived you?" said the *Arrabbiati*. "Behold the happiness that he predicted for you!" Everyone assumed that there would be an uprising before the election of the next Signoria and that the new government would reach an agreement with the emperor, Ludovico's agent in Bologna told him.

Seeing no hope of human succor, on Wednesday, October 26, the incumbent Signoria voted to bring the Madonna of the Impruneta into the city the following Sunday, and ordered Savonarola to preach on Friday.

He entered the cathedral that morning surrounded by his bodyguard and followed by the thousands of boys who, like so many flies, now buzzed about him whenever he left San Marco.

As the spokesman of the popular faction, he knew that he was expected to assure the people that God and His merciful mother would help them and to urge them to lay aside the idea of changing the government and making surrender. He went considerably further, however, announcing "good news from heaven," and offering to forfeit his very robe if "by uniting together and casting out all dissension," they did not drive off their enemies. And he reminded them of the Friday two years earlier when he had prevailed upon King Charles to leave Florence, and how when the king returned from Naples, he had gone at full speed to the French camp and threatened his majesty so that Charles left them unharmed. "Have faith in my words," he told them. "Arrange this procession and trust in the Lord....And I want no women standing in the streets like whores. If anyone can't take part in this procession, let him or her remain indoors."

Now it so happened that at about this time, the mail from Lyons included three letters from King Charles assuring the Florentines that help was on the way. Although the friar did not mention these letters in his sermon, it could have been the knowledge of what they contained that led him to speak so boldly. Nor would he feel uneasy about withholding this knowledge from his audience, for by then the need to keep his hold on them had made such equivocation second nature to him.

Shortly after the singing of the *Ave Maria* the following evening, the miraculous hidden image of the Madonna of Santa Maria dell'Impruneta began its 6-mile journey to Florence accompanied by the confraternities and the canons of the village. Day was just breaking when the candlelit procession reached the Porta San Piero in Gattolino, where the Signoria and all the confraternities, religious orders, and guilds of the city were waiting to pay homage to the merciful Mother. Taking their prearranged places behind the great cross of the Duomo, they marched in solemn silence in the direction of the Ponte Vecchio, followed by the Madonna and her retinue. As the sacred tabernacle was slowly borne across the bridge between rows of kneeling marchers, those facing south saw a lone horseman gallop across the Ponte alla Carraia at breakneck speed, then wheel in his horse and head down the Lungarno in their direction waving what appeared to be an olive branch.

He brought the most wonderful news, he told the great throng that pressed in upon him when he reached the Ponte Vecchio: seven ships from Marseilles carrying supplies of corn and reinforcements had arrived at Livorno that morning. Moreover, the same wind that had brought them safely into the harbor had compelled the Venetian ships blockading the port to withdraw. As a result, the Livornese had routed the emperor's forces, killing about forty soldiers and taking many more prisoner, including, among others, Maximilian's own herald.

"The friar's sermons have saved us again!" the people told one another as they flocked to the churches to give thanks.

Although he at first cautioned them against being "so easily overcome by joy or grief," two weeks later, when the city learned that the storm had "dispersed and battered the ships of the League," he was as euphoric as everyone else. And he could not resist taunting his enemies.

"First laughter, now tears," he declared. "First the wicked are gay, then they are saddened. Only a little while ago, they were rejoicing and saying 'Do you see how we have been deceived?' Now they keep quiet....Well, what do you see now? The noose was in the rope, but it didn't go in. What do you say now, you wicked ones?"

It was at this time, when his hold on the city seemed once again assured, that a new brief arrived from Rome.

VI

THE BATTLE GOES ON

Being a prudent man, Alexander VI liked to do unpleasant things in a pleasant manner whenever possible. The pope's new brief was called *Reformationi et Augmento*. It had been suggested to him by Francesco Mei, a onetime brother of San Marco who had since become procurator of the Dominican order and one of Savonarola's most dogged adversaries. In the interest of religious reform, it proposed to unite San Marco and fifteen other convents in a new Tuscan-Roman congregation. Should anyone object to this reshuffling of convents or seek to impede it, he would be subject to excommunication. And the beauty of the whole scheme was that although the brief was not addressed to Savonarola nor did it so much as mention him, it was his freedom of action that it would curb.

After the pope had (so foolishly, it now seemed to him) removed San Marco from the Lombard congregation, he had allowed the friar to be permanently affiliated to the convent and had given him the powers of a provincial over the newly constituted Tuscan congregation. As such, he had no immediate superior and could do more or less what he pleased. In the Tuscan-Roman congregation, on the other hand, he would no longer be a provincial but simply one prior among sixteen, subject to the close supervision of a vicar general, who could transfer him to another convent at any time.

Given Savonarola's imperious and power-loving nature and

the freedom he had enjoyed for the past three and a half years, he would have found such an arrangement intolerable under any circumstances. As it was, he could tell himself that since God had sent him to Florence and Christ had ordered him to remain there, he had no alternative but to object, even if by doing so he laid himself open to excommunication. He sought to dilute the risk, however, by having the first challenge to the new brief come from his friars. That way, he could use their opposition as an excuse for his.

During the five and a half years he had been prior, San Marco had grown from a convent housing 50 monks to one that housed 250, including, said Guicciardini, "noble youths from the first families of the city, older men of reputation, such as Pandolfo Rucellai, a member of the Ten and ambassador to King Charles; Messer Giorgio Antonio Vespucci and Messer Malatesta [Sacramoro], canons of the cathedral; Pietro Paolo da Urbino, a physician of reputation and good life; Zanobi Acciuoli, who was very learned in Latin and Greek; and many others like them." Among this company were some who heard spirits everywhere, one who foamed at the mouth and saw men in the shape of crows, and a few, including Savonarola's former secretary Fra Ruberto Ubaldini, who took exception to the way Fra Girolamo and his two closest associates, Fra Domenico da Pescia and Fra Silvestro Maruffi, lorded it over everyone else. As if, said Fra Ruberto, the rest of them were there "only to give assent to what these three *gran maestri* proposed." But not even Fra Ruberto was prepared to cross the *gran maestri* by refusing to sign the letter which the brethren of San Marco sent to Rome that November. The new brief was irregular, they told the pope. Furthermore, they did not wish to pass from the close observance under which they lived to what they assumed would be the more lenient observance of the new congregation.

Although it could not have taken Alexander long to divine the real purpose of this letter, he was too busy trying to subdue his rebellious vassals, the Orsini, to force the issue. On November 30 Savonarola, who by then was used to ignoring papal briefs and getting away with it, began a new round of sermons based upon the Book of Ezekiel, a prophet as given to elaborate and terrifying visions as Savonarola himself. Like so many of his sermons, his first one on Ezekiel took the form of a dialogue. "You are not a Jew, you are a Christian," he had the prophet tell him. "And the veil of the temple was rent when Christ was crucified; so you must not speak *sub nube;* you must speak the truth openly, though some may take it ill."

Although this seemed to presage new attacks on the pope and the clergy, there was little mention of either in the sermons that Advent. And if the preacher appeared to have forgotten the pope, the pope for his part seemed once again to have lost interest in the preacher. But this lull in hostilities was not destined to last, for though Alexander still wished to avoid a direct confrontation with the friar, he was also determined to quash pro-French sentiment in Florence—and so was his close ally Ludovico Sforza.

On November 7, Ludovico's agent Paolo Somenzi had had a long talk with Savonarola, promising rich rewards for both him and the city if he would undertake to bring Florence into the Holy League. Although Somenzi was encouraged, or at least pretended to be encouraged, by the friar's response, Ludovico's agent in Bologna warned him that Savonarola was "bound hand and foot to the French alliance." However, said this agent, many people in Florence believed that if the League acted with vigor, the designs of the *Frateschi,* or friar's party, would come to nought.

That autumn, Ludovico had begun a passionate love affair with Lucrezia Crivelli, one of his wife's ladies-in-waiting. Dazzled by the beauty of his teenage mistress, he had asked Leonardo da Vinci to paint her portrait. To one observer it seemed as if the 47-year-old lover found all his pleasure in the company of this young girl. But neither his infatuation with Lucrezia nor his grief at the unexpected death of his 15-year-old illegitimate daughter Bianca was allowed to interfere with his resolve to thwart the *Frateschi.* Young Bianca Sforza had been in her grave little more than a month when Ludovico summoned the papal legate to his chambers. Since Charles VIII was expected to invade Italy at any moment, he told the legate, it had become more necessary than ever for the states of Italy to present a united front. To that end, he and the ambassadors of the League at his court wanted the pope to assume responsibility for the affairs of Florence. And they were prepared to grant the Holy Father full power to use any means he considered suitable to bring the city into the League, including restitution of its former possessions (that is, Pisa).

On January 3, the pope discussed this proposal with the League's representatives in Rome. Since with the exception of Venice, they were enthusiastic, he invited the Florentine envoys to the Vatican. Like a good pastor, he had always sought the union of his sheep, he told them. But never had this union been more necessary than now when a new invasion seemed imminent. And he urged the Florentines to be good Italians and no longer to allow themselves to be seduced by the words of Fra Girolamo. Rather than commit themselves, the envoys promised to relay the pope's message to the Signoria. The Signoria had not yet drafted a reply when Alexander learned that the assault of the papal army on the Orsini stronghold at Lake Bracciano led by his son, the duke of Gandia, was going badly. As a result, the pope decided to postpone action on Florence.

Although Ludovico Sforza might have been expected to chafe at the postponement, he did not. Since the early hours of January 3, the duke of Milan had been lying on his bed in a darkened room "quite prostrate," and he would lie there for the next fortnight "more overcome with grief," said the Ferrarese ambassador, than anyone the ambassador had ever seen.

Ludovico had married Beatrice d'Este, the youngest daughter of Duke Ercole of Ferrara, when he was 40 and she was 15. Although he had had a mistress at the time and had been reluctant to give her up, until Lucrezia Crivelli caught his eye he had been a combination of lover and indulgent parent to his rambunctious young bride. As his infatuation with Lucrezia grew more open, Beatrice, who was then pregnant with her third child, grew increasingly despondent. More than once, her ladies-in-waiting saw tears in her eyes, though whether these were caused by her husband's neglect or grief over the death of her stepdaughter Bianca, they could not say. That December, Beatrice began making daily visits to her stepdaughter's tomb in the church of

Santa Maria delle Grazie, where Leonardo was working on his *Last Supper*. Seemingly oblivious of the masterpiece taking shape on the convent wall, this normally vivacious young woman, whose cruel pranks had once so delighted her husband, spent hours praying at Bianca's tomb. After passing the morning of January 2 on her knees before the tomb, she returned to the Castello Sforzesco to dress for a ball that was to be held in her chambers. At eight o'clock that evening, while dancing with her ladies-in-waiting, she was suddenly taken ill. Three hours later, she was delivered of a stillborn son. At half past midnight, she died.

It was Ludovico's unassuageable guilt at the heartache he had caused her during the last months of her life that made him take to his bed. If he had not behaved as he should toward his wife, if he had wronged her in any way, as he knew he had, he begged Duke Ercole's pardon and hers, he told the Ferrarese ambassador. And, said the ambassador, "he lamented her in language so true and natural, it would have moved the very stones to tears." Rather than being concerned about events in Florence, it seemed to one correspondent that the duke had "ceased to care for his children or his state or anything else on earth and could scarcely bear to live."

A few days before Ludovico took to his bed, the *Piagnone* majority in the Great Council chose Francesco Valori as gonfalonier for the months of January and February. Until then, said one chronicler, the *Piagnoni* had been "a tail without a head," whereas Valori had been "a head without a tail." Since the new head of the *Piagnoni* was known to act "without respect for others, hustling and abusing anyone who opposed him," the *Arrabbiati* considered his election as gonfalonier a catastrophe. Even Savonarola's enthusiasm was tempered by the fear that Valori's spiny tongue and imperious manner would eventually drive off all his friends. On the other hand, he was one of the few politicians who had never sought to enrich himself at the expense of the state. Though there could be little doubt that he had initially chosen the friar's side because "it was stronger and would give him easier access to office and greater public favor," unlike others who had made the same choice for the same reasons, Valori could be counted on to pay more than mere lip service to a program of moral reform.

No sooner did he take office than he rammed through a bill giving legal sanction to the political organization of the *fanciulli* and another regulating the dress of women and girls, which even the *Piagnoni* had hitherto refused to consider. At the same time he announced a redoubling of the war against sodomy and gambling.

Nor was this all. Convinced that Florentine citizens in Rome who visited the palace of Cardinal Giovanni were conspiring with him for the return of Piero, Valori demanded passage of a law making all commerce with Piero and his brothers illegal. Because the friar's Advent sermons had stressed the need to "polish and readjust" the Great Council, Valori also pushed through a bill excluding all who were delinquent in their tax payments. When this reduced the pool of citizens eligible for membership well below the number required by law, he decided to make up the difference by lowering the age of eligibility from 30 to 24.

Until he did this, young men between the ages of 24 and 30—or *giovani*, as they were called—had lived in a sort of limbo, old enough to join the priesthood or marry but too young to vote or hold office. By giving them the opportunity to serve on the council, Valori hoped to swell the *Piagnone* majority. But perhaps because he was childless himself and had little contact with men under 30, he failed to realize that there was no group in society which found the friar's reforms more irksome; no group more devoted to gambling, drinking, whoring, and sodomy; no group more resentful of the pieties of the carnival and the elimination of the horse race from the feast of San Giovanni.

On January 17, a wealthy young blood by the name of Francesco Cei was banished from the city for publishing a popular ballad, in which he asked God for what sin He had consented to ruin Florence:

> At the request of four citizens
> Ambitious and astute
> Who have subtly fashioned an idolatry
> Only to usurp this nation.

The day before Cei was banished, Giovanni Dicomano had undertaken to distribute copies of a ballad written by his friend Girolamo Muzi. It began:

> O ungrateful people
> Thou art caught by a cry
> And follow a guide
> All full of hypocrisy.

Muzi had to pay a fine of 70 gold florins and was prohibited from holding public office for five years. After being forced to spend over two hours in the pillory, Dicomano was sentenced to jail for two months.

At the time of his sentencing, carnival was in full swing. While his fellow *giovani* continued to fume at what they regarded as the hypocritical proscription of sex, drink, and all the other diversions that had once made the weeks between Epiphany and Lent so glorious, Fra Domenico was sending the *fanciulli* from house to house to confiscate "lascivious and shameful" articles, or *anathemae*, as they were called. Humbly pointing out that such articles were accursed of God and the canons of the holy church, the boys demanded that the ladies of the house surrender rouge pots, eye shadow, and perfume; ribbons, false hair, and pearl-studded hairnets; cameos, necklaces, and pendants, as well as any other superfluous adornments they might own. When out of fear of eternal damnation or of the downy-cheeked inquisitors on their doorstep, as the case might be, the ladies dropped the accursed stuff into the waiting baskets, the boys recited a short blessing composed for the occasion by Fra Domenico. If while moving on to the next house they chanced upon some fashionable dame with a smooth and shaven forehead visible beneath her provocatively transparent veil, two daubs of red on her cheeks, and ribbons and pearls entwined in the tureen-shaped edifice that was her hair, they would form a circle around her. "Gentle lady," they told her, "remember that you too must die. Give up this pomp and luxury." And they would refuse to let her pass until she had deposited the offending articles in their baskets. If, as often happened, she was accompanied by some musk-scented *signore* with rings on every finger, parti-colored hose, and an embroidered vest, he too was asked to surrender his finery.

Nor was personal adornment the boys' only target. Cards, dice, and gaming tables; chessboards, and ivory and alabaster chessmen; harps, guitars, and horns; books by Boccaccio, Plato, Luigi Pulci, and even Dante; carnival masks and costumes; terra-cotta Cupids and other "indecent" statues; lascivious tapestries and paintings—all had to be given up. Even pictures of the Virgin were fair game if they did not meet the friar's standards. "Do you imagine the Virgin Mary went about dressed as she is depicted?" Savonarola had asked in a sermon the previous Lent. "I tell you, she went about dressed as a poor person—simply, and so veiled that her face could hardly be seen. You would do well to blot out pictures so unsuitably painted. You make the Virgin Mary look like a harlot."

On the last day of carnival, all the "vain and useless articles" the boys had collected would be transferred to a gigantic pyramid of vanities to be erected in the Piazza della Signoria and then burned. The pyramid was 60 feet high and reached a diameter of over 270 feet at its base. At its center was an immense fir tree from whose summit eight wooden beams extended downward. Encircling these beams at regular intervals were fifteen steps, or tiers. Upon these, the boys placed the contents of their baskets—not haphazardly, but in a fashion calculated to please the eye: women's ornaments, toilet articles, scents, mirrors, veils, and false hair on one tier; paintings, especially paintings of female beauties, including courtesans, on another; lutes, harps, chessboards, and playing cards on a third. In the empty space behind the beams was a pile of old brooms, kindling wood, and bundles of twigs, along with enough gunpowder to ensure a roaring blaze when a torch was applied. Having heard the friar "shout every day in the pulpit…that it was not good to keep paintings of male and female nudes in a house where there were children," Baccio della Porta brought the drawings of nudes he had to be burned, as did Leonardo's old friend Lorenzo di Credi and many lesser artists.

Although such bonfires had been part of the Franciscan repertory for over fifty years, the brothers of Saint Francis were not at all happy to see their colleagues in the order of Saint Dominic appropriate the idea. Fra Jacopo da Brescia, a Franciscan preacher in the church of San Lorenzo, warned the people that they were being deceived "under cover of good"; and his cry was taken up by Franciscans preaching in three other churches. The Valori-dominated Signoria retaliated by demanding that the Franciscans explain in what way the people were being deceived or cease preaching. But when Fra Jacopo showed up at the palazzo to plead his case, Valori called him and the friars who accompanied him "seditious and wicked men" and drove them from the premises without giving Fra Jacopo a chance to say a word. Thoroughly intimidated, all four preachers retired to the suburbs.

At about the same time, a group of *giovani* decided to divert attention from the proposed bonfire by announcing plans for a soccer game on the last day of carnival. They divided into two teams, one team dubbing its leader "king" and the other calling its leader "duke." But the Signoria refused to allow the teams to play one another, insisting that it would be too dangerous.

Meanwhile, the city's corn supply had dwindled still further, and the price had risen to 3 lire 14 soldi a bushel. On January 25, a woman died in the crowd in the Piazza del Grano, the market behind the palazzo where the government sold bread and corn at what was considered a fair price. On February 6, the day before the vanities were to be burned, the crush in the marketplace was so great that several women suffocated and others were carried out "half dead." Rather than burn all the beautiful things the boys had collected, some people thought that the commune ought to sell them and use the money from the sale to help the poor. But when a Venetian merchant offered the Signoria 20,000 ducats for the pyramid and its contents, he was reprimanded and his picture placed at the summit of the pyre to reign over the proceedings alongside a figure of King Carnival so monstrous and deformed that "it would be difficult to imagine anything more grotesque."

That evening it seemed as if all Florence was either in the Piazza della Signoria or at the windows of the nearby buildings when, to a fanfare of trumpets and fifes and a clanging of cymbals, the four *custodi*, or neighborhood leaders of the *fanciulli*, applied lighted torches to the ungainly wooden structure. As the tiers began to blacken and collapse, and the orange-yellow flames reached up toward the figure of King Carnival, the clangor of the palace bells echoed and reechoed in the cold night air, while the music of trumpet, fife, and cymbal grew ever more jubilant, and the white-clad *fanciulli* on the platform in front of the palace and in the Loggia dei Lanzi sang hymns and lauds.

"Should anyone regard this as a childish affair," said Girolamo Benivieni, who had composed many of the lauds, "let him as a Christian put off the spectacles of Satan's pride and assume those of Christ's humility before passing judgment." The poet who had once shared Lorenzo's love of all those beautiful artifacts of "secular humanism" appeared to derive great satisfaction from seeing paintings and statues worth several thousand ducats on the tiers and holding in his own hand a painted head for which 10 ducats had been offered, as well as a chessboard said to be worth 40 ducats without its men.

But for Savonarola, this was only the beginning. The *fanciulli* had taken away many old things; they must ferret out the others, he declared in his Ash Wednesday sermon. "You women," he cried. "Rid yourselves of these vain articles, these ugly faces you have. And I give you permission on Christ's behalf to cast them into the fire."

"What are you doing with Hercules and Anteus?" he continued. "Put the Virgin Mary, the cross, and the saints everywhere." Turning to the *fanciulli*, he urged them to confiscate every anathema they had not confiscated during carnival.

Saint Paul had burned many curious volumes and other articles, he declared in his sermon the next day. Saint Gregory had smashed the beautiful figureheads of Rome and set fire to the first ten books of Titus Livius. Was Saint Gregory a madman? If he was, "I want such madmen here, and the bark of Peter will be the better for them!"

Although the last important French-held fortress in the kingdom of Naples had surrendered a few weeks earlier and Charles VIII was said to still be too grief-stricken over the death of his infant son to care, the friar was convinced that the king would soon return to Italy. In his sermons that February he alternated

pleas for moral reform and faith in God with attacks on the prof-
ligacy of Rome and predictions of a great scourge. Just as Ezekiel
had foretold the scourge of Jerusalem, so he foretold the scourge
and renovation of the church, Savonarola declared on February
13.

God had lifted him up and said, "Go look at Italy, friar. Behold the idols everywhere; behold Rome where they sell all
things," he told his audience on February 19. "Is it not written
in their canons that every sin is as nothing compared to the sin
of simony?"

Although there had been no word from the Vatican since November, he was careful to take the edge off the accusation of
simony by denying that he spoke ill of the pope. He named no
one, he declared. Resorting to the dialogue form he found so con-
genial, he launched into a spirited defense of his attacks on the
priests and the *tiepidi*. There was much more he had planned
to say that morning, but preaching three hours each day and
preparing a new sermon each evening was proving more exhaust-
ing than he had anticipated. Using the lateness of the hour as
an excuse, he suddenly cut short his sermon with a promise to
take up where he had left off the following day. Twice during
the past week he had curtailed his sermons with the same promise. Soon after he cut short his sermon that Sunday, peasants
waiting to buy grain in the Piazza del Grano broke through the
fence and began looting the commune's supply. Although the
town criers and mace bearers sent by the Signoria repeatedly
ordered the looters to disperse on pain of death, no one paid any
attention to them. More than one onlooker reported hearing cries
of *Palle! Palle!* from the mob, "as if things had been better under the Medici." And many blamed the friar and the Valori government for the shortages.

Although the looting of the grain supply was still on everyone's lips when Savonarola entered the pulpit the following morning, he did not mention it in his sermon. Instead, he launched
into a rambling exegesis of Chapter 9 of Ezekiel. But once again,
he lacked the energy to finish what he had started. On February
21 he appeared refreshed. The prophet never grew discouraged,
he told the crowd in the cathedral that Tuesday. Even when he

was mocked and scorned, he remained firm. All true prophets behaved thus, and so would he. He ended his sermon with a reminder that just as the things that Ezekiel had foretold had happened in the lifetime of his audience, so the scourge which he had foretold would happen in theirs.

Only a few hours after he made this prediction, the Florentines learned that Philip of Spain, acting on behalf of the Holy League, had negotiated a one-year truce with Charles VIII. What now was to be made of the prophetic light by which the friar had foretold the king's imminent return to scourge and renovate the church? And what of all the money that had been lavished on Charles because of the friar's assurance that if they remained loyal to the king, they would have Pisa "despite all the world"?

Although Savonarola refused to disavow any of his prophecies, to the *Arrabbiati* chronicler Piero Parenti, who heard his next two sermons, he seemed to be "changing cloaks, but cautiously and subtly under the guise of comforting the people and doing good."

"Florence, I have told you many things absolutely and many conditionally," he declared on February 22. "The scourge of Italy, the renovation of the church, and the conversion of the Turks: these are all absolute and must arrive no matter what." But he denied having asked them to hold with the king of France. He had never asked them to make a league with anyone but Christ, he declared. As for Charles, had he not warned the king that he would have many tribulations if he did not keep faith? "And he has had many tribulations and his son has died....If he does not do what he has to do, he will be rejected; God will kill him and he will lose his temporal and spiritual reign and God will quickly elect someone else."

But despite his efforts to justify himself, the truce, coming as it did so soon after the looting of the Piazza del Grano, encouraged his enemies and increased their number. Because, said Guicciardini, Bernardo del Nero, the leader of the *Bigi*, or Medici faction, was "elderly and enjoyed high reputation as a wise man," and because "there did not seem a more suitable man in Florence to oppose Francesco Valori," everyone who had a grievance against the *Frateschi* rallied behind him. On February 26, the Great Council named del Nero gonfalonier for March and April.

Upon hearing the news, Paolo Somenzi immediately wrote to Ludovico. "It is believed that the friar and his faction will fare ill," Somenzi told his employer. "He has been preaching against the French king, so that it is easily seen that he has been preaching in accordance with the wishes of the Valori government and not by divine inspiration. Consequently, he will lose his reputation, and all will go according to your highness's wishes."

Although by then Ludovico had left his bed, his rooms were still draped in black, and out of respect for Beatrice he insisted upon taking all his meals standing up. To keep alive his wife's memory, he had decreed that 100 requiem masses be sung each day in Santa Maria delle Grazie where she was buried, and that 100 wax tapers be kept burning around her tomb. Wearing a suit of black fustian and wrapped in a long black cloak, he made a point of being present at two or three of these masses each day. There was, of course, no thought of resuming his liaison with Lucrezia Crivelli. "The duke was very religious, recited the offices daily, observed fasts and lived chastely and devoutly," said the Venetian chronicler Sanuto. And this chastity combined with his constant self-reproaches and his wild laments at Beatrice's funeral soon made the world forget that there had ever been any other woman in his life.

The role of grieving widower, though demanding, was not, however, so demanding as to preclude other roles. After the battle of Fornovo, Ludovico had boasted that Pope Alexander was his chaplain, the emperor Maximilian his condottiere, the Signoria of Venice his chamberlain, and the king of France his courier who came and went at his pleasure. No sooner was he up and about than the old zest for masterminding the affairs of Italy returned. With the threat of a new invasion by the French temporarily out of the way and the friar's party no longer in control of the Signoria, he told the pope, the time had come for a new effort to bring Florence into the Holy League. And he proposed that the Holy Father use the return of Pisa as the bait with which to snare their prey.

Since Alexander had signed a treaty with the Orsini on February 5, there was no longer anything to keep him from resuming negotiations. Rather than negotiate with Ricciardo Becchi, the pope asked the Ten to send a special envoy to Rome to discuss the matter. Unlike the new Signoria, the Ten, who had been elected in January, were still loyal to the friar. And they did not trust either Ludovico or the pope. Nor could they see how the pope could give them Pisa, since the Venetians controlled the city and clearly had no intention of turning it over to anyone. On the other hand, it would be foolish to antagonize the Holy Father. On March 4, the Ten named their secretary, the corpulent and cautious Ser Alessandro Bracci, as special and secret envoy to Rome. Besides dealing with the question of Pisa, Bracci was to urge the friar's cause. The task would not be an easy one, for rather than being chastened by his reverses, the friar had grown more vehement. As usual, his sharpest barbs were directed at the church.

"Come here, thou ribald church," he cried on March 4. "Thou hast dedicated the sacred vessels to vainglory, the sacraments to simony. Thou hast become a shameless harlot in thy lusts....Once anointed priests called their sons nephews, but now they speak no more of their nephews but always and everywhere of their sons!"

Not content with this clear reference to the pope, all three of whose sons were then in Rome, he denounced the church as a prostitute who had displayed her foulness to the whole world and stank unto heaven. Nor was he intimidated by the ensuing hullabaloo. Instead, he poked fun at those who took exception to his language.

"O you said the church is a harlot!" he had an imaginary interlocutor tell him on March 5. "O Father, the Holy Church! What have you said!"

Assuming his own persona, he called his questioner a fool. "Look at Saint Jerome on this point in Ezekiel where he says, 'We may apply this to the church,'" he shouted. "Now go study and then speak of these things."

But the anger and the audacity that were his in the pulpit deserted him when he left it. Alone before the high wooden desk in his cell with a new sermon to prepare, he realized how vulnerable he was now that the *Frateschi* were out of power and there was no longer the threat of a French invasion to keep the pope from excommunicating him. On March 7 he sent a confidential letter to Duke Ercole of Ferrara, the only Italian ruler who still professed a belief in his prophecies. Being careful to refer to King Charles only as "the friend," he asked Ercole to send a trusty person to the king to open his eyes to the duty which God had imposed on him to once more invade Italy. He could not bring himself to admit, though, that Ercole would be doing him a favor. Instead, he told the duke that he was confiding this "secret of the Lord" to him because Ercole's faith had merited it. And in his sermons that week he continued to deny the loneliness of his position.

He was not alone, he declared on March 10. In every city, castle, and village, in every order, there were some with the same fire within. But he advised them to remain hidden until they heard the words "Lazarus, come forth!" And he was waiting for the day when the Lord would give him a mighty blow so that he might proclaim that message in a voice that would be heard not only in Italy but all over Christendom. Nor would he admit to any fear of excommunication. "Bear it aloft upon a lance, open the gates to it!" he shouted, "and I will answer it....I will cause so many faces to turn pale that you will be well pleased and we shall utter a great cry like that of Lazarus and you will see the whole body tremble....Lord, cause me to be persecuted. I ask Thee this favor that I may not die in my bed but that I may shed my blood for Thee as Thou hast for me."

Soon afterward, Alessandro Bracci had his first audience with the pope. Never had the Holy Father seemed more cordial or more genuinely solicitous. He was aware of how greatly Florence had suffered and was still suffering as a result of the French invasion, he told Bracci in his wonderfully rich and melodious voice. A new invasion would send a fresh wave of suffering washing over the peninsula, especially if the Italians were not united. For this reason, as God knew, his principal aim was to unite Italy and to make it into one body. Moreover, because he had always embraced their city with paternal love and affection, he

Portrait of Savonarola by Fra Bartolomeo, Museo di San Marco, Florence (*Art Resource*)

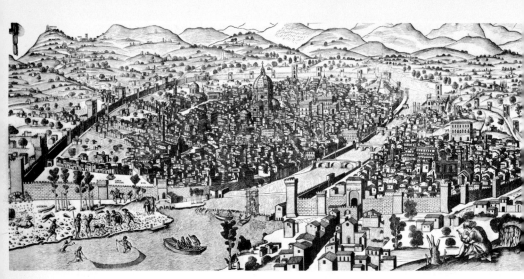

View of Florence, c. 1490 (*Art Resource*)

Lorenzo dei Medici (second from left) with three members of the Sassetti family painted by Domenico Ghirlandaio for the Sassetti Chapel in Santa Trinità, Florence (*Art Resource*)

Death mask of Lorenzo the Magnificent at the Palazzo Riccardi, Florence (*Photo Alinari/Art Resource*)

Portrait of Pico della Mirandola in the Uffizi Gallery, Florence (*Art Resource*)

Detail of a fresco by Ghirlandaio in Santa Trinità of Angelo Poliziano with Giuliano dei Medici (*Art Resource*)

Façade of the Villa Medicea at Careggi (*Art Resource*)

Bust of Piero di Lorenzo dei Medici by Andrea del Verrocchio in the Museo Nazionale (*Art Resource*)

RIGHT AND BELOW: Savonarola in the Luther Monument in Worms (*Bildarchiv, Foto Marburg/Art Resource*)

Woodcut of Savonarola preaching (*British Museum*)

Bronze medals of Savonarola, with the sword of God on the obverse, by Fra
Luca and Fra Ambrogio della Robbia at the Museo Nazionale (*Art Resource*)

ABOVE: Charles VIII by anonymous Florentine artist in the Bargello, Florence (*Art Resource*)

BELOW: Savonarola's cell at the Museo di San Marco (*Art Resource*)

Ludovico Sforza, detail of the Pala Sforzesca (*Photo Alinari/Art Resource*)

Portrait of Niccolò Machiavelli by Santi di Tito in the Bargello, Florence (*Photo Alinari/Art Resource*)

Pope Alexander VI, fresco by Pinturicchio, Borgia apartments, the Vatican (*Art Resource*)

Piazza della Signoria, Florence (*Art Resource*)

was prepared to return Pisa to Florence. And he intimated that it had required no small amount of cunning on his part to induce the Venetians to agree to this. All he asked in return for his labors, however, was that the Florentines be good Italians, leaving the French in France. Besides giving him their word that they would do this, they must also give him the necessary guarantees.

Ever since antiquity, the Florentines had been not only good Italians but the very best, Bracci protested. Hence, there was no need for any guarantee save their simple good faith. He went on to explain why Florentine commercial interests made union with France vital, but insisted that this union was in no way harmful to any of the other Italian powers.

Because the pope was self-conscious about his weight, he was quick to notice the weight problems of others. As he listened to this portly secretary the Florentines had sent him offering the same excuses he had heard so many times in the past, he grew increasingly restive until finally the temptation to call attention to the gentleman's girth got the better of him. "Mr. Secretary," he said in a voice that was no longer either cordial or solicitous, "you are as fat as we are, but if you will pardon me for saying so, you have come with a mighty thin commission, and if you have nothing better to say, you may as well return whence you came."

He knew that as a result of the truce the Florentines were "mutilated and broken," with famine in their homes and discord between citizens, he continued. He could not understand how they came to be so obstinate. He suspected it arose from their trust in the prophecies of that windbag of theirs. If he, their Holy Father, could speak to the people in person, he felt certain he would be able to cure them of the blindness and madness into which the friar had led them. "But what pains us even more and gives us just cause for complaint against you," said the pope, growing ever more indignant, "is that your Signoria and citizens permit him to rend and insult, to threaten and trample upon us who occupy *licit immeriti* [however unworthily] this Holy See." As always happened when he grew angry, his eyes began to blink, and nothing Bracci said could pacify him.

A few days later, Ricciardo Becchi warned the Ten that Cardinal Caraffa, until then one of the friar's staunchest advocates, was determined to excommunicate him if he did not consent to the union of San Marco with the Tuscan-Roman congregation. Nor was Caraffa the only one to favor excommunication. Everywhere at Rome, said Becchi, the indignation against Fra Girolamo was increasing to the point where "it was no longer possible to defend him." Speaking in consistory, Savonarola's old enemy Fra Mariano da Genazzano had urged the pope to "cut off this monster from the church of God." But despite the constant pressure from those around him and his own resentment of the friar, Alexander continued to hope for a less drastic solution.

Meanwhile, unemployment among the Florentine *popolo minuto* was growing, and famine was driving whole families of peasants and beggars into the city. By the time they arrived there, many were so weak and gaunt it was impossible to restore them. "Men, women, and children were falling down exhausted from hunger," said Luca Landucci. Despite all the provisions for their care made by the government and private charities, thousands died, many in the street or in the doorways of the shops. Although the friar urged every Florentine with leftover grain to donate it to the poor, the speculation of wealthy *Arrabbiati* merchants such as Lorenzo Popolani (né Medici) drove prices ever higher. When the price of corn rose to 5 lire a bushel, even so dedicated a *Piagnone* as Landucci could not resist selling a small quantity he had left over at a profit.

During Holy Week, there was a rumor that on Good Friday, Piero dei Medici would secretly enter the city bringing with him a guarantee of cheap grain for all. After distributing beans and bread to the common people, he would stir them to revolt. Others said Piero planned to enter Firenzuola and to give flour and corn to the people, forcing them to cry *Palle!* Fearing an uprising that could end with Piero's reinstatement, the leaders of the three parties decided to seek ways to reconcile the divided city. To this end the Signoria established a twelve-member tripartisan body known as the *Piaciali*, or peacemakers. But the *Arrabbiati* on the new commission thought that the only way to bring peace was to exile the friar; whereas the *Piagnoni* would not hear of it. Encouraged by their bickering, Piero sent Fra Mariano to Florence. Besides preaching against Savonarola and in favor of the League, Mariano was to ascertain the extent of pro-Medici sentiment in Florence. "Although," said Guicciardini, "Mariano's arrival and his private talks with Piero's friends aroused suspicion, the divisions in the city were such that he was neither investigated nor punished for his activities." This, of course, further encouraged Piero.

After the collapse of his plans to enter Florence the previous winter, Piero had returned to Rome. There he had sought solace in wine, women, and food, gorging himself at the palace of his mother-in-law's family, the San Severini, and passing the time between meals with one or more of the numerous courtesans he frequented. But the cries of *Palle!* during the looting of the Piazza del Grano on February 19 changed all that. On hearing the news, he and his brother Giovanni announced that they hoped to be in Florence in two months. A few days later, when they learned that Bernardo del Nero had been made gonfalonier and two of Piero's staunchest supporters were members of the new Signoria, the hope became a conviction. With the tacit approval of the pope and the Venetians, both of whom expected him to bring Florence into the Holy League, and with thousands of florins supplied by the Orsini, as well as between 500 and 600 ducats smuggled out of Florence by his cousin Nofri Tornabuoni, Piero was able to raise an army of 1300 men.

On April 20, he and his army set out for Siena, being careful to travel by night and to avoid the main roads so as not to be recognized. After picking up new recruits in Siena, they headed for Florence on the evening of February 27. If they marched all night, they would reach the suburb of San Gaggio near the Porta San Piero in Gattalino by daybreak when few would be around to notice them. As soon as the gate opened, they would enter the city. What with the help Piero's friends had promised him and the enthusiastic support of the common people, it would be a simple matter to regain control of the government. Or at least that is what Piero told himself. But it was not for nothing that history would call him "Piero *lo sfortunato*" ("Piero the unlucky one").

Just as his troops reached Tavernelle, a hamlet 16 miles from San Gaggio, they were caught in one of those torrential downpours so common in Tuscany during April. While the drenched and exhausted men waited for the storm to subside, Piero set up a roadblock to prevent any of the local people from warning the Florentines of his approach. But one of the peasants who was turned back knew of another road to Florence. By the time Piero and his men reached San Gaggio, not in the half light of dawn as they had planned, but, because of the delay at Tavernelle, in broad daylight, they found the Porta San Piero in Gattolino locked and the artillery on the walls about to open fire. Not knowing what else to do, Piero ordered his men to seek shelter behind the wall of a nearby fountain. Although they were within bowshot of the gate, he realized that they were not strong enough to take it without help from his supporters in the city. Thanks to the peasant's warning, however, the fifty men considered most likely to help Piero had been rounded up and were being detained in the palazzo. The common people, who Piero had expected to rise in his favor, were quietly waiting to see how things turned out. Nor were the residents of San Gaggio eager to help him. Instead, they stood around the fountain watching him and his men "almost as if they were at a show." They continued to stand and stare until Piero finally decided that if he waited any longer, Florentine troops diverted from Pisa would cut off his retreat.

His enterprise had turned to smoke, wrote the elders of Pisa. It served him right, said the pope, for he had managed this as badly as he managed all the rest of his affairs. However, the Florentines were not prepared to take the matter so lightly. Because, said Guicciardini, "public opinion in Florence was sure that Piero's arrival had been arranged by his Florentine supporters," the Signoria for May and June established a secret committee of eight citizens with special powers to find out exactly who those supporters were. Besides engaging spies to watch the comings and goings of likely suspects as well as the activities of Piero himself, the eight placed guards at all the gates to keep track of letters entering or leaving the city. It would be more than three months before any evidence was forthcoming, and those three months were unusually hectic ones for the friar and the city.

The same day that Piero and his men waited at San Gaggio, the Great Council met to elect both the new Signoria for May and June and a new gonfalonier. As a result of Valori's decision to admit young men between the ages of 24 and 30, what the *Piagnone* chronicler Jacopo Nardi called "the ill-mannered youth" had multiplied in the council. Because, said Nardi, like most young men they were "sensual and not easily disciplined," even those who favored the council and liberty opposed the friar and had no faith in his prophecies. This made them natural allies of the *Arrabbiati*. With the help of their votes, the *Arrabbiati* leader Piero degli Alberti was selected gonfalonier and four of the priors in the new Signoria were also *Arrabbiati*. Of these, the most outspoken was Benedetto dei Nerli, whose millionaire father Tanai was at that very moment using his money and influence to have the friar excommunicated.

Ostensibly to prevent the spread of plague but actually to silence the friar, dei Nerli and another of the *Arrabbiati* priors introduced a resolution forbidding all preaching after May 4, Ascension Day, and ordering the removal of all benches and tiers erected in the churches. No sooner was this resolution passed than the friar's enemies demanded that Savonarola not be allowed to preach on Ascension Day. They intimated that if he did preach, there was bound to be violence. Because tempers rose to such an extent that "everyone thought an explosion was imminent," Francesco Valori sent his lieutenant Andrea Cambini to San Marco to ask the friar whether he was determined to preach. To Savonarola, such a question showed a complete ignorance of his obligation to his flock. He would not dream of leaving the people without a sermon on the very day when Our Lord bade the apostles preach his doctrine to all men, he declared. Nevertheless, many were willing to wager whatever money they had on them that when the time came, he would be too frightened to enter the pulpit. The betting grew so frenzied that the only way the Signoria could stop it was by invalidating all bets and making it a crime to interfere with any sermon delivered on Ascension Day.

This did not prevent Benedetto dei Nerli's rowdy younger brother Jacopo from going ahead with plans to disrupt the friar's sermon. Jacopo had no more difficulty finding disaffected and angry *giovani* to help him on Ascension Eve than he had had on that tumultuous Sunday when he had shut the door of the Palazzo della Signoria in Piero's face. Francesco Cei could not forget that he had been temporarily exiled for writing a ballad critical of the friar. Others wished to keep the friar from preaching simply because he interfered with their good times. A few considered the whole undertaking a lark—on a par with harassing tavern keepers and seducing the young wives of elderly husbands.

The group's first plan was to set fire to the cathedral pulpit and to the benches and tiers where the *fanciulli* sat. When Tanai dei Nerli heard of this plan, he forbade Jacopo to go ahead with it. Since Jacopo would not disobey his father, another way to silence the friar had to be found. By chance, one of the young men in the group had come across a dead ass two days earlier, and this ass became the focal point of their new plan. After being admitted to the cathedral by a priest who had agreed to help them, they draped the animal's skin over the pulpit, then smeared its putrefying flesh over the column against which the high wooden balcony housing the pulpit was built and at the base of the crucifix the friar was in the habit of taking in his hands. That done, they placed what remained of the carcass on the lectern "as a decoration" and drove iron spikes into the ledge which the friar struck with his fist when he wished to emphasize a point.

"Turks and Moors would have been ashamed to profane a Christian church as they did," said Jacopo Nardi. And perhaps he was right. In any case, the stench made it easy for the sacristans who opened the church the following morning to discover what had happened. Long before the friar arrived, all traces of the profanation had been removed. But Jacopo and his band of well-to-do ruffians were not so easily foiled. On learning that their work the previous evening had been in vain, they armed themselves and returned to the cathedral. Because the *Piagnoni* expected trouble, not only the men but many of the women, including a number of "venerable matrons," had come to church with scythes, Turkish scimitars, and other weapons hidden under their clothing. There was also the armed guard which had accompanied the friar down the Via Cocomero and now surrounded the pulpit, not to mention the weapons that had been stored in the houses of *Piagnoni* who lived nearby.

As the text for his sermon that Ascension Day, the friar had chosen a portion of the seventh psalm: "O Lord my God, in Thee do I put my trust: save me from all them that persecute me, and deliver me." The sermon was about two-thirds over, and he had just warned the wicked that in combating him they made war on the Lord when Francesco Cei picked up one of the heavy metal alms boxes used to collect money for the *Monte di Pietà* and sent it crashing to the pavement. To Luca Landucci, it sounded as if someone in the choir were knocking a stick against a box. Giovanni di Borromeis thought someone was beating a drum. Piero Parenti thought a rock was being struck against a table. To Giovanni Cambi, it sounded more like a sledgehammer. And, said Landucci, "everyone believed it had been done on purpose" by the same men who had defiled the cathedral.

"I hear someone making a noise!" the friar cried, as certain of who the culprits were as everyone else. "The wicked refuse to hear their fate. Have a bit of patience, because if you knew what I know, you would weep. Don't be afraid, for God is with us, and there are many thousands of angels here."

By then the commotion was so great that, except for Lorenzo Violi, who was transcribing the sermon, no one had any idea what he was saying. Startled by the noise, the entire congregation has risen to its feet, and cries of *Jesu!* and *Misericordia!* filled the air. Some took out their brass crucifixes and raised them heavenward; others took out their weapons. Shouting "Long live Christ our king!" they sought to block the doors so that those responsible for the disturbance would not escape.

While this was going on, Bartolomeo Giugni, one of the *Arrabbiati* members of the Eight of the Ward, was strolling in the Piazza San Giovanni. Hearing the commotion in the cathedral and seeing the doors flung open, he decided to find out what was wrong. To both Piero Parenti and his fellow *Arrabbiato* Giovanni di Borromeis, it seemed obvious that all Giugni intended to do was to calm the crowd. Since he was unarmed, they were probably right. But seeing him approach the pulpit and knowing how he felt about Savonarola and his party, those guarding the friar feared that Giugni wished to seize the friar and hurl him to the pavement. To prevent this, a man by the name of Lando Sassolini struck Giugni with the flat of his sword.

This unprecedented assault upon an officer of the law increased the tumult in the cathedral. Although the gate at the foot of the spiral staircase leading to the pulpit was locked, Savonarola seemed frightened by the uproar. Falling to his knees, he began to pray. Apparently taking heart from his brief communion with God, he then held aloft a small crucifix he always carried with him and called on the faithful to remain firm. Finding it impossible to understand what he was saying and seeing him with the crucifix in his hand, the people began to shout; many took out their own crucifixes and held them aloft once more.

When the tumult had first begun, about sixty of the friar's supporters had rushed out of the door leading to the Via Cocomero to fetch the weapons stored nearby. Virtually beside himself with rage, Giovambattista Ridolfi, whom Guicciardini called "one of the gravest and most esteemed citizens of his time," emerged from the house of the Lorini carrying a pruning hook on his shoulder and shouting *Viva Cristo!* Thus armed, he returned to the cathedral with the others to escort the friar to San Marco. They were accompanied by a great multitude of the faithful so that the Via Cocomero seemed a vast sea of people all shouting, *Viva Gesù Cristo! Viva il signore!* and holding aloft their crucifixes.

The time of tribulation had arrived, the time when it would be manifest who believed in the truth and who was only pretending to believe, the friar had told them shortly before the tumult began. In their faces could be seen their joy at being among the true believers who would defend God's chosen prophet, as well as their hatred of the "Sons of Satan" who had disrupted his sermon. At that point, says one *Piagnone* chronicler, "The entire city was in arms, some in defense of the servant of God, some against him."

To Paolo Somenzi, it seemed that Florence had returned to the days of the Guelphs and the Ghibellines. This time, the friar had made clear what sort of man he was, Somenzi told Ludovico. If he had been a man of good will and a Catholic, on being warned that his sermon might give rise to disorder, he would have refused to preach that morning. Instead he wished to show what a great scoundrel he was. And it was this view of the Ascension Day riot that both the Sforzas and the *Arrabbiati* sought to impress on the pope.

That April, Fra Mariano had introduced one of his protégés, Giovanvittorio Camerino, to the Holy Father. After spending a month in prison for criticizing the friar, Camerino, whom Piero Parenti thought "rather learned," had been banished from Florence. From him, Alexander received a detailed account of the manifold ways in which Fra Girolamo continued to "lacerate and threaten" him. Although by then the pope was beginning to realize that he could not allow the vilification to continue without undermining the authority of the Holy See, he was still not ready to sign a writ of excommunication. On May 1, he asked Alessandro Bracci to inform the Ten that His Holiness wished them to use whatever means seemed best to keep Fra Girolamo from speaking ill of him. In view of the great love he bore their city, he did not deserve such treatment, he continued. And he did not want to be forced to use the measures he had at his disposal to put a stop to the abuse.

Whoever had informed the pope that the friar was disparaging him was not speaking the truth, the Ten told Bracci. Had Fra Girolamo said the things he was supposed to have said, neither they nor the Signoria would have tolerated it. The friar carried out the tasks of a good preacher modestly and without offending or naming anyone. Nevertheless, when he returned to the pulpit, he would be reminded not to speak ill of the pope.

By the time this reply arrived in Rome, the entire city was talking about the Ascension Day riot. Fra Mariano was calling the friar "an instrument of the devil and the perdition of the

Florentine people." Cardinal Caraffa was demanding that he be excommunicated for his part in the riot and for refusing to allow San Marco to join the Tuscan-Roman congregation. A host of other prelates were also insisting on excommunication, either because they had been paid to do so by agents of Tanai dei Nerli and his fellow millionaire Alfonso Strozzi or because they wished to oblige Cardinal dei Medici. Had the reply of the Ten been less equivocal, Alexander might have been more disposed to wait. As it was, he could only conclude that further delay was pointless. On May 13, the pope signed the brief *Cum soepe a quamplurimus*, which declared the friar excommunicate.

VII

THE EXCOMMUNICATION

o Piero Parenti, the hard feelings, the charges and count-
ercharges unleashed by the Ascension Day riot were
"questo guazzabuglio." Alongside the gloriously onomato-
poetic *guazzabuglio*, no English equivalent—whether mess, mud-
dle, confusion, or disorder—seems adequate. The *Piagnoni* were
outraged because the *Arrabbiati*-dominated Eight of the Ward
had not punished Jacopo dei Nerli and his band of hooligans for
desecrating a Christian church. The *Arrabbiati* for their part
were equally indignant because Lando Sassolini, who had had
the temerity to strike a member of the Eight with the flat of his
sword, had avoided banishment by asking for and receiving asylum in San Marco. Almost every evening when the brethren
were at prayer, a mob gathered outside the convent to howl insults at the friar, and sketches of him wearing a habit that exposed his private parts were found lying in the street. The
Piagnone demanded that the Eight put a stop to the vituperation;
the Eight, of course, refused to budge.

Meanwhile, the law against preaching during the summer
months went into effect, and the friar promised the Ferrarese
ambassador he would not contest it. "We have resolved to imitate the Lord, who on many occasions bent before the rage of
the Scribes and Pharisees," he wrote in an epistle "To All God's
Chosen and Faithful Christians," which he published on May
8. However, "in order that the Lord's work not be overthrown

nor the wicked made to rejoice," he would express in writing what he could not say by word of mouth. With the zest for martyrdom so typical of him, he thanked the Lord for having in those "utterly faithless times" chosen him to suffer for the faith.

The *Piagnoni* found his courage inspiring. The *Arrabbiati* were convinced that the only way to end the *guazzabuglio* was for him to leave the city. On May 20, the Signoria convened a *pratica* to discuss the matter. Although the four *Arrabbiati* priors and the *Arrabbiati* gonfalonier insisted that exiling the friar would sweep away the divisions which were "a hurt and a dishonor to the public in general and to every citizen in particular," the majority of the *pratica* feared that rather than bring peace, exiling him would give rise to more hatred and dissension.

By then, both Bracci and Becchi had warned the Ten that a brief declaring the friar excommunicate was on its way. "Bear it aloft on a lance, open the gates to it, and I will answer it!" Savonarola had shouted that March. When it arrived, he had promised to utter a great cry like Lazarus, so that they would see "the whole body tremble." But these were mere words of the sort that sometimes emerged unbidden when he was in the pulpit with a great crowd looking up at him. Rather than stand by them now that the excommunication was expected momentarily, he panicked and sought to appease the pope.

"For what reason is my Lord angry with his servant?" he asked the Holy Father in the letter he sent to Rome on May 22. "Have I done wrong because my enemies accuse me? Why does not my Lord interrogate his servant and listen to his reply before believing the charges against him?" He either forgot or chose to forget that when Alexander had sought to interrogate him, he had found excuses for not going to Rome.

His enemies accused him of "having ceaselessly carped at the pope with injurious words," he told the Holy Father. But he wondered that Alexander did not see through their malice. In a clear reference to Fra Mariano, he asked how that "high and mighty preacher" could have the face to charge him with a fault of which—as many could testify—he was himself guilty. In fact, Savonarola had once had occasion to reprove him for the insolent words he had dared to utter against His Holiness from the pulpit. As for himself, he would soon publish a work, *The Triumph of the Cross*, from which it would be apparent whether he was a sower of heresies (that might he never be!) or of the Catholic truth.

The pope had addressed one copy of the excommunication to the Signoria and other copies to various churches and convents in Florence, and he had asked Giovanvittorio Camerino to deliver them. Camerino was on his way to the city when some of his *Arrabbiati* friends warned him that despite the change in the composition of the Signoria and the Eight, the ban against him was still in effect. Consequently, he risked being sent to jail the instant he set foot in Florence. Rather than take the risk, Camerino stopped off in Siena. The pope, who knew nothing of his envoy's problems, wondered what had become of him. On May 27, the Holy Father asked Alessandro Bracci whether the briefs had been delivered; Bracci, however, was as much in the dark as he was.

The Florentine ambassador had sought an audience with the pope that day in order to plead the friar's cause, but Alexander was not in the mood to listen. It was no wonder that Fra Girolamo would not confess to having spoken ill of him, His Holiness told Bracci, seeing how strongly he was supported by the Ten. All the same, Alexander was just as certain that the friar had maligned him as he was that he was pope, for he had it on the testimony of many trustworthy witnesses, and he would grant no further audiences until he received the Signoria's reply to his brief.

Three days later, however, Cardinal Caraffa told Ricciardo Becchi that the Holy Father regretted having sent the brief and especially having done so by an enemy of the city and of Fra Girolamo. If Camerino were wise, said the cardinal, he would never set foot in Florence. Although the friar had brought discord to the city, some other means must be taken to discipline him. Soon afterward, Alexander received Savonarola's letter. The pope was so moved by its conciliatory tone that he had it read aloud in consistory. However, he made no move to revoke the excommunication.

On June 16, Camerino wrote to the Signoria from Siena to demand a safe conduct "in order to put certain matters before them." When the Signoria denied his request, he sent a substitute to Florence with a packet of briefs to be distributed to the various churches. Because this substitute had not been sent by the pope, only five churches—Santa Maria Novella, Santo Spirito, San Francesco del Monte, the church of the Badia, and the church of the Servi—would accept briefs from him. On the evening of June 18, 1497, a feast day and a Sunday, the briefs were read aloud from the chancels of these churches by readers standing between lighted tapers. A company of friars surrounded each reader, and as he read, small bells tolled incessantly. When he finished, the tapers were extinguished, the bells stopped ringing, and the friars filed out of the darkened church in silence.

Because Savonarola had ignored not only the pope's first brief summoning him to Rome, but also the brief of November 7, 1496, which had commanded him under pain of excommunication to unite San Marco with the Tuscan-Roman congregation, he had ipso facto incurred censure and was to be held excommunicate by all men. Inasmuch as he was an excommunicated person suspected of heresy, they were forbidden under pain of the same penalty to assist him, hold intercourse with him, or approve him. That, in essence, was the message of the brief. It was, of course, immediately relayed to the friar.

He could have written another begging letter to the pope. But Alexander had not answered his first letter, and he was no longer in the mood to grovel. Nor was he in the mood to spend much time thinking about what he ought to do instead. Rather, he seemed to feel an indomitable urge to rebut the charges against him as quickly as possible. The "Epistle against Surreptitious Excommunication," addressed to "all Christians and beloved of God," which he wrote that night and had printed the following day, was a pastiche of arguments hastily culled from old sermons and writings. Describing himself as "the servant of Jesus Christ sent by him to the city of Florence to announce the great scourge which is to come on Italy and especially upon Rome and which is to extend itself all over the world," he assured his "dear friends" that inasmuch as the excommunication was based on false insinuations devised by his enemies, it had no value in the eyes of God or the church. He had always submitted and even still submitted to the authority of the church, he declared. Nor would he ever fail in his obedience. But it was monstrous to suppose that he was bound to obey his superior when that superior demanded what was contrary to God.

> For we ought to obey our superior insofar as he holds the place of God; but he does not hold the place of God and is not our superior when he commands what is contrary to God. Accordingly in cases such as this, I have not obeyed knowing that neither God nor the church wishes me to obey.

Those who had induced the pope to promulgate the order uniting San Marco to the Tuscan-Roman congregation had done so not out of zeal for religion, he declared, but to find an excuse to proceed against him, having foreseen that he would not consent to a union which they knew to be pernicious. He then alluded to twelve irrefutable reasons he had given them to demonstrate that the proposed union was "contrary to the honor of God and the good of souls." Perhaps because he was not as sure of those reasons as he claimed to be, he did not rest his case on them. As he had planned to do from the very beginning, he hid behind his friars. Since it was they who had declared in writing that they would not consent to the union but would rather suffer excommunication and even martyrdom, why did his enemies impute the disobedience to him, he asked. Could it be that they sought only one man whom they hated because he told the truth?

Having demonstrated to his own satisfaction that the excommunication was unjust, he then published another letter in Latin in which he cited a number of experts on canon law, including the fourteenth-century French theologian Jean Gerson, to prove that no one was obliged to honor an unjust excommunication. Though he did not do so publicly, within the confines of San Marco he continued to celebrate mass and to carry out his other priestly duties as if no brief had come. Nor did he seem to fear the consequences of his defiance. God would not suffer one of his elect to perish, he told the chancellor of Duke Ercole of Ferrara. Inevitably he took the news that the pope's favorite son, Juan, Duke of Gandia, had been murdered as a sign that the Almighty was already "wielding the stick" against the Holy Father for having excommunicated His chosen prophet.

Juan was reported missing on the morning of June 15. At about the hour of vespers on the evening of June 16, his body, still fully dressed with his gloves under a belt containing 30 ducats, was fished from the Tiber. His throat had been cut, and he had been stabbed eight times in various parts of the legs, head, and trunk. For the pope, the anguish was at first unendurable.

> Upon learning that his son had been thrown like dung into the river [said the papal master of ceremonies Johann Burchard] the pope shut himself away in a room...weeping most bitterly....From Wednesday evening until the following Saturday morning, the pope ate and drank nothing; whilst from Thursday morning to Sunday, he was quiet for no moment of any hour. At last, however...after being exhorted by friends, His Holiness agreed to begin ending his mourning insofar as he was able, since he understood that otherwise he would bring greater harm and danger to himself through it.

His eyes were still red and swollen from weeping when, on June 19, he appeared before a papal consistory. "The blow which has fallen upon us is the heaviest that we possibly could have sustained," he told the assembled cardinals and ambassadors. "We loved the Duke of Gandia more than anyone else in the world. We would give seven tiaras to be able to recall him to life. God has done this in punishment for our sins, for the duke has done nothing to merit this mysterious and terrible death."

In his despair, he saw the loss of his son as God's way of chastising him for the worldliness of his reign and vowed to reform both himself and the church that he headed. "No longer can we tolerate the way in which the former salutary measures instituted by our predecessors to keep sensuality and avarice within bounds have been violated so that we fall headlong into corruption," he told the consistory. "We will begin the reform with ourselves and so proceed through all the ranks of the church till the whole work is accomplished." To preside over the work of reform, he appointed a commission of six cardinals headed by Cardinals Caraffa and Costa. On June 22, Ricciardo Becchi informed the Ten that the pope had put everything, including the affairs of Fra Girolamo, into the hands of this commission.

Like the friar, his supporters took it for granted that the murder of the Duke of Gandia was a sign that God wished to show the pope his error in excommunicating their preacher. Savonarola himself seemed to consider it his duty as one of God's elect to point out to the conscience-smitten old man the path that the Lord now wished him to take.

"Faith, most Holy Father, is the one and true source of consolation for the heart of man," he told the pope in the letter of condolence he sent him on June 25.

"Let your Holiness then help forward the work of faith wherein I suffer trouble as an evil doer even unto bonds (Paul II Timothy 29) and let him not give ear to the impious. Then shall God give you the oil of gladness for the spirit of grief. For the things which I have predicted are true and come from God. And what mortal can resist Him and prosper? (Job 9:4)"

He wrote these words in all humility and, moved by the spirit of charity, he told the pope, "desiring that His Holiness find consolation in the Lord in truth rather than in appearance, for the Lord's anger was kindled in an instant, and happy were those who put their trust in him. (Psalms 2:12)"

Whether Alexander found this letter presumptuous or touching, or merely self-serving, or perhaps a mixture of all three, is not known. In those first agonizing days after his son's death, the pope seemed to regret the excommunication. It came at a bad time, and it went beyond his intentions, he told one of his cardinals. Before the friar's letter of condolence had even been posted, however, the Holy Father was given a copy of the "Epistle against Surreptitious Excommunication." Although still in mourning for his son, he summoned Alessandro Bracci to his chambers.

As God was his witness, he told the ambassador, he had begun to be well-disposed toward Fra Girolamo. After reading this latest epistle, however, he was determined to proceed against the friar with all the rigors canon law reserved for the contumacious and the rebellious. Was the ambassador aware that excommunicate as the friar was, he had celebrated the mass of the Holy Spirit. Without giving Bracci a chance to reply, the pope then began speaking of how well-disposed he was toward the Florentines and of his desire to give them Pisa if only they joined the Holy League. Even as he spoke of these matters, however, the question of Fra Girolamo was still at the back of his mind. After mentioning a letter he had received from the king of France that morning, he suddenly asked Bracci to write to the Ten on his behalf. The ambassador must tell their excellencies that His Holiness would be content if Fra Girolamo came to Rome to justify himself, said the pope. Nor need the friar fear for his safety, for Alexander would see to it that not a hair of his head was touched. If he were found to be innocent, the pope would give him his blessing. If not, the Holy Father would accord him justice with mercy. In a gesture which could only cast doubt on the sincerity of this sudden about-face, the pope then asked two of the Florentine businessmen who had come with Bracci to thank Jacopo dei Nerli for all he had done for the satisfaction of the Holy See in this matter of Fra Girolamo.

Jacopo's father had paid a number of clergymen to put pressure on the pope to sign the brief of excommunication. Now that it had been signed and delivered, several wealthy *Frateschi* were said to be offering large sums to any clergyman who could induce the Holy Father to revoke it. Hearing this, Cardinal Piccolomini, the future Pope Pius III, indicated that his good offices could be had for 5000 ducats. But Savonarola made it clear that he would consider it "a greater censure" were his absolution to be obtained in this manner. Consequently, Piccolomini, who was the father of twelve illegitimate children, had to look elsewhere for the additional revenue he needed to support his brood.

Because the pope refused to absolve Fra Girolamo, said Piero Parenti, the friar and his supporters were "ostracized like Jews." On learning that the brethren of San Marco intended to march in the annual procession in honor of the city's patron saint, John the Baptist, the brothers of Saint Francis and the brothers of Saint Augustine announced that they dared not incur the pope's wrath by marching alongside friars who associated with an excommunicated person. If either Fra Girolamo or his brethren marched in the procession, the others would stay away, they told the Signoria.

Rather than allow this to happen, the Signoria ordered the friars of San Marco to remain indoors that day. Meanwhile, the church of Santo Spirito and a number of other Augustinian and Franciscan churches began ejecting worshippers who continued to visit San Marco and converse with Fra Girolamo, calling them enemies of the Holy Church and excommunicate for ignoring the papal brief. Even before the brief arrived, the Signoria had begun chipping away at the friar's program of moral reform. Saying, "Let us cheer up the people a little; are we all to become monks?" the priors gave permission for the horse race of Santo Barnabo, which had not been run since Piero's time. They also reopened the Frascato, a place of amusement near the Mercato Vecchio, whose principal attractions were a brothel and an ancient and celebrated tavern where men had always gathered to drink and gamble.

To Ludovico Sforza this sudden reversal in the fortunes of Fra Girolamo was cause for rejoicing. Because the friar had defied the excommunication, Ludovico felt certain that when the Great Council elected a new Signoria for July and August, the *Arrabbiati* would again be in the majority. If they were, they would surely force the friar to leave. Or at least that is what Ludovico's agents told him.

But Fortune's wheel, which had so abruptly sent the friar plummeting, just as abruptly sent him to the top once more.

Contrary to expectation, the majority of those elected to the new Signoria belonged to the friar's party, Paolo Somenzi told his employer on June 29. As a result, Fra Girolamo probably would not have to leave after all. Somenzi blamed this unexpected reversal on Piero's friends, those who called themselves

Bigi. Because they held the friar's enemies responsible for detaining them in the palazzo on the day Piero was at the Porta San Piero in Gattolino, the *Bigi,* who until then had lent their support to the *Arrabbiati,* had gone over to the friar's side.

Jean Gerson, on whose writings the friar had relied to demonstrate that no one was obliged to honor an unjust excommunication, had also said that the Christian does not commit a sin in accepting the aid of the secular power to escape from such disfellowship. Two days after the *Piagnoni*-controlled Signoria took office, they sent Alessandro Bracci a letter thanking him for all he had done on the friar's behalf and urging him to persevere. Three days later, they convened a *pratica* to discuss the advisability of writing to the pope. Since the majority approved, the Signoria sent a letter to Rome on July 8.

A little over a week before this letter was dispatched, Bracci's son-in-law told the friar of a petition accusing him of preaching false doctrine and heresy, which "certain citizens" had sent to the pope. With Valori's approval, the brethren of San Marco drew up a counterpetition in which all 250 of them assured the pope of the soundness of their prior's doctrine and beseeched the Holy Father to revoke the censures against him. Fearing that the pope would not find their signatures sufficient, they appended another petition signed by 358 Florentine laymen ranging from patricians like Valori and the *Bigi* leader Lorenzo Tornabuoni to barbers and clerks whose names Fra Silvestro Maruffi thought "unsuitable for the purpose." Before the petitions could be sent to Rome, however, opponents of Fra Girolamo reminded the Signoria that it was unconstitutional for private citizens to address a foreign power. Not sure they were right, yet unwilling to add to the dissension in the city by saying they were wrong, the Signoria convened a *pratica* to discuss the matter. There were so many conflicting opinions that in the end the *pratica* adjourned without recommending anything. Meanwhile, several cases of plague were discovered in San Marco, and one of the friars died. Faced with the need to guard against contagion and terrified at finding themselves in the valley of the shadow of death, the surviving brethren lost all interest in the petition.

When the first cases of plague had appeared in the city that

May, the principal victims had been the hungry and the home-less. To check the spread of the disease, the Signoria had pro-vided shelter for the destitute in the pope's stables on the Via della Scala and had arranged for each of them to receive a loaf of bread every evening. But perhaps because "spiritual discour-agement and physical weakness" made the poor "indifferent as to dying," those measures proved insufficient. At the end of May, in the "last days of the waning moon," 120 cases of plague were reported "at the hospitals and in the city together," and many died of fever after being ill only a few days. In the middle of June, "whilst the moon was full," 100 people were said to have died in a single twenty-four-hour period. By the time the new Signoria took office at the beginning of July, numerous private dwellings were "infested with plague," so that everyone "was thinking of fleeing the city." When the plague reached San Marco, Savonarola immediately sought accommodations for the novices and the younger friars in villas in the nearby hills. How-ever he himself chose to remain in the city with the older friars.

They saw nothing in Florence but "crosses every day and corpses," he told his brother Alberto in a letter he sent to Ferrara on July 24. Nevertheless, he was staying on because he wished to console the afflicted; and he was not afraid, hoping as he did that God's grace would be with them. A few days before he wrote this letter, Ricciardo Becchi informed the Ten that unless Fra Girolamo consented to the union of San Marco with the Tuscan-Roman congregation, or the Signoria guaranteed that he would come to Rome within two months, neither the pope nor the commission of cardinals would consider absolving him. But the same confidence in God's grace that kept the friar in the plague-ridden city led him to dismiss this latest reversal as merely tem-porary. "Our persecutions do not discourage me nor dampen my spirits in any way," he assured Duke Ercole of Ferrara on Au-gust 1, "for I know that they will end well. When human means have failed, God will help us with a mighty hand and a stretched-out arm."

As to what ought to be done until then, his thinking seemed to go no further than a resolve not to submit to the pope's de-mands under any circumstances and a continuing reliance on the Signoria and the Ten to uphold him. "It had been far easier in the days of the apostles, for they at least were not bound to respect an authority with which they were at war," he had said in one of his sermons the previous year. But he was a man governed by sudden epiphanies, not a deep thinker; and it never occurred to him as it had occurred to John Wycliffe and would occur to Martin Luther to ask himself by what right the pope held his authority or how far that authority went. As long as the Holy Father did not command what was contrary to God, he must be obeyed and that was that. Who besides the Almighty and Fra Girolamo was qualified to judge when the pope's commands were contrary to God, and what would happen to the authority of the Holy See if every man were to judge this for himself, the friar did not say.

Instead, he devoted himself to working on *The Triumph of the Cross*, the exposition of the Catholic faith which his letter of May 22 had assured the pope would make it apparent whether he was a sower of heresy or of Catholic truth. Impelled by his urgent need to demonstrate his own orthodoxy, he forgot his numerous attempts to qualify the pope's authority, forgot his rage at having to obey a pope whom he considered simoniacal and unworthy, forgot that he had defied that pope's order to unite San Marco with the new congregation. "The words 'Thou art Peter and on this rock I will build my church' must be held to apply to Peter and the successors of Peter," he declared. "Wherefore it is manifest that all the faithful should be united under the pope as the supreme head of the Roman church, the mother of all other churches; and that whoever departs from the unity of the Roman church unquestionably departs from Christ."

Nor was this the only time that summer when he would find it politic to sidestep a seemingly crucial issue. Caught in what George Eliot called a "tangle of egoistic demands, false ideas, and difficult outward conditions," except for his desire to effect a great moral renovation, he had never been all that clear about where he was going or how he planned to get there. Under pressure, he seemed ever more inclined to suit his words to the needs of the moment. And like apocalyptic preachers before and since, he expected others to be as blind to his inconsistencies as he was.

Because of the danger of infection, the Great Council did not meet in July. Whatever government business there was was handled by the Eight, the Ten, and the Signoria with the help of the various committees and civil servants under their jurisdiction. With the exception of priests and tradesmen, the only other people left in the city were those who had nowhere else to go. As the plague grew more virulent, many collapsed in the street from exhaustion. All day long, the stretcher-bearers moved through the narrow cobblestoned *vie* and the even narrower *vicoli*, or *chiassi*, as they are called in Florence, gathering up the fallen and carrying them off to the hospitals, where the majority soon died. On July 20, the Eight arrested a priest officiating in Santa Maria Maggiore for declaring that Fra Girolamo, Fra Domenico, and the other *frati* at San Marco were sodomites. After admitting that he had done so because he had a grudge against them, the unfortunate cleric was compelled to mount a pulpit placed on the steps of the cathedral alongside the campanile. There, in the presence of all the people, he confessed that he had lied. His confession and subsequent imprisonment in a cage provided a diversion of sorts. Other than an eclipse of the sun on July 29, nothing else of moment occurred until the beginning of August when there were rumors that Piero dei Medici had gone to Bolsena to mobilize his troops.

Besides dispatching spies to determine whether the rumors were true, the Signoria called a meeting of the Great Council. Most of the council members had already returned to Florence for the meeting when, on August 5, the committee set up to unmask those responsible for Piero's previous assault on the city arrested Lamberto dell'Antella.

Before the revolution, Lamberto and his brother Alessandro had been members of the circle of wealthy young patricians around Piero. After Piero's overthrow, they had been sentenced to life imprisonment in the Stinche, the vast windowless jail

on the Via del Diluvio (now the Via dei Fossi). They had somehow managed to escape and make their way to Cardinal Giovanni's palace in Rome. Once there, what they came to think
of as Piero's "mad wish to return to Florence" kept them constantly on the move. Since instead of appreciating their efforts,
Piero treated them "worse than dogs," the brothers began looking for a way to get even. When Francesco Valori was elected
gonfalonier, they wrote to him, but Valori never replied, and they
remained with Piero. That April they accompanied him on his
flight to Siena, following the debacle at the Porta San Piero in
Gattolino. By then, however, Piero had grown suspicious of
them. After finding an excuse to leave them behind when he
set out for Rome, he persuaded Pandolfo Petrucci, the tyrant of
Siena, to imprison the dell'Antelli in the Carnaio, a dungeon
few ever left alive. The brothers had been in the dungeon twelve
days when Petrucci relented. He would release them on condition that they agree to pay a fine of 2000 florins if they ever left
Sienese territory, he told them. Although they agreed immediately, they did not regard the agreement as binding since it had
been obtained under duress. Once free, they were more determined than ever to get back at Piero.

Lamberto's brother-in-law Francesco Gualterotti was a member of the Ten and a devoted *Piagnone*. After Lamberto's release
from the Carnaio, he wrote to Gualterotti several times asking
for a safe conduct so that he might reveal certain matters of importance regarding Piero's affairs. Since Gualterotti never answered any of these letters, at the beginning of August Lamberto
decided to slip into Florentine territory without a safe conduct
and give his wife a letter to deliver to her brother in person. It
was this letter that was found on Lamberto when he was arrested at his country home of dell'Antella some four miles from
Florence.

He was taken to the Palazzo della Signoria where, after being given four turns of the pulley, he was examined by the Eight
of the Ward. His letter had hinted at a conspiracy in Piero's favor and had offered to name names. So that none of those named
would be tempted to leave the city, the seven gates of Florence
were locked during the examination. The first to be implicated

were Giannozzo Pucci, whom Guicciardini called "a very capable young man of excellent means but completely devoted to Piero," and Giovanni Cambi, "a man of little authority, who was a friend of the Medici not because of his forebears or because he owed them his position, but because he had been involved with them in some Pisan business affairs and had been impoverished by the Pisan rebellion." Both Pucci and Cambi were arrested that same evening and taken to the Palace of the Bargello for questioning. The following morning, Piero's cousin Lorenzo Tornabuoni was summoned to the palazzo. Guicciardini called Lorenzo "probably the most beloved young man his age in Florence." Although a leader of the *Bigi*, he seldom missed any of the friar's sermons, and he had insisted on signing the petition which the brothers of San Marco had planned to send to Rome. But Piero was his first cousin, and under Piero's rule he had enjoyed great power.

Soon after his arrest, Niccolò Ridolfi and the ex-gonfalonier Bernardo del Nero were brought in for questioning. Niccolò's brother was that devoted *Piagnone* Giovambattista Ridolfi, who had wielded a pruning hook in the friar's defense on Ascension Day. Had Niccolò's son Piero not married Lorenzo dei Medici's daughter Contessina, Niccolò too might have become a *Piagnone*. But, said Guicciardini, "the marriage had made him so powerful in the old regime that his ambition could not be satisfied by anything the new had to offer."

Bernardo del Nero was 75 years old and childless. Either because he was too old to adapt to the egalitarian ways of the new regime or because he had been burdened with an extra tax of 400 ducats, which he considered unfair, he too wished to see the end of popular government in Florence. He had originally hoped to replace it with an oligarchy headed by Piero's cousins Lorenzo and Giovanni Popolani (né Medici), but Niccolò Ridolfi had convinced him that this was not feasible.

Also arrested was Piero's older sister, Lucrezia Salviati, of all Lorenzo's children the one who most resembled him in character and temperament. Her brothers had not been expelled for their faults, she told the examiners, and she had desired and still desired their return. So that they would want for nothing, she had given them more than 4500 ducats in cash and over 500 ducats worth of clothing. Because her husband, Jacopo, was a devoted *Piagnone* and because Francesco Valori thought it unseemly to harm a woman, she was allowed to return to her villa in the country after being questioned. But the five men were tortured to make them confess and then tried by a committee of twenty that included five private citizens, seven representatives of the Ten, and the Eight of the Ward. The committee found all five conspirators guilty: Bernardo del Nero because although while gonfalonier he had been told of the plot by Niccolò Ridolfi, he had not revealed it to the Signoria; the others because they had been actively involved. However, the powerful family connections of the condemned men made the Eight of the Ward, whose task it was to pass sentence, reluctant to do so. Finally, Domenico Bartoli, the gonfalonier, suggested widening the area of responsibility by referring the case to the Great Council. Ostensibly because they thought it unwise to communicate secrets of state to so great a multitude but actually because they wished to delay the sentencing as long as possible, four of the priors opposed this. Since a plurality of six was needed for it to pass, that ended that. As a compromise, the Signoria then voted to submit the case to a *pratica*.

On August 17, the 136 members of the *pratica* voted unanimously to cut off the heads of the accused and to confiscate their worldly goods. But the voting was by benches, which meant that one member of each bench spoke for the majority seated thereon. In an attempt once again to delay the verdict, counsel for the defense asked that every member of the *pratica* be allowed to vote separately. Whereupon Francesco Valori, who had made himself the leader of those favoring immediate imposition of the death sentence, summoned the notary to record publicly his words and in a loud voice cried out that the five deserved to die. Spurred by his example, his supporters created such an uproar that the Signoria decided to refer the case back to the Eight. When the Eight voted 6 to 2 to confirm the sentence of the *pratica*, the condemned turned to the celebrated *Arrabbiati* lawyer Guidantonio Vespucci. He advised them to take advantage of the law of the six beans to demand that the Signoria grant them the right to appeal to the Great Council against the verdict of the Eight. He pointed out that the right of appeal had been granted in two previous cases of suspected treason. But when the Signoria voted, the four priors who had originally opposed an appeal supported it and the gonfalonier and the four priors who had originally supported it opposed it.

No sooner did the Signoria's inability to obtain a plurality become known than everyone in the city took sides. The friends and relatives of the condemned men stressed the need to abide by the law. Some even hinted that Francesco Valori was pressing for the death sentence because he wished to be rid of Bernardo del Nero, "the only man capable of opposing him and impeding his power." The people, on the other hand, were "universally determined to take revenge on these proud aristocrats." The news that Piero was preparing to launch a new attack on the city increased their determination. A flood of handbills sought to inflame them further by exhorting lovers of liberty to deal with the five as those traitors had planned to deal with the republic.

In 1494, when the people had demanded the blood of all who had supported the Medici, the friar had called for a universal peace that would wipe out past offenses. "I tell you and I command you in the name of God," he had cried, "pardon everyone." And that January he had exhorted the people to grant political offenders the right of appeal from the verdict of the six beans. It was not mercy per se that had impelled him to speak thus, but mercy as a politically expedient course, for many of the leaders of the popular faction, including Francesco Valori and Paolantonio Soderini, had once served the Medici, and Giovambattista Ridolfi's brother was related to them by marriage. The following July, when the position of these men was more secure and it was a question of ridding Florence of the *parlamento*, mercy no longer found a place in his vocabulary.

"People, if you hear the bell summoning you to a *parla-

mento, draw forth your swords!" he cried. He also urged them to "cut to pieces" any prior who set foot in the palazzo with the intention of pulling the bell cord.

"I tell you that Christ intends to rule here," he declared that autumn, "and any who fight against this government fight against Christ." As the opposition to him grew more vehement, so did his conviction that the sword was the best recourse against his opponents. Although in the *Compendium Revelationum* he had referred proudly to "the appeal from the six votes advocated by me for the greater security of the citizens," he did not speak out in favor of an appeal in August 1497.

In the matter of the five citizens, he was content that they should die or be expelled, he would say later, and he saw no reason to involve himself in the particulars of the case. True, he thought Bernardo del Nero's guilt relatively minor, and he would have preferred to see him live. But he did nothing to save him. He advised his friend Giovambattista Ridolfi, if it turned out to be God's will that his brother should die, to think only of his brother's soul, for by gaining his brother's soul, Giovambattista would gain him forever and nothing would be lost. "Perhaps," wrote Savonarola, "God has ordained this penance for his [Niccolò's] salvation. Often, tribulations save those who would be ruined by prosperity."

In the case of Lorenzo Tornabuoni, however, he found it impossible to remain so dispassionate. Ignoring his decision not to involve himself in particulars, he sent a letter to Francesco Valori. Experience had taught him that in seeking something from Valori that the latter opposed it was best not to press him. And so he recommended Lorenzo coldly, in a manner that would create the impression that he did not care. In this case, however, the ruse had no chance of succeeding, for although Valori too was pained to see this charming young man die, he considered him guiltier than almost anyone else. And he knew that he could not spare him without sparing the others.

Strictly speaking, now that the Eight had condemned Lorenzo and his coconspirators, only the Great Council had the right to spare any of them. Because the Signoria was still unable to decide the question of an appeal to the council, the priors and the gonfalonier again sought the advice of the *pratica*. A small minority of those consulted held that the right of appeal against the death sentence was sanctioned by law and ought to be granted. But the vast majority went along with Valori in saying that any hesitation in carrying out the sentence of the Eight might bring the risk of a popular uprising. "And if tumults are feared, according to common law all appeals are denied."

When this argument failed to convince the other side, the gonfaloniers of the sixteen districts of Florence threatened to sack the houses of all who favored an appeal, and one of the *Piagnone* leaders began to shout, "Let justice be done!" The commotion continued until seven that evening when everyone returned to his bench to vote. Although the majority of the benches voted against an appeal, even such a confirmed *Piagnone* as Francesco Gualterotti seemed reluctant to impose a decision on the Signoria. But Valori would have none of their shilly-shallying. Seizing a ballot box, he slammed it against the table. "Let justice be done," he shouted, "or there will be a revolt!" And he extended the ballot box to the Signoria. When the president for the day took the vote, though, it was no different from what it had been on August 17.

"Why then have your Excellencies summoned all these citizens, who every one of them as recorded by the notary has already voted against these plotters of novelties, these subverters of our country and destroyers of freedom?" Valori shrieked, virtually beside himself with rage.

Reminding the Signoria that they had been placed there by the people of Florence to defend the city's liberty, he again extended the ballot box. In the ensuing tumult, one of his supporters grabbed Piero Guicciardini, the father of the historian and spokesman for the four priors who favored an appeal, and threatened to throw him out of the window if he did not change his vote. Although Guicciardini refused to be intimidated, when a new vote was taken, one of the other priors who had favored an appeal was sufficiently frightened to change his vote, giving the opposition the plurality it needed.

In an effort to arouse compassion for the condemned, counsel for the defense then led the chained and barefoot prisoners through the meeting hall. But the Eight had already left for the adjoining palace of the Bargello to arrange for the executions. There, at the foot of the staircase in the palace courtyard, workmen erected the scaffold, then spread straw on the pavement to absorb the blood of the victims. At four o'clock that morning, by the flickering light of torches fixed in iron rings attached to the stone pillars that framed the courtyard, the five were beheaded in the presence of a few *cittadini principali,* and their corpses consigned to their relatives for burial. Seeing the headless corpse of Lorenzo Tornabuoni carried past the Canto dei Tornaquinci on a bier shortly before dawn, Luca Landucci could not refrain from weeping. But he consoled himself with the thought that everything happens "in accordance with God's will. May all be to his glory!"

At the time this was happening, Niccolò Machiavelli was a 28-year-old unemployed *giovane,* too distrustful of what he saw as the friar's "partial and ambitious spirit" to become a *Piagnone,* yet too much of a popular republican in his sympathies to make a good *Arrabbiato* or a *Bigi.* In *The Discourses* Machiavelli wrote that the executions

> did more than anything else to diminish the influence of Savonarola, for if the appeal was useful, then the law should have been observed, and if it was not useful, it should never have been made. And this circumstance was the more remarked as Fra Girolamo in his many subsequent preachings never condemned those who had broken the law and rather excused the act in the manner of one unwilling to condemn what suited his purpose yet unable to excuse it wholly.

Guicciardini too thought that the heated refusal of Valori and his faction to grant an appeal was not without shame for the friar "that he should have failed to dissuade especially among his followers the violation of a law which he himself had proposed a few years earlier as very salutary and almost necessary for the preservation of liberty."

*   *   *

Although the executions brought Valori a host of enemies among the friends and relatives of the executed men, the people hailed him as a new Cato. Since there was no leader of stature to oppose him now that Bernardo del Nero was dead, he became the virtual head of the city. While that made it necessary for Savonarola to use even more guile in dealing with him, it also ensured the victory of the friar's party in the elections that September. "Now one can say that the friar's party holds the government of the state freely in its hands without any opposition," Paolo Somenzi told Ludovico soon afterward.

Ever since the excommunication, both Bracci and Becchi had been urging Cardinal Caraffa to put in a good word for Savonarola. But the friar's refusal to unite San Marco with the Tuscan-Roman congregation had alienated the cardinal. He probably would have remained alienated had not the death of the five conspirators unexpectedly provided a way to bring him around.

Among the many Florentines besides the five who had been implicated in the conspiracy was Nofri Tornabuoni, who had been accused of smuggling between 500 and 600 gold ducats into Rome for Piero's use. Rather than answer the charges, Nofri had fled. As a result, his property was confiscated along with that of the executed men.

Some time before this happened, he had borrowed a large sum from Cardinal Caraffa. When Caraffa wanted it back, Nofri referred him to the Signoria. They would be only too happy to ask the commissioners in charge of confiscated property to satisfy him, the Signoria told Caraffa, if in return he agreed to work for the absolution of Fra Girolamo. To make his task easier, the cardinal suggested that the friar write a conciliatory letter to the pope.

In his conversations with Bracci and Becchi, Alexander had repeatedly made it clear that he would not absolve Fra Girolamo until he came to Rome. Hence, if the friar wrote to the pope, he would either have to agree to go to Rome or offer some good excuse for not going. The only excuse he could think of was the one he had used so many times before, namely, that because of his enemies it was unsafe for him to make the trip. But he was careful to sandwich this in between abject pleas for forgiveness.

Just as a son grieved by the anger of his father constantly seeks ways to placate him and will not allow any rebuff to make him despair of regaining the love that once was his, so Savonarola, more afflicted by the loss of His Holiness's good graces than by any other misfortune, sought to throw himself at the feet of the pope in order to cleanse himself of every false accusation, he told the Holy Father. He would go to Rome at once, he continued, if on the journey he could be sure of being safe from the malice and plots of his enemies. He wished with all his heart that he could go so that he might at last clear himself of every calumny. In conclusion, he beseeched the pope not to spurn one whom he would find not less devoted to him than sincere.

He hoped that his affairs with the pope would soon be arranged, Savonarola told the Ferrarese ambassador that November, since the groundwork had been laid and his Holiness seemed so inclined. To the ambassador, it seemed obvious that the friar thought this would redound to his credit, "all the more so because he had not yielded to the pope's demands."

But as it turned out, the pope had no intention of absolving him just yet. At the time he received the friar's letter, the truce with Charles VIII was about to end. To prevent a new invasion of Italy, Alexander considered it essential that Florence, the one Italian state still loyal to France, join the Holy League. As he had done previously, he planned to use Pisa as the bait. This time, however, he decided to make the bait even more alluring by throwing in the friar's absolution. If Florence joined the Holy League, the Florentines could have Pisa and the absolution of Fra Girolamo into the bargain. If they didn't, Alexander would give them neither. As far as is known, he did not bother to answer the friar's letter.

It was then over six months since Savonarola had preached his last sermon. That September, the children had gone to the palazzo to ask the Signoria to rebuild the tiers in the cathedral. At the time, the friar had been optimistic enough to believe that they would soon be needed. As week followed week with no reply to his letter, he grew increasingly restive. A medal had just been struck in his honor. On one side, it showed his likeness; on the other, Rome with a disembodied hand holding a dagger over the city and the inscription *Ecco gladius Domini super terram cito et velociter.* When, if ever, would he once again be able to proclaim that warning from the pulpit? An hour after sundown on the first Sunday of Advent, he asked his friars to meet him in the convent hospice wearing their copes and chasubles. Although he had given innumerable reasons to prove the truth of his doctrines, men were growing harder and harder to convince, he told them. Since men could not be convinced by reason alone, he begged his friars to pray for a miracle, and he warned them to speak of it to no one.

Two weeks later, the Ten sent Domenico Bonsi, whom Piero Parenti described as "in every way the friar's man," to Rome to discuss the Pisan question and to use his ingenuity to secure the absolution of Fra Girolamo.

Since the chief business of all the wealthy *Frateschi* and of many of the *Arrabbiati* was with France, the government also continued to negotiate with the French. To Parenti it seemed obvious that those in power wanted Fra Girolamo to speak out because they needed him to keep the people loyal to King Charles.

Although the friar had celebrated mass and performed his other priestly functions after being excommunicated, he had not as yet done so in public. On Christmas morning, he publicly celebrated the three solemn Christmas masses in the church of San Marco and gave Holy Communion to 300 men and women of the congregation. This was followed by a procession in the piazza, which Machiavelli described as, "first the cross, then the boys, then the friars, then the men and women with red crosses in hand shouting '*Viva Cristo!*'"

The astonishment at the friar's boldness had scarcely subsided when on January 6—the Feast of the Epiphany—he again officiated in San Marco. Although the cold was then so bitter that the Arno seemed a solid cake of ice, the eight priors and the gonfalonier donned their ermine-trimmed red jackets and, as had always been the custom of the Signoria on that day, brought gifts to the church. After leaving their gifts at the door, they went up to the altar to kiss the hand of their excommunicated friar. Luca Landucci, who had always been devoted to Fra Girolamo, noted "the great surprise of thoughtful men, not only his adversaries but also among his friends."

By then, however, there were others among his friends who, as he later put it, "hungered for the word of God." These friends kept asking him when he intended to preach again, saying that they were "starved for his sermons." At the end of January, the Signoria suddenly ordered the tiers rebuilt. This gave substance to the rumor that he would preach on Candlemas, February 2.

Perhaps because he needed a quiet place in which to think things over, he was then staying in the convent of San Domenico in Fiesole. On February 1, the Ferrarese ambassador visited him there. He had quite made up his mind to preach during Lent or perhaps sooner should those who had a right to command him give him a sign, he told the ambassador. Not sure what he meant by this, the ambassador asked him if he was awaiting orders from the pope or the Signoria. He could not be induced to undertake the work by the command of the Signoria nor even by command of the pope, given the continuance of the latter's style of life, the friar replied. Moreover, he was well aware that the pope made no secret of his determination not to withdraw the excommunication. The commission he awaited was the commission of One who was superior to the pope and to all creatures. Later, under oath, he would say that he had been awaiting a letter from Domenico Bonsi. When Bonsi informed him that the pope was not inclined to allow him to preach, he decided that the work of reform for which God had sent him to Florence would be ruined if he continued to obey the Holy Father. And he made up his mind to return to the pulpit.

When the commission to reform the church the pope had appointed after his son's death had suggested increasing the power of the College of Cardinals and convening a General Council to discuss further measures, the pope had tactfully but firmly ignored its suggestions. After that, there was no further talk of reform. Because Cesare was eager to replace his murdered brother as captain general of the church, Alexander was then considering releasing his son from his ecclesiastical vows. He was also said to be looking for a wife for Cesare. As if this were not bad enough, on December 22, Lucrezia's marriage to Giovanni Sforza was annulled. Although Sforza's impotence was the ostensible reason for the annulment, many believed that the real reason was that Alexander wanted his daughter for himself. Cesare and Juan were also rumored to have enjoyed their sister's favors.

To the friar, this catalog of papal iniquity would seem ample justification for the step he was taking. As usual when confronted with stories of the pope's evil life, he would make no attempt to sort out what was true from what was merely hostile gossip. Nor did it seem to trouble him that, according to Bonsi, the pope regarded his defiance of the excommunication as a serious matter touching on the honor of the Holy See. After all, Alexander had spoken like this so many times before. Surely He who had stayed the Holy Father's hand in the past would stay it once again.

VIII

THE POPE DEFIED

raditionally, Florentine preachers began their Lenten sermons on Septuagesima Sunday, the third Sunday before the fast began. No sooner did Savonarola announce that he would preach in the cathedral that day than what Guicciardini called "the evil humors and divisions" which had died down somewhat during the nine months he had kept silent were resuscitated. Because the canons of the cathedral feared they would lose their benefices if, excommunicated as he was, he returned to the pulpit, they sent a delegation to the Signoria to demand that he not be allowed to do so. At the same time, the vicar of the archbishop of Florence forbade the canons to celebrate mass in the cathedral if the friar preached there and asked every parish priest to warn his flock that anyone who went to hear Fra Girolamo would be denied the sacraments and not receive a Christian burial.

But the city magistrates were almost all *Piagnoni*, and they were determined that the friar should preach and the people should hear him. Upon learning of the vicar's directive, the Signoria sent a member of the Eight to demand that he vacate his post within two hours. His replacement was an ardent *Piagnone* who, of course, put nothing in the way of the friar's return to the pulpit.

"The will of God had prevailed over the malevolent intentions of men," said Jacopo Nardi. However, as befitted a good

Arrabbiato, Piero Parenti took a more cynical view. Realizing that a new Signoria would be elected at the end of the month, said Parenti, "the magistrates were counting on the friar's sermons to ensure a *Piagnoni* majority."

Despite the numbing cold on Septuagesima Sunday, "so great a concourse of men and women of every class," from *cittadini principali* in ermine-lined cloaks to threadbare and shivering *sottoposti*, escorted Savonarola and his brethren from San Marco to the Duomo that the Via Cocomero and the surrounding streets seemed one great undulating mass of people. When at last they had all found places in the cathedral and Savonarola mounted the steps to the pulpit, they joined the *fanciulli* in singing the *Te Deum*. But though the cathedral was full, it was not as full as it had been in the past, for, like Luca Landucci, many who had once made a point of attending the friar's sermons had stayed away for fear of being excommunicated, saying "Just or unjust, it [the excommunication] is to be feared."

Appropriately, the friar chose as his text the words of the third psalm: "Lord, how are they increased that trouble me. How many are they that rise up against me."

"My enemies say Thou art not with me!" he cried in the brief prayer with which he opened his sermon. "I beg Thee stay with me and grant me the natural light of reason that I may not be deceived by those who oppose me. Grant me also the supernatural light to know things that are hid that I may not deceive myself nor deceive the people as I have not deceived them hitherto."

It was because his teaching had led and still did lead men to a good life that the devil had stirred up so many persecutions against him, he continued. To explain why some who had once come to hear him were absent that morning, he compared the excommunication to a winnowing fan which God had sent to separate the tepid from the good. "Now," he told the good, "let us inquire into its validity."

So that even the lowliest workingman would be able to follow his argument, he drew an analogy between the prince (Alexander VI) and an iron saw. If the workman cast away his saw among other bits of broken iron, it became like them and was no longer a saw, for there was no hand to guide it. So it was with the prince. If he was not guided by the superior agent (God), he was a broken tool, and they had the right to tell him so. And if, said the preacher, "he should reply, 'I hold the power,' you may answer: 'This is not true because you are moved by no guiding hand, you are a broken tool!'"

Those who had induced the pope to excommunicate him wished to do away with a virtuous life and all good government for the commonweal. Hence, if he was banned on earth, it should be clear that he was blessed in heaven. Who had told him so, he asked. "God has told me so," he replied. "Mind what I say, God himself has told me so."

As for the excommunication, which was said by some to be null and void in the sight of God but externally binding, it was enough for him that he was not bound in the sight of Christ. "O my Lord!" he cried, suddenly wheeling around to address the great wooden crucifix in the choir. "I turn to Thee and I say: 'If ever I should seek absolution from this excommunication, send me to hell!'"

It is possible that in the grip of the frenzy into which he had driven himself, he did not appreciate how greatly he had compromised himself by this outburst. Nevertheless, he was enough of a showman to sense the need for some comic relief after so dramatic a high. Alluding to those friars who refused to absolve anyone who came to hear him, he asked the congregation if they would like him to tell them who would absolve them. "Well, no," he replied, "it is better that I should say nothing about it. I will only say—just do this." And here, wrote Lorenzo Violi, who was transcribing the sermon, the preacher "jingled his keys one against the other, whereby everyone understood his meaning to be: 'Give them money, and they will absolve you.'"

After urging the congregation to drive the bad priests out, he turned next to the question of his supernatural light. "Brother, I don't believe you. You have worked no miracles that I should be bound to believe you against the church," he had an imaginary interlocutor tell him.

True, it had not yet pleased our Lord to grant a miracle, he replied. True, the excommunication had not been borne aloft on the point of a lance as he had predicted, but not everything had yet come to pass. However, if they had eyes, they must see that many signs had followed. In a clear reference to the pope, he reminded them that in Rome one had lost his son. "And you have seen who has died here," he continued, referring to the execution of the five conspirators the previous summer. "And I could tell you and I would who is in hell."

Although he had not yet been compelled to work a miracle, when he was compelled, he assured them that God would open His hand according as His honor would require. As a doctor of theology and a student of the writings of Jean Gerson and Thomas Aquinas, he knew, of course, that the church frowned on such reckless invocations of the supernatural. But by then, the need to enlist the "mixed multitude" that faced him in the Duomo in what he had convinced himself was a holy war against an unjust excommunication outweighed all other considerations. That this indiscriminate catering to the public thirst for miracles might one day redound to his discredit seems never to have occurred to him.

The following Sunday, the cold was so intense that many feared the young sprouts would die in the outlying regions and the harvest be ruined. Although the cold may have had something to do with the further shrinkage of the friar's audience, he chose to explain it as yet another sifting of the good from the bad. He was not going to preach to them, he told those who had come to hear him that frosty morning. Instead, he would undertake to prove that whoever obstinately maintained the validity of the excommunication was himself a heretic. And he reminded them that even a pope could err, either out of malice or because he had been circumvented. In the present case, a review of all that had transpired between him and Alexander would demonstrate that the pope had indeed been circumvented. Those whose false arguments had persuaded the Holy Father to excommunicate him were like a night walker bent on evil who, seeing a light approach and fearing to be recognized, cries: "Put out that light!" "O priests!" he roared. "This flame will never be extinguished; blow on it as hard as you wish!"

That February, his sermons were being printed immediately

after they were transcribed. Moreover, the use of woodcuts, which had begun in 1490, made it possible to include illustrations. And these brought the message of the sermons to many who would have been unable to read them. But this rapid dissemination had one drawback: If the sermons were quickly brought to the attention of the people, they were just as quickly brought to the attention of the pope and the cardinals. On February 17, Ludovico, who was then making a great show of being a friend and protector of the Florentine republic, had the Milanese envoy in Rome warn Domenico Bonsi that the enemies of Florence were using the friar's words to stir up the pope and the cardinals. As a counterweight, the envoy suggested that the Signoria write a conciliatory letter to the Holy Father.

The situation was serious, Bonsi told the Ten in the dispatch he sent them that evening, and he awaited their instructions. He was still awaiting their instructions on February 22 when he and Alessandro Bracci had an audience with the pope. He wished to know if Florence would be willing to obligate itself to oppose the king of France should Charles again invade Italy, said Alexander.

Since the Signoria had just informed its ambassador in France that despite papal inducements to drop the alliance with the French crown, they were convinced that only from France could they hope for security, the return of Pisa, and other favors, Bonsi and Bracci had no alternative except to repeat the usual generalities about being good Italians. The pope, however, had heard this formula too often not to be aware of what lay behind it. He well knew that, as the Venetian ambassador had warned him, they had no intention of breaking with France and would do nothing without the French king's consent, he told the two ambassadors. Rather than give them a chance to reply, he indicated that the audience was at an end and rose to leave. At the door, he suddenly turned to address Bonsi. "Let Fra Girolamo preach forsooth," he declared. "I should never have believed you would treat me so!"

"And," said Bonsi in the letter he addressed to the Ten later that day, "away he went, leaving Ser Alessandro and myself quite nonplussed."

Nonplussed though Ser Alessandro may have been, he was by then used to such outbursts. Moreover, as a civil servant of the Florentine republic and a good *Piagnone,* he seemed content to go on pleading the friar's case without ever asking himself whether the arguments the Ten gave him were having any effect. Domenico Bonsi, on the other hand, was no mere civil servant but a former gonfalonier and one of the most astute lawyers in Florence, a man whose legal training had accustomed him to weighing the pros and cons of every action. Although he had come to Rome filled with enthusiasm for the friar's cause, it had not taken him long to realize that the arguments which had seemed so convincing in Florence were not going to work at the papal court. As if this were not discouraging enough, the 68-year-old ambassador was finding life in the Holy City both expensive and dangerous.

Late the previous Monday evening, three men had been surprised attempting to scale the wall surrounding his residence. Two had managed to escape, but the third had broken a leg and been apprehended. From the answers he had given the sheriff, it was obvious that the three had powerful friends behind them and that robbery had not been their only motive. "So," Bonsi told the Ten, "you can see in what security I live."

Despite his concern for his own safety and the growing suspicion that nothing would come of his efforts on the friar's behalf, on February 25 he requested another audience with the pope. Having heard that Alexander had spoken "honorably enough" about the Florentines in a conversation the previous day, he and Bracci expected to find the Holy Father more cordial than he had been the last time they had seen him. Hence, neither of them was prepared for what occurred.

They knew how favorably disposed he was toward their Signoria, the pope told the two ambassadors. However, in view of what Fra Girolamo was saying about him, he marveled that the priors and the gonfalonier allowed the friar to go on preaching. The Holy Father then quoted at length from the friar's sermon on Septuagesima Sunday. "Neither Turk nor infidel would tolerate such conduct," he declared. Bonsi must send a special messenger to Florence immediately to warn the Ten that unless an effective means to stop the sermons were found, His Holiness would place a universal interdict on the city. Since this would mean that no merchant in Christendom could either buy from or sell to the Florentines, the two ambassadors immediately protested. They were so constantly interrupted they could make no headway. Taking out some sonnets critical of the Holy See which had just come from Florence, the pope asked one of the cardinals to read them aloud. "Am I to be derided thus in sonnets?" he exclaimed after hearing them.

Nor would he listen to the Florentines when they sought to explain that it was Fra Girolamo's enemies, not the friar himself, who were responsible for the sonnets. "In fact," Bonsi told the Ten, "it is quite beside the point to insist upon the friar's virtues or his reasons and arguments, for they make no impression in Rome." As for the Ten's insistence that the friar's case "surpassed the limits of mere nature," no one in Rome could be persuaded of the supernatural character of his work. Nor was it any use to try to obtain the support of anyone in the Holy City, especially of such as had heard what he had said against the pope.

But the Ten were in Florence, and in Florence the supernatural character of the friar's work was the issue for friend and foe alike. "We await the outcome of the affair whereby it will be possible to form a better judgment as to the grounds of his action whether human or divine," the Ferrarese ambassador had told Duke Ercole when the friar had first announced his decision to return to the pulpit.

"What was needed," said the *Arrabbiato* millionaire Leonardo Strozzi on February 24, "was a speedy clarification of whether Fra Girolamo's work was inspired by God or the devil."

Although at first the friar had been content to have a "supernatural guarantee" of his prophetic mission come "in God's good time," by then talk of an interdict, as well as rumors that the new Signoria was likely to be unfavorable to him, had convinced him that only an immediate sign from heaven could unite his dwindling flock and restore his ascendancy over the Florentines. "O Lord, I would that Thou shouldst make haste, we can do no more!" he cried in his sermon on February 25.

That God might be "the more ready to hasten matters," he proposed that on February 27, which was the last day of carnival, they should all join in earnest prayer. "And I will say mass, and I will take the sacrament in my hands," he told the congregation. "And if I am deceiving myself, I bid ye all pray fervently that Christ will send down a fire from heaven which will then and there swallow me in hell!"

He invited the *tiepidi* to be present and to deliver up the same prayer. "Write this everywhere," he cried. "Bid mounted messengers ride posthaste to Rome and bid them pray that if this thing be not of God, destruction may fall upon me!"

With a confidence in the outcome that could have just as easily sprung from fakery as from faith, he announced that afterward they would have the procession of the children. And he warned the children to be grave and not to cry *Gesù Cristo!* until he told them to, for now they were going to make war on the devil and his carnal pomp. As part of that war, the children had once again gone from house to house gathering up "vain and beautiful things" to be burned, and the Eight had forbidden the wearing of masks during the carnival season. "Matters had come to such a pass," said the anti-*Piagnoni* chronicler Bartolomeo Cerretani, "that this small cause had a huge effect."

Among the wealthy *giovani* in the city were ten from aristocratic families who had been drawn to one another by their mutual distaste for the friar and his work of moral reform. When these ten learned that they would not be allowed to wear masks during carnival, they invited other idle and wealthy youths to join them in forming a company called the *Compagnacci*, or boon companions. In all, some 300 *giovani*, whom Simone Filipepi described as "the most ill-mannered in the city...young men of ribald and dissolute life," joined the new company. Among them were Jacopo dei Nerli and most of the other wellborn hooligans responsible for the Ascension Day riot. As their "governor," the *Compagnacci* chose Doffo Spini, a 50-year-old wastrel whose preference for the company of younger men led many to suspect that he was a homosexual. As Spini's chancellor, the group elected another high-living ne'er-do-well, Ser Francesco de Ser Barone, commonly known as Ser Ceccone, an ex-Medici supporter who had been imprisoned at the time of the revolution and had later been disowned by his father.

With the dues collected from their well-to-do membership, the new officers rented a sumptuous residence near the Arno known as the Casa del Patriarca. There the *Compagnacci* had a banquet every Wednesday. There they discussed how best to harass the friar. Using what Filipepi called "the filthiest language," some of them paraded up and down outside San Marco at night ringing cowbells. Others slipped into the pulpit before the friar was scheduled to preach and, with an onion stuck on the tip of a sword, pretended to bless the congregation. Still others donned skirts and sat in the women's section. When the *Compagnacci* learned that carpenters were constructing the framework for a new pyramid of vanities "modeled after the one the previous year but bigger," they made up their minds to destroy it. After their first foray into the Piazza della Signoria, however, the Eight stationed an armed guard there each night.

On Shrove Tuesday, the completed pyramid rose intact at the center of the piazza, with Lucifer in effigy at its summit, surrounded by the seven cardinal sins looking down on tiers laden with dice, lutes, women's hair, great quantities of perfume, copies of Luigi Pulci's *Morgante,* and other "heretical" books, including an illuminated Petrarch, as well as mirrors, rouge pots, combs, and marble busts of such famous beauties of yore as Cleopatra and Faustina, the whole estimated to be worth many thousands of florins.

Before those vanities were incinerated, however, the friar would seek to elicit a response from God, and on that last morning of carnival, 1498, the prospect of "seeing signs" drew all Florence to the Piazza San Marco. With his customary disdain for the excommunication, Savonarola insisted on first saying mass in the church. With his own hands, he then gave the sacrament to all 250 of his brethren and to "several thousand men and women." Seeing this, said Luca Landucci, the *tiepidi* (among whom Landucci was wont to include the *Compagnacci*) "laughed and mocked, saying, 'He is excommunicated and he gives the communion to others.'" But the friar was too preoccupied with what lay ahead that morning to notice. Removing a silver pyx containing the sacrament from the altar, he walked slowly up the nave with it and then out into the piazza, followed by his friars and the entire congregation. Still carrying the pyx, he entered an ornate wooden pulpit, which had been erected to the right of the church door, and addressed the vast multitude in the square.

"Citizens of Florence," he told them. "If I have said anything to you in the name of God which was not true; if the apostolic censure pronounced against me is valid; if I have deceived anyone—pray to God that He will send fire from heaven upon me that will consume me in the presence of this people. And I pray our Lord, three in one, whose body I hold in this blessed sacrament, to send death to me in this place."

With that, he sank to his knees, apparently lost in prayer. Those who believed in him also sank to their knees and prayed, while those who, like Piero Parenti, considered this whole elaborately staged appeal to the Almighty "food for blockheads" remained standing. In George Eliot's *Romola*, after the friar has prayed for half an hour, the sunlight, which has been trying to break through the gray winter sky, finally effects "a wider parting, and with a gentle quickness like a smile" pours itself upon the pyx and then spreads itself over Savonarola's face. Whereupon, an instant shout rings through the piazza: "Behold the answer!" However, not one of the contemporary chroniclers mentioned this incident. In fact, Parenti tells us that when nothing happened, many of those who had come in the hope of seeing the friar perform a miracle began to speak against him. But for the faithful it was sufficient that a fire had not come down from heaven to consume their prophet.

After lunch, they returned to San Marco for the solemn procession to the Piazza della Signoria where the bonfire of vanities would be ignited. Carrying red crosses and olive branches and wearing garlands of olive leaves on their heads, the *fanciulli* were grouped according to neighborhood: first came Santo Spirito, then San Giovanni Battista and Santa Maria Novella, and finally, Santa Croce. Each district had its own insignia and its own tabernacle carried on the shoulders of four neighborhood boys. Behind them in size places, the other boys walked two by two singing hymns and lauds. After the district of Santa Croce came the adult men, then the girls and great multitudes of women, and finally the black-manteled friars of San Marco.

The vanguard of the procession had just reached the half-finished palace of the Strozzi where workmen were putting in the first row of mullioned windows when about sixty *Compagnacci* suddenly appeared. While some began spitting at a tabernacle representing the Virgin and child with the twelve apostles, others snatched the red crosses out of the hands of the smaller boys, broke them in two, and stomped on them, telling the people that they were mandrakes in the service of the devil.

Still singing hymns and lauds and apparently undaunted by their encounter with those whom they had been taught to think of as "sons of Satan," the *fanciulli* continued on their way, past the old Gothic church of Santa Trinità and the narrow crenellated palace of the Spini to a point opposite the bridge of Santa Trinità known as La Pancaccia. There, said the chronicler Burlamacchi, many idle and wellborn youths were in the habit of passing the time of day. There too could be found many *Compagnacci*. No sooner did the latter catch sight of the procession than some of them began tearing the red crosses out of the hands of the *fanciulli* and flinging them into the Arno, while others sought to impede the marchers by throwing stones. Seeing this, Luca Corsini, an eminent doctor of jurisprudence and a member of the Signoria that had rejected Piero, cast off his cloak and picked up a fistful of stones. Without further ado, he proceeded to hurl them at those who would disrupt the procession, all the while shouting that he was prepared to die for the faith. Inspired by his example, many other leading citizens, including, said Burlamacchi, the gonfaloniers of the companies, members of the Ten, and a number of foreign ambassadors joined the fray. And they soon prevailed over the *Compagnacci*.

After that, there were no further incidents until the procession reached the Piazza della Signoria, where the *Compagnacci* began throwing dead cats and other garbage on the bonfire and those in the procession picked up the cats and hurled them at their tormentors. Machiavelli, who was a spectator, spoke of "dead cats and chickens flying." But with the help of the armed guard keeping watch over the pyramid, the *Compagnacci* were again driven back and the vanities ignited with as much panache as the previous year.

To Savonarola, the battle between his followers and the *Compagnacci* was a battle between good and evil. That Lent, he would expound the Book of Exodus, he told his audience on Ash Wednesday. Just as God's people had been persecuted by Pharoah in biblical times, so in their own time were Christians being persecuted by Pharaoh and the *tiepidi.* Yesterday, for example, during the procession and devotions of the God-fearing, the wicked had behaved worse than if they had been Turks or pagans, breaking the crosses in two and throwing them away. Nor, in the friar's opinion, were the clergy any better. "O clergy, clergy, O Rome, Rome," he cried. "You say you are the blessed and we are the excommunicated, and yet you fight as the damned and the infidels....Write to Rome and say that that friar who is in Florence with his followers will fight against you as against the Turks and pagans and that we desire to die and be martyred by you."

As if in answer to his challenge, that same afternoon two briefs arrived from Rome: one addressed to the canons of the cathedral, the other to the Signoria. Referring to the friar as "that son of iniquity Fra Girolamo Savonarola of Ferrara," the brief to the Signoria reviewed the Holy Father's futile efforts to correct Fra Girolamo's many "grave and pernicious errors," then proceeded to list the numerous ways in which the said Girolamo had defied the excommunication as well as the signs of favor and support shown him by the citizens. "And this with the permission of the Signoria, from whom better things might have been expected." To put an end to such flagrant disregard of his orders, the pope demanded that Savonarola either be sent to Rome or be "confined as a rotten member in some private place where he may be cut off from all communications with others." If this demand was not met, the Holy Father threatened to lay the city under interdict or proceed to even sterner measures.

One reason for Alexander's unaccustomed severity was that he had just learned that not only had Charles VIII not renounced the idea of invading Italy, but he had also signed a truce with Ferdinand of Spain. No longer able to count on support from Ferdinand, the pope was determined to have Florence join the Holy League as soon as possible. An even more pressing reason for silencing the friar was the need to assert the authority of the church over one who had dared to call the duly elected successor of Peter a "broken tool" and his writ of excommunication heretical. Though determined to brook no further abuse, Alexander was not inclined to be vindictive, perhaps because despite everything he continued to respect what he had once called the friar's "misguided zeal for the vineyards of the Lord." "If Fra Girolamo will prove his obedience by abstaining from preaching for a reasonable time," the pope told Bonsi, "I will absolve him from the censures he has brought upon himself. But if he persists in his disobedience, we shall be obliged to proceed against him with the interdict and all other lawful punishments to vindicate our own honor and that of the Holy See."

The brief the pope sent to the canons of Santa Maria dei Fiore bade them shut the door of the cathedral on Fra Girolamo and not allow him to preach there under any circumstances. When the canons delivered this brief to the Signoria on the afternoon of February 28, the latter refused to accept it. The following day, however, a new Signoria would take office. Since the names of those elected to this new Signoria had already been made public and since the friar judged two-thirds of them to be hostile to him, either on his own or on the advice of the leaders of his party, he decided to leave the cathedral before he was asked to leave.

In his sermon on March 1, he sought to put the best possible face on what he was doing. "Briefs have come from Rome, have they not?" he asked. "They say they call me *filius perditionis*, that is, the son of perdition," he continued. And he advised his audience to write to the authors of those briefs as follows: "He whom you call by that name keeps no concubines or boys for pleasure but devotes himself to preaching the faith of Christ. He works to exalt the church; you work to ruin it."

Resorting to one of his favorite metaphors for the church of Rome, he announced that the time was drawing near to open the casket. "If we do but turn the key," he cried, "there will come forth such a stench from the Roman sink that it will spread through all Christendom and everyone will perceive it!"

Since what he said could be proved by natural reason and supernatural signs, he feared nothing, he told them. Because he wished to imitate Christ, who gave way to ire, however, he would no longer preach in the cathedral. "Please understand I was not commanded to do this," he declared. "I will preach in San Marco to men only because the times require this....Should you wish to drive us away, I tell you that as long as this head remains on this body, this tongue will never be silent."

These last words were, of course, addressed to the new Signoria and his other enemies in Florence. Because he was uncertain of just what they had in mind, at about this time he endeavored to strengthen his hand by yet another test of his unique relationship with God. In letters to the pope, the general of the Dominican order, and the head of the observant Franciscans, he proposed that all three accompany him to a cemetery where they would strive to raise one of the dead. He who succeeded would be accepted as God's chosen by the others. Hearing of this, Pico's nephew offered his uncle's corpse for the experiment. However, the Franciscans refused the invitation, and the pope and the general of the Dominicans ridiculed it.

Meanwhile, Savonarola began his sermons in San Marco. Although the pope's brief to the canons had threatened to excommunicate anyone who attended the friar's sermons, almost every man who had gone to hear him in the cathedral on March 1 went to hear him in San Marco on March 2. Among others, this included the Ferrarese ambassador, all the members of the Eight and the Ten, most of the other principal magistrates of the city with the exception of the Signoria, and, although no one took any notice of him at the time, Niccolò Machiavelli.

Since the friar's return to the pulpit on Septuagesima Sunday, Machiavelli had been keeping track of his activities for Ricciardo Becchi. Although Becchi no longer represented the Ten at the Vatican, he was still in Rome, and he desired "full information about matters concerning Fra Girolamo." Whether Machiavelli supplied this information because he and Becchi were friends or because this was one way to prepare for the post in government he sought is not known. Whatever the reason, it offered the as yet untried young man an opportunity to exchange opinions with one whose judgment he considered superior to his own.

As the text for Savonarola's first sermon in San Marco, he had chosen a verse from Chapter 1 of Exodus: "But the more they afflicted them, the more they multiplied and grew." Although filled with admiration at how audaciously the friar began his sermon and with what boldness he continued, Machiavelli thought his arguments most apt to convince those who did not consider them carefully; for, as was his custom, the friar called his followers the very best of men and his opponents the very worst, and touched "only those points which served to weaken the opposing party and strengthen his own." Obviously, he feared that the new Signoria was preparing to attack him and "had decided that many citizens should be brought down with him in his ruin."

This fear of what the new Signoria would do, as well as the wish to bring others down with him, was also evident to Machiavelli the next morning when the friar expounded those verses in Exodus in which Moses slays an Egyptian for smiting a Hebrew. To Savonarola, Egypt represented wicked men and Moses the preacher who killed them by uncovering their vices. "O Egypt, I wish to give you a stab!" he cried. And here, Machiavelli told Becchi, "he commenced to flip through your books, O priests, and treat you in such a fashion that dogs would not have eaten you."

The point of all this ferocity became apparent when he added that he wished to give Egypt another wound and a large one, then confided that there was someone in Florence who hoped to set himself up as a tyrant. "Do you know the meaning of interdict, interdict, interdict?" he asked. "It means tyrant, tyrant, tyrant. Do you know the meaning of 'drive out the friar'? It means drive out you and you and you; cut off the heads of this one and that one and that other one." He was so prolix, said Machiavelli in his letter to Becchi, "that later that day men made public conjectures about one who is as close to being a tyrant as you are to the sky."

The one they were conjecturing about was Piero's cousin Lorenzo Popolani (né Medici). Among the *Arrabbiati*, there had always been a faction that wished to establish an oligarchy with Lorenzo and his brother Giovanni as leaders. However, this faction posed no more of a threat that March than it had earlier. What had changed, as Machiavelli saw it, was that the friar was now faced with a hostile Signoria and wished to "unite his own party by frightening them with the name tyrant."

Piero Popoleschi, the new gonfalonier, was a confirmed *Arrabbiati*, more averse to the friar, said one rhymester, "than the Germans are to water." But contrary to expectations, the *Arrabbiati* could count on only five votes in the Signoria. Even if they had had the six-vote plurality necessary to do as they pleased, they probably would have thought it advisable to first summon a *pratica* to discuss the pope's demands. As it was, they had no alternative.

The majority of those consulted were devoted to the friar. Partly because they believed in him and partly, no doubt, because they realized that their political future was at stake, they begged the republic not to abandon "that saint, that servant of God, that liberator of the people, that man of good life and impressive doctrine, that spiritual benefactor of Florence, that infinite treasure." Since the Signoria was legally bound to abide by the will of the *pratica*, it had to comply. Perhaps, as Paolo Somenzi told Ludovico, the *Arrabbiati* majority hoped that by complying it would instigate the pope to take more effective measures.

The letter which the Signoria sent to the Holy Father on March 3 began by telling him that after the arrival of his brief calling the friar a son of iniquity, Savonarola had withdrawn from the cathedral to his own monastery in the hope of mitigating the anger of His Holiness. However, the Signoria regretted that it could not ask him to abstain from preaching. For one thing, there was the debt of gratitude which the republic owed to a man who had done so much for their city. For another, there was the greatest danger of popular disturbances should it take steps against him.

When the friar learned that the Signoria had "written favorably of him to the pope," said Machiavelli, he "changed his tactics." Where he had once made mention of a tyrant and dwelled on the wickedness of his adversaries, now he sought "to alienate everyone from the supreme pontiff...saying about him what one can say of the most depraved man who exists." And so, Machiavelli concluded, Savonarola adapted himself to the times and shaded his lies.

"At this time," said Piero Parenti, "the friar persisted in slandering the pope, calling him Pharoah and similar indecent names."

Buoyed by the unexpected support of the Signoria, on March 3 the friar also wrote a letter to the pope. In this letter he accused the Holy Father of having always listened to his calumniators and detractors, thereby opening the way to wolves and giving them the strength to hinder the work of Christ. He warned the pope that God, who chose the humble of this earth to confound the strong, was ready to prove the truth for which the friar and those who believed in him were suffering by "natural proofs and supernatural signs." "These things will be shown in this manner and proved with these arguments to those who hinder God's work," he declared. "Therefore, Holy Father, delay no longer in looking for your salvation."

Nor did he stop there. Rather than continue to use the metaphor of the key and the casket, he now spoke openly of the need to summon a council. "Tell me, Florence, what does *concilium* mean?" he asked in his sermon on March 9. "In the *concilium* reformers must be appointed who shall reform what is rotten. Likewise in the *concilium* the wicked priests are punished, the bishop is deposed who has been guilty of simony and schism."

In a meeting with the pope on March 1, the Venetian ambassador had told him that he might judge from the license accorded to Fra Girolamo in what esteem His Holiness and the League were held by the Florentines. But the ambassador's efforts to stir up bad blood had been to no avail, Bonsi told the Ten. His Holiness was determined that no insult to himself personally should cause him to oppose the common good of Italy, especially since he took it for granted that the Signoria would obey his commands as set forth in the brief.

Since Bonsi also took this for granted, he was not prepared for the Signoria's letter upholding the friar, and it must have been with considerable trepidation that he and Bracci sought an audience with the pope. They were admitted to the Camera del Pappagallo, where they found the Holy Father seated on his throne conferring with the Milanese envoy. Seeing the two Florentines, Alexander demanded to know what answer their Signoria had made to his brief. Rather than give him a direct reply, Bonsi handed him the Signoria's letter, and the pope asked the Milanese ambassador to read it aloud. "This is a wretched letter," the Holy Father exclaimed when the ambassador had finished, "one that gives the lie to its own expressions of loyalty."

As for the oft-repeated charge that he was misinformed, he continued, the sermons were in print. Moreover, he had read the passages in which Fra Girolamo made light of the excommunication and described him as a broken tool and said that he would rather go to hell than seek absolution, as well as that other passage in which the friar reproached him for the death of his son. Nor was the pope impressed by the friar's withdrawal to San Marco, since it had not been made at the behest of the Signoria and could not have any effect as long as he continued to preach. Furthermore, there was no guarantee that he would not return to the cathedral tomorrow. In view of all this, said the pope, he would be justified in declaring an interdict then and there. He had decided, however, to give them one more chance. If the Signoria did not obey this time, he would impose an interdict immediately.

Not knowing what else to do, the ambassadors sought to defend Savonarola by praising his life and work. He found fault not with sound doctrine but with obstinate disobedience, said the pope. After ridiculing the friar's reasons for questioning the validity of the excommunication, he suddenly asked to have the Signoria's letter read aloud once more. Obviously, it had been written by Fra Girolamo, he told the ambassadors, for the style was precisely his.

What displeased him even more than the letter of the republic, Alexander told the Milanese envoy after dismissing the Florentines, was the letter of an evil nature which he had received from Fra Girolamo. In the first flush of anger, the pope drew up the brief *Numquam Putavimus* in which he accused the Signoria of not only encouraging the friar in his disobedience but of making him their Delphic oracle, shutting out all other preachers so that they might worship him alone. "Wherefore," said the pope, "we will never desist from our efforts until reparation be made to the honor and dignity of the Holy See for the insults of this vile worm ye have fostered." He threatened to lay the entire city under interdict and never to remove it so long as they continued to favor that "monstrous idol" of theirs.

But after he had had a chance to calm down, he decided that such intemperate language would accomplish nothing, and the brief was either never sent or recalled before it reached Florence. In its place, the pope dispatched another brief, in which he condemned the friar for his obstinacy, his pride, and his mischievous boldness and sought to explain why, having tolerated him thus far, he could do so no longer. "Wherefore," said the pope, "for the last time, we warn and command you either to send him to us forthwith or to confine him in his monastery in such a fashion that he shall hold no intercourse with anyone until brought to a better mind he shall deserve absolution. If you act otherwise, you will not be consulting either your own interest or that of Fra Girolamo."

The brief was delivered to the Signoria on March 12. On Wednesday, March 14, the largest *pratica* yet convened to discuss the friar's affairs met in the palazzo. In this assembly, which, in addition to all the principal magistrates of the city, included twenty-five citizens from each of the four districts of Florence, there were some who, like Paolantonio Soderini, either believed or pretended to believe that the friar was to be cherished like "a rare and precious jewel." But there were many more who agreed with Guidantonio Vespucci that since they could not be certain that Fra Girolamo had been sent by God, they had more to gain by satisfying the pope. "We in Italy are what we are," said Vespucci speaking on behalf of five of the nine lawyers on his bench. "We desire a tithe on church property; we desire Pisa; we desire the absolution of Fra Girolamo. Whether Fra Girolamo is wrong or right, we will obtain none of these things from the pope without giving him satisfaction. Moreover, if the interdict is imposed, our commerce will be ruined. Already many merchants are not sending out goods, and safe conducts are being denied."

In vain did Enea della Stufa, speaking for one of the citizen's benches, protest that the friar spoke by divine inspiration and that interdict or no interdict, trade would go on as before, with bales of wool being packed and unpacked. "If Messer Enea had anything to lose, he would speak in a different tone," said Giuliano dei Gondi. "As for me, I have wine all over Italy and elsewhere. If the interdict comes, it will bankrupt me."

In all, Paolo Somenzi told Ludovico, two-thirds of those who spoke for their benches favored silencing Savonarola. Among that amorphous majority were *Piagnoni* who wished merely to ask him not to preach for a while and *Arrabbiati* who wished to have the brief read aloud in the Great Council. Because the two sides could not agree, the Signoria decided to convene a new *pratica*, composed of nineteen outstanding citizens, the so-called *cuor civitas*, or heart of the city, selected from the leadership of the *Piagnoni* and the *Arrabbiati*.

When the friar had first begun preaching in San Marco, the women in the congregation had been sent to the church of San Niccolò in the Via Cocomero to hear Fra Domenico. Later, in answer to their urgent pleading, Savonarola had agreed to reserve Saturdays for them. So uneasy was he about the deliberations in the palazzo that Friday, however, that he announced he would speak to the women the next morning "if something else was not determined." And when he tried to compose a sermon, he could think of nothing to say. As was invariably the case when this happened, he was convinced that God had abandoned him because of some sin, and he begged Fra Silvestro to hear his confession and to pray for him. Apparently, the confession provided the necessary catharsis, for that Saturday he preached what Silvestro later described as "a very beautiful sermon."

Rather than a verse from Exodus, he chose as his text a portion of the eighty-fourth psalm: "How amiable are Thy tabernacles, O Lord of Hosts! My soul longeth, yea, even fainteth for the courts of the Lord." Many people complained that they never had a chance to speak to him, he told the women, and he too complained that he never had a chance to speak to himself. That was why he had chosen this psalm as his text. Instead of speaking to the congregation, he was going to pretend that he was alone in his cell. "O Lord, it is with you I would speak," he cried. And he pleaded with God to show His love for the faithful by working the miracle for which they had waited so long.

> Sleep no longer on Thy cross. Act, O Lord, so that the unbelieving will not be able to say, "Where is the God of those who have offered up so many prayers and fasts, so much penitence?"...Have compassion on Thy sheep. Can't you see how afflicted and persecuted they are?...If I am no longer of any use for this work, take my life. If I am a hindrance to it, take Lord my life and slay me. But what have these little sheep done? They have done no evil. I am the sinner, look not upon my sins but upon Thine own compassion and show us mercy. O Lord, mercy!

"And here," said Lorenzo Violi, "the preacher was so carried away and the audience so fervid and tearful that, unable to contain themselves, they began to sob and cry, 'Mercy! Mercy! O Lord, mercy!' And the father gave them his blessing and left."

At eleven that evening the Signoria sent two mace bearers to inform Savonarola that he must quit the pulpit. But pride would not permit him to give his consent immediately. "Come ye from your masters?" he asked the mace bearers. When they said they had, he told them that he too must consult his master. Tomorrow they would have his reply.

In his sermon the next morning, he compared himself to Jeremiah, who had preached against Jerusalem and been struck down by Phassur, the high priest. The Lord was the master. He turned the tool to His own ends, and when He needed it no longer, cast it aside as He had cast aside Jeremiah, who was stoned to death, he told his audience. "Even so will it be with us when we have served His end."

After describing the visit of the mace bearers the previous evening, he announced that God had granted and not granted the Signoria's prayers. Granted them in that he would abstain from preaching, but not granted them in regard to their salvation. "Ye fear an interdict from the pope, but the Lord will lay one upon ye that will deprive the wicked of life and of substance," he roared. "Lord, I pray Thee have mercy on the good and delay Thy promises no longer."

Although the Signoria had ordered him to leave the pulpit, on the advice of the *pratica*, it decided not to keep the citizens from going to San Marco. Taking advantage of this partial victory, Savonarola sent Fra Domenico to preach in his stead each morning. In the evening, another of his friars, Fra Mariano Ughi, preached in the cathedral. And, Paolo Somenzi told Ludovico, these other friars spoke no less freely than he had done, but perhaps more so against the pope and the clergy.

Meanwhile, in Rome, the pope, acting on the advice of Cardinal Ascanio Sforza, had decided that merely barring the friar from the pulpit was not enough. In view of his repeated attacks on the Holy See, the Signoria must send him to Rome immediately. If it didn't, His Holiness threatened to imprison all Florentine merchants in Rome and confiscate their goods. Alarmed, the merchants dispatched a letter to the Signoria complaining of the special favor the republic was showing Fra Girolamo and begging for help. By the time this letter arrived in Florence, many of the city's merchants had also received letters "which made them fear their places of business in Rome would be sacked."

The excommunication had already alienated many who had once followed the friar and made enemies of all those middle-of-the-roaders who, said Guicciardini, "considered it a very serious and unseemly thing for good Christians to disobey the orders of the pope." On March 25, signs plastered on the doors of Santa Croce and Orsanmichele told these citizens that it was not the *frate* who was their undoing. If they wished to live in peace and quiet, they must first get rid of Soderini and Valori. "Go and set fire to their houses."

Along the main thoroughfares and in the more important piazzas, the *Compagnacci* could be seen walking back and forth carrying candle ends with which they pretended to search for the little key the friar had lost. When they grew tired of this, they would grab hold of three or four passersby and force them to kneel before a lighted lantern, saying, "Adore the true light." Because, thanks to Valori's edict lowering the age for admission to the Great Council, many of the *Compagnacci* were now council members and because everyone feared them, most people did as they were told. In fact, said Guicciardini, just to be on the safe side in case the *Compagnacci* should win out, "Paolantonio Soderini, though a passionate supporter of the friar, had his son Tommaso join them."

The friar's answer to all this was to organize processions in San Marco and to walk at their head with a cross in his hands. All those taking part would repeat prayers with tearful devotion, "some of the citizens having come in unknown to others." But only a handful of those who so earnestly beseeched the Lord to come to the aid of their friar knew that he was also seeking human aid.

In January 1497, Charles VIII had asked the doctors of the Sorbonne whether in their opinion he had the right to summon a council to depose the pope. After discussing the matter, the learned gentlemen had decided that he did. Although Charles had as yet made no move, Savonarola felt sure that if the king were reminded of his duty, he would act. So too, in the friar's opinion, would the emperor Maximilian, Ferdinand of Spain, Henry of England, and Ladislaus of Hungary. That March, when the pope was threatening Florence with an interdict, Savonarola wrote the first draft of a circular letter addressed to these princes.

The moment of vengeance was come, he told them, and the Lord desired him to reveal new secrets which would make clear to the world the danger which, thanks to their indifference, beset the bark of Peter. This Alexander was no pope, said the friar. "Because to say nothing of his most wicked crime of simony, I affirm that he is not a Christian and does not believe in the existence of God." And Savonarola urged the princes to set their hand to the work of assembling a council in a suitable place. God, he assured them, would send signs and portents to attest to the truth of his words.

Before dispatching this letter, however, he thought it best to prepare the way by writing to a Florentine contact at the court of each of the rulers in question. Rather than do this himself, he gave rough drafts of the letters he wanted sent to five trusted friends. By the end of March, all five had sent out their letters. To be absolutely certain that Giovanni Guasconi, the Florentine ambassador at the court of King Charles, received the letter intended for him, Domenico Mazzinghi dispatched two separate copies by two separate messengers. One of the letters reached its destination; the other was intercepted by hired assassins in the employ of Ludovico Sforza.

On March 28, Ludovico's ambassador in Rome had told Sforza that it had been judged desirable "to repress and annihilate Fra Girolamo." To this end, said the ambassador, certain Florentines resident in Rome had assured His Holiness that the present Signoria would not fail in its duty to him. At the same time, efforts were being made to induce the Holy Father to send a prelate to Florence with full powers to chastise and imprison the friar and to deliver him into the hands of the pope. Because Alexander was still not persuaded, it was with a sense of having finally sealed Savonarola's doom that Ludovico forwarded the intercepted letter to his brother Ascanio and asked him to deliver it to the pope. By the time Alexander saw it, however, Fra Girolamo was being faced with ruin from a different—and totally unexpected—quarter.

IX

THE TRIAL BY FIRE

When Savonarola's friend and confidant Fra Domenico Buonavinci da Pescia replaced him in the pulpit for the first time, the *Arrabbiati* dubbed the new preacher *Il Fattoraccio*, the Rotten Bailiff. The name had stuck so that in time, forgetting his real surname, people called him Domenico *Fattoraccio*. To Paolo Somenzi, Domenico seemed a bumptious and ignorant preacher lacking in prudence and generally unfit for his task. Savonarola's erstwhile secretary Fra Ruberto Ubaldini found Domenico "a man of perfect integrity but exceptionally stubborn and too willing to believe in the revelations of weak-minded and foolish persons." And if one or another of his brethren chose not to believe those revelations, Domenico would make the skeptic's life "a continual martyrdom."

"Fra Domenico was a simple man," said Bartolomeo Cerretani. "And he was reputed to be a good man. However, of one thing they could be certain; he firmly believed that whatever issued from Savonarola's lips had been placed there by God."

In 1497, Domenico had preached the Lenten sermons in the Dominican church in nearby Prato. Also delivering sermons in Prato at the time was a Franciscan preacher, Fra Francesco da Puglia, who "spoke up boldly against Fra Girolamo." When Domenico defended his chief, Fra Francesco volunteered to go through a blazing fire to prove the truth of what he had said, and he challenged Domenico to do the same.

Going through the fire to prove a point was nothing new in Florence. In 1068, the Florentine saint and reformer Giovanni Gualberto had encouraged one of his monks to go through the fire to prove that the then archbishop of Florence was guilty of simony. The monk, who was later canonized under the name of San Pietro Igneo, made the trip before a huge crowd and emerged unscathed. Or at least that is what legend would have people believe. Although no one had ventured into the fire since then, challenges to do so were a staple of monkish rhetoric. During the Lenten season of 1496, Fra Gregorio da Perugia, the preacher at Santo Spirito, had challenged Savonarola to enter a fire and remain there for one-eighth of an hour. But whereas Savonarola had ignored Gregorio's challenge, Domenico immediately agreed to play the part of San Pietro Igneo and go through the fire to prove the truth of his mentor's teaching. The test, or *sperimento*, as it was called, was set for the Tuesday morning before Easter. On Monday evening, however, Fra Francesco was suddenly called back to Florence to attend to "a matter of stupendous importance."

When Domenico began preaching in San Marco at the end of March 1498, Fra Francesco was preaching in Santa Croce. As he had done the year before, he spent much of his time attacking Fra Girolamo, calling him, among other things, a heretic and a schismatic. Then on Sunday, March 25, which in those days was not only the Feast of the Annunciation but also the beginning of the Florentine year, he again announced that he would be willing to enter the fire with anyone who wished to prove the truth of Fra Girolamo's prophetic calling and the invalidity of his excommunication. He expected to burn, said Fra Francesco. If his opponent did not burn, they could believe in Fra Girolamo.

When Savonarola had returned to the pulpit on Septuagesima Sunday, he had assured his congregation that although he had not yet been compelled to work a miracle, if he was compelled, God would open His hand "according as His honor would re-

quire it." To the ingenuous Fra Domenico, a trial by fire must
have seemed the ideal way to demonstrate this. In his sermon
on March 27, he announced his willingness to enter the fire and
listed five propositions he intended to prove. Three of them were
the usual ones about the need to reform the church and the
scourge that would precede reform. One reaffirmed Savonarola's
promise that after being scourged, Florence would be renewed
and would flourish. The last called his excommunication invalid
and said it was no sin to ignore it.

The following day, Domenico announced that most of the
men in his congregation were eager to enter the fire with him.
Turning to the women, he intimated that they too would be
willing to undertake the *sperimento*. What with all the talk of
supernatural signs and miracles that Lent, any number of them
found nothing exceptional in the idea, and they rose to their
feet shouting, "I am one of those!"

It was astounding how many wished to enter the fire, said
Girolamo Benivieni, not only priests and other religious but ordinary men and women and young boys, "almost as if they were
being invited to a wedding." What made them so enthusiastic,
of course, was their absolute faith in Fra Girolamo and his ability to produce the necessary miracle. They would have been
pained and surprised to know how unwelcome their enthusiasm was to him.

He deeply regretted Domenico's action in provoking the affair, and he would have paid a great sum to prevent him from
doing so, Savonarola would later say. The way his friends "embraced the matter" also grieved him. Had he been preaching, he
would have done his best to put a stop to the whole business by
showing that the conclusions to be proved could be demonstrated by natural reason. Since he was not preaching, he was
forced in the end to consent to the trial in order not to lose all
credit with the people by giving the impression that he was
afraid. But he rebuked Fra Domenico for placing him in a position of great difficulty and danger.

Like Machiavelli and many other persons in Florence, he
seems to have realized that the trial was a snare. "Those who
guided the dance," said Lorenzo Violi, "were the *Compagnacci*

and their chief, Doffo Spini." Burlamacchi speaks of a banquet in the Pitti Palace at which the friar's mortal enemies discussed how they might use the proposed trial to get rid of him. It may have been at their instigation that the Signoria invited Fra Domenico and Fra Francesco to the palazzo on March 28.

Domenico arrived with a written statement obliging him to enter the fire and listing the propositions he intended to prove. By virtue of God the Savior and in confirmation of the truth of the aforementioned propositions, he hoped to emerge unharmed, he declared. Since Fra Francesco had never had any intention of going through the fire with Domenico or anyone else, he was compelled to think of how he could worm his way out of the affair. When the Signoria asked him to provide a statement of intent, he announced that he would enter the fire only with Fra Girolamo. He had no quarrel with Fra Domenico, said Francesco, but he would be willing to supply another Franciscan to enter the fire with him. Although Fra Mariano Ughi then signed a statement indicating his willingness to enter the fire with whomsoever the Franciscans provided, Domenico was still intent on entering the fire with Francesco. Because Savonarola was destined to be the actor in other greater works, it was perhaps against the will of God to obligate him to enter the fire, said Domenico. He urged Francesco to cross out the name of Fra Girolamo wherever it appeared and substitute the name of Domenico. Not only was he prepared to enter the fire, Domenico told the Signoria, but he was also prepared to undergo an even more dangerous ordeal if one could be devised.

That the "greater work" for which Savonarola was destined was the renovation of the church became clear when he indicated his willingness to enter the fire if the ambassadors of the Christian princes and the papal legate were present and agreed to reform the church "in its head and members" if he emerged unscathed. But his enemies accused him of trying to gain time, and Francesco continued to insist on his terms. He would not presume to compare himself to Fra Girolamo either in learning or in virtue, he told the Signoria. Nevertheless, Fra Girolamo was the principal actor, and Francesco had chosen him in order "to put an end to all this evil." Were Francesco and Domenico to die, everything would remain in the same state of confusion. Francesco then offered a lay brother of his order, Fra Giuliano Rondinelli, to go through the fire in his place. Whether things would be any less confused if Domenico and Giuliano died, Francesco did not say.

Two days later Fra Giuliano arrived at the palazzo to signify his willingness to enter the fire with Fra Domenico. Like Fra Francesco, Fra Giuliano declared that although he knew that he would burn, he was content to do so "for the salvation of souls." According to Lorenzo Violi, however, the *Compagnacci* had assured Giuliano that they had no intention of letting him burn. All they wanted, they told him, was to keep up the game long enough to put an end to "this business of the friar."

Before setting the date and establishing the conditions under which the ordeal would take place, however, the Signoria thought it best to convene a *pratica*. Among Savonarola's opponents on this *pratica* were some who found the very idea of a trial by fire an embarrassment. Their forefathers would have blushed to see them discuss a matter which made them the laughingstock of the whole world, said Giovanni Canacci.

Girolamo Capponi said he had no particular desire to see a miracle. The Signoria should turn the matter over to the vicar and let the city reform itself and put a stop to the nocturnal lawlessness of some of its young men. Others thought the matter ought to be settled by the pope. Surely, said Braccio Martelli with tongue in cheek, one who was not afraid to go through the fire ought not to make a fuss about going to Rome.

Like Martelli, several speakers assumed or pretended to assume that Fra Girolamo was the instigator of the ordeal and that he planned to go through the fire himself. "It would be well if one who laid claim to supernatural powers could prove them without committing homicide," said Guidantonio Vespucci. The affair was a fad of the friars whose busy tongues were the cause of a great part of the dissension in the city.

Fire seemed a strange thing, said Filippo Giugni, and he for one would be reluctant to pass through it. A trial by water would be less dangerous, and were Fra Girolamo to go through it without getting wet, Giugni would certainly join in asking his pardon.

For the declaration of the truth, one miracle was as good as another, said Antonio Strozzi. So they might as well choose one unattended by risk of life, for example, crossing the Arno without getting wet.

However, many of the *Arrabbiati* welcomed the ordeal as one way to end the uncertainty over the friar with which they had been living for so long. If Savonarola was victorious, it would be an honor for the city to possess such a treasure, said Luigi Corsi. If, on the other hand, both friars perished, the citizens would know they had been deceived. The *Piagnoni* also favored going ahead with the ordeal. Like Domenico Mazzinghi, a number of them made ringing speeches about how the miracle would tend to the glory of God and the peace of the city. Since to say otherwise would be to cast doubt on Fra Girolamo's supernatural powers, they really had no alternative. Although some undoubtedly believed what they said, others, like Giovambattista Ridolfi, were prompted by the secret conviction that Fra Giuliano would never enter the fire and that Domenico would win by default. Although there is no official record of how the *pratica* voted, the majority must have endorsed the trial, for that night the Signoria established the penalties for each side. If the Dominican champion perished, Savonarola would be exiled. If the Franciscan perished, Fra Francesco would be exiled. If both champions perished, only Savonarola would be exiled.

By then, an all-consuming excitement pervaded the city. At Fra Domenico's sermon in San Marco on April 1, several thousand people, including many women and children, began shouting, "I will enter this fire for Thy glory, Lord!" That evening in Santa Maria dei Fiore, Fra Mariano Ughi knelt in the pulpit and, with eyes fixed on the crucifix, reiterated his promise "to enter the fire for the truth," begging whomever it concerned "to proceed with the work." His 279 brethren at San Marco prepared to send a letter to the pope informing him of their wish to enter the fire.

Their eagerness made Savonarola's reluctance all the more puzzling. Ever since he had let pass Fra Francesco's invitation to enter the fire with him, the *Compagnacci* had been spreading the rumor that he was afraid. To put an end to what he called their "slanders," he composed a brief apology in which he sought to justify himself. It could not have been an easy piece to write, for like so many of his beliefs, his conviction that this was the wrong miracle at the wrong time in the wrong place was instinctive; and he had to search for ways to explain it.

His first thought was to address his apology to an imaginary correspondent. "Magnificent Signore," he began, "I am replying briefly to your objections," then crossed the sentence out and started over, this time directing his remarks to the public at large. He had no need to prove that the excommunication was invalid by entering the fire, he told them, since he had already proved this by natural reasons which no one in Rome or Florence had yet refuted. Moreover, to enter the fire with only one friar would not have the utility for the church which the great work that God had confided to him demanded. If, on the other hand, his adversaries would publicly bind themselves to make the reform of the church and the validity of his doctrines the issues, he would not hesitate to enter the fire and would feel confident that, like Shadrach, Mesach, and Abednego when they entered the fiery furnace, he would emerge unharmed. He pointed out that not only his friars but religious from many other orders in the city and even some secular priests, as well as several thousand people assembled in San Marco that morning, were willing to enter the fire with Fra Francesco. Should even one of them burn, the entire undertaking would have to be abandoned. Hence, there was no need for Fra Francesco to ask for anyone but Domenico. Savonarola then cited the example of San Giovanni Gualberto, who although a man of great sanctity, had allowed another to enter the fire in his place because that had been God's will. As for himself, though he had proposed to manifest great things with supernatural signs, he had not proposed to do these things to annul the excommunication but for other reasons when the time came.

Like the arguments Machiavelli had heard in San Marco, these were most convincing to anyone who did not examine them closely. That Savonarola shrank from entering the fire because, as George Eliot put it, "it was impossible for him to believe that he or any other man could walk through the flames unhurt," seems clear. That he realized he could not keep his followers from entering the fire without losing his hold over them seems equally clear. Very likely, he also realized that his own sermons, with their ever more extravagant promises of supernatural signs, had produced this mad upsurge of faith. Caught in a trap for which he himself had laid the groundwork, he found solace in the assumption, which he shared with many others, that Fra Giuliano would never enter the fire. Even as he secretly longed for this happy outcome, however, he was compelled by the force of circumstance to assure the great multitude clamoring to go through the flames that their champion would emerge unscathed. He may even have hoped that the fasts he urged upon them and the processions he was organizing in San Marco would persuade the Almighty to help His chosen prophet.

The day after he wrote his apology, said Luca Landucci, Savonarola "formed a procession within the monastery with all his friars and many citizens; they came out of the cloisters, went all around the piazza and then returned to the church, Fra Girolamo carrying the crucifix and singing psalms."

That afternoon Fra Ruberto Salviati and Fra Malatesta Sacramoro both went to the palazzo. They had had a call from the Lord, they declared, and they wished to sign in alongside Fra Mariano Ughi and Fra Domenico as champions of San Marco. The Salviati were part of that inner circle of *cittadini principali* who took for granted their right to rule the city. Giuliano Salviati had been gonfalonier for January and February; Jacopo Salviati was married to Lorenzo dei Medici's daughter Lucrezia. The Malatestas were the lords of Rimini. Before becoming a friar of San Marco, Fra Malatesta had been a canon of the cathedral. So impressed were the Ten by the social standing of the would-be champions that they immediately wrote to Bonsi and asked him to inform the pope.

A few days earlier, the Ten had asked the ambassador to tell the Holy Father of the arrangements for the ordeal. When Bonsi did so, Alexander appeared incredulous. To him, the very idea of such a contest was abhorrent—the inevitable outcome of giving fanatics like Fra Girolamo free rein. "You see where these things lead," he told Bonsi. Although the pope's close friend Cardinal Lopez hastened to add that it was not a good idea to allow something like this to go forward without the permission of a superior, neither he nor Alexander gave any indication that they planned to stop it. After being told of the many men, women, and children who wished to enter the fire, the pope asked what sort of man Fra Domenico was, then demanded to know whether Bonsi thought the trial would really take place. If His Holiness were to absolve Fra Girolamo, it might not, said Bonsi. Otherwise, it was necessary in order to end the dissension within the city. However, there was always the chance the Franciscans would withdraw.

Burlamacchi says that the pope refused permission for the ordeal because he feared that if it succeeded he would lose his miter. Actually, although Alexander eventually let the Signoria know he disapproved of the ordeal, he never forbade it. More than likely, he realized that if he were to do so, the vast superstitious multitude that hungered for such outlandish spectacles would immediately assume that he feared the outcome.

Originally, the ordeal had been set for Friday, April 6. At the last moment, however, the Signoria moved it ahead to April 7. Most people still didn't believe that it would really take place, said Piero Parenti. Savonarola, of course, continued to hope that it wouldn't, and Giovambattista Ridolfi had twice reassured him on this score. However, the double role he was then playing required that he use a special dispensation to preach given him by the Signoria to announce that he was prepared to let his friars pass through the fire in defense of his prophetic truth. Not only some but all of his friars were ready to do so by acclamation, he declared, as were several thousand secular men, women, and children. So stirred was the congregation by his words that in the middle of the sermon all rose to their feet with a cry "offering their lives for the truth."

Meanwhile, in the Piazza della Signoria, workmen had begun constructing a platform for the bonfire. That Friday the Signoria decreed that if Fra Domenico perished in the flames, Fra Girolamo would be declared a rebel and be given three hours to leave Florentine territory. At the same time, the terms of the contest were revised. Under the new terms, should either party refuse to enter the fire or hesitate to do so, that party would be declared the loser. To give the Franciscans ample reason to hesitate, Savonarola wished the blaze to be as huge and terrible as possible, and he sent Fra Malatesta to the Signoria with instructions concerning its form. Nevertheless, there was always the possibility that something or someone would force Fra Giuliano to enter the flames. In that case, Fra Domenico would be obliged to follow. To protect him, Savonarola insisted that Domenico carry the Host. Since Domenico was certain that he could pass through unharmed without the Host, he probably would have refused had it not been for a dream which Fra Silvestro Maruffi had that night.

Except for Fra Girolamo, no friar of San Marco was so constantly reviled as Fra Silvestro. The *Arrabbiati* spread the rumor that he was not above revealing the secrets of the confessional. Fra Ruberto Ubaldini complained that he spent whole days jabbering with groups of citizens. Savonarola himself thought Silvestro "an inconsiderate and not very good man who was also much too talkative." None of these shortcomings, however, detracted from what Savonarola firmly believed to be the divine origin of this sleepwalking friar's dreams. Fra Domenico too was convinced that Silvestro's dreams were visions sent by God. This conviction had been reinforced by a dream in which Silvestro's guardian angel appeared to him together with the guardian angels of Fra Girolamo and Fra Domenico. Using a chain of gold, the angels had bound the three friars together, instructing them to remain united, for God had ordained that they have but one heart and one soul. The angels then told Silvestro that his revelations were being given to him not for his own sake but for the sake of Fra Girolamo.

In the dream he had the night before the ordeal, Silvestro beheld the fire in the Piazza della Signoria. And he saw Fra Domenico, dressed all in red, enter the flames carrying the Host with him. Whereupon the fire divided in two, and to the singing of the *Te Deum*, Domenico emerged unscathed. Immediately thereafter, universal peace was proclaimed.

The Signoria had wanted the trial to begin at four in the afternoon. Savonarola, however, asked that it begin at one so that his friars might be "soberminded." Since most of them had been living on bread and water in preparation for the ordeal, this may have been an excuse to get the affair over with as quickly as possible. The long, narrow wooden platform on which the fire would be kindled began at Donatello's *Marzocco*, the august stone lion seated on his haunches to one side of the *ringhiera*. From there, it extended 90 feet into the vast irregular piazza in the direction of the Tetti dei Pisani, a loggia at the far end of the square directly opposite the palazzo. To prevent the platform from catching fire during the ordeal, a 12-inch-high double layer of unbaked bricks had been placed over the timber. This was covered with giant logs, in between and over which was piled a vast quantity of boughs and brushwood soaked with oil and resin to ensure a crackling blaze. Down the center, a path barely 2 feet wide had been left for the friars. As part of Savonarola's campaign to terrorize the Franciscans into withdrawing, he had asked that the fire be lit at the far end of this path before the two champions entered, then lit behind them to prevent their turning back.

Ostensibly for reasons of security, but perhaps also out of a sense of the utter madness of what was being permitted, the Signoria had ordered all foreigners to leave the city on pain of the gallows. On the morning of the ordeal, all nine gates of Florence were locked. The Signoria also decreed that no one was to bear arms that day and that women and children were to be barred from the piazza. In the case of the women, said Piero Parenti, "to avoid giving occasion for scandal and to spare their feeble and ignorant sex."

To make sure that these proscriptions were observed, all but three of the approaches to the piazza were blocked off, and foot soldiers of the Signoria guarded these approaches. Five hundred additional infantrymen guarded the *ringhiera* and the entrance to the palazzo. As a further precaution, each of the sixteen gonfaloniers of the companies patrolled the city with the twenty armed men under his command. At nine o'clock that morning, still fearful of a riot, the Signoria sent for the heads of both the *Arrabbiati* and the *Piagnoni* and detained them in the palazzo.

The ordinary men of the city had begun streaming into the piazza long before that, the *Piagnoni* carrying little red crosses to show where their sympathies lay. As always when there was some great spectacle, every available spot at the windows and on the balconies and rooftops of the surrounding palaces and houses was occupied. About the only empty space was the Loggia dei Priori (now the Loggia dei Lanzi), which had been partitioned down the middle to accommodate the friars.

The first to arrive were the gray-robed brothers of Saint Francis. Since most of them knew nothing of the *Compagnacci's* promise not to permit Fra Giuliano to enter the fire, they expected him to perish in the flames. All that week, said a contemporary chronicler of their order, they had remained in their cells fasting and praying so that the very walls of Santa Croce seemed to melt into tears along with them. When the day of the ordeal finally arrived, "there was not as much terror in the whole world as there was in that church." A little after noon, they set out for the Piazza della Signoria "not in any sort of procession but all mixed together in a bunch." Without any fanfare, they took their places in the loggia on the side nearest the *ringhiera*, and Fra Giuliano and his mentor, Fra Francesco, went into the palazzo to pray. Immediately afterward, the Signoria sent two mace bearers to San Marco to fetch the Dominicans.

That morning, great crowds of the faithful had come to the church to hear Fra Girolamo celebrate mass and to receive communion from his hands. In contrast to the Franciscans, "so much gladness was in their hearts," said Burlamacchi, "that the face of all things smiled out of the certainty of victory." While they knelt in silent prayer awaiting Savonarola's arrival, Giovambattista Ridolfi was once again assuring him that the Franciscans would never enter the fire. It was for this eventuality that he sought to prepare his congregation. So far as had been revealed to him, he told them, if the ordeal took place, the victory was theirs, and Fra Domenico would come out of it unhurt. But whether it would in fact take place, the Lord had not revealed to him.

In the past when he had deceived his audience, he had also been deceiving himself. This time, however, he knew exactly what he was doing. In the brief prayer which he addressed to the Lord that morning, he seemed to be trying to convince the Almighty of the purity of his intentions and his desperate need for divine justification.

> Thou knowest Lord that I did not undertake this mission out of my own pride. Thou knowest that it was Thy doing. This people has believed in me because I was sent by Thee. I ask Thee therefore this morning that Thou wilt show to this people that Thou reignest in heaven and on earth, so that they may believe that Thou hast sent me and change their ways, and everything may be to Thy praise and glory. Lord fulfill this morning our prayers and show that we have told the truth.

After that, there was barely time for him to bless the congregation before the mace bearers arrived to summon them to the ordeal.

Preceded by the cross bearers and the candlestick holders, the friars left the church two by two. Behind that double line of black and white walked Fra Domenico wearing a flame-red cope and carrying a 4-foot-high wooden cross, "in the fashion of a martyr," said one chronicler. Next came Fra Ruberto Salviati and Fra Malatesta Sacramoro, with Savonarola walking between them carrying the Host in a silver ostensory. They were followed by the entire congregation, the men carrying lighted torches and little red crosses, the women crying and sobbing, so that, said Piero Parenti, "they aroused feelings of great tenderness in all who beheld them." Since the women were barred from the ordeal, on reaching the piazza, most of them returned to San Marco to pray for a successful outcome.

The friars entered the piazza chanting the first line of the sixty-eighth psalm: "Let God arise, let his enemies be scattered." To which the thousands of laymen who accompanied them replied with the next line: "Let them also that hate Him flee before Him." What with the great sound of all those voices, said

Burlamacchi, "the earth underfoot appeared to tremble and great fear and terror filled the hearts of the enemies."

To protect the friars of San Marco from those enemies, Fra Ruberto Salviati's brother Marcuccio, a young man famous for his swordsmanship and his bellicosity, was stationed at one side of the loggia with 300 armed men, all loyal followers of Fra Girolamo. While the friars prepared to sing a mass, Doffo Spini and 300 of his *Compagnacci* rode into the piazza, sitting astride their richly harnessed mounts "like paladins." All were armed; many had armed infantrymen in tow. Thrusting aside any who blocked their path, with a great fracas they stationed themselves near the Tetti dei Pisani. One Franciscan chronicler said that God had sent "these noble and rich young men" to defend the brothers of his order. Simone Filipepi said that on receipt of a prearranged signal from the palazzo, Spini and his men intended to attack the Dominicans and slay Fra Girolamo. Although this would seem to explain why, after forbidding the carrying of arms, the Signoria allowed the *Compagnacci* to enter the piazza, it doesn't explain why that same Signoria also allowed Marcuccio Salviati and his men to enter. In any event, the two groups seem at first to have ignored one another. While Fra Giuliano Rondinelli and Fra Francesco da Puglia lay prostrate before the altar in the tiny second-floor chapel of the Signoria, the friars of San Marco sang their mass; and, said Luca Landucci, "the people awaited the great spectacle."

From the ranks of the leaders detained in the palazzo that morning, the Signoria had chosen four—two *Piagnoni* and two *Arrabbiati*—to oversee the event. Before it could begin, the four told Savonarola, the Franciscans wanted Fra Domenico to strip himself of all his outer garments, including his cope, as they suspected that these garments were bewitched. After much discussion, Savonarola allowed Fra Domenico to go into the palace to undress, and one of the Franciscans entered the Dominican side of the loggia to select the friar with whom Domenico would exchange clothes. When he finally emerged in his new habit, the Franciscans sent word via one of the four that Domenico's underclothes were bewitched, and the ordeal could not begin until he changed those. Rather than being satisfied when Savonarola allowed him to do so, the Franciscans then declared that his crucifix might be bewitched and insisted that he discard that. No sooner did he surrender the crucifix than the Franciscans turned their attention to the Host. To carry the Host into the fire was sacrilegious, they declared, for it made the most sacred mysteries of the Christian faith rather than Domenico's theses the subject of the experiment.

To Luca Landucci, who like everyone else in the piazza was eagerly awaiting the ordeal, all these objections seemed proof that the Franciscans "were desirous to avoid the test." Had Domenico agreed to surrender the Host, they would have undoubtedly raised some other objection. But how consent to give up the Host when Fra Silvestro's dream had made it clear that God wished Domenico to carry it through the flames with him? Even if Savonarola had been willing to discard it, and there is no evidence that he was, Fra Domenico would never have agreed.

While the two sides were debating the question of the Host, the friars of San Marco continued to sing hymns and psalms, and the vast crowd in the piazza grew increasingly restive. Many had not eaten since early morning. Others had fasted in preparation for the ordeal. As they watched the comings and goings between the palazzo and the loggia, a murderous irritation took hold of them. Since it was Savonarola from whom they were expecting a miracle, and since it was he with whom everyone was conferring, it was at him that the irritation was directed. To many, his insistence on the Host seemed a mere subterfuge— a way of avoiding the test—which on one level it undoubtedly was. Seeing a throng of disgruntled citizens make a rush for the Dominican side of the loggia, Marcuccio Salviati traced a line on the red brick pavement with his lance and announced that anyone crossing the line would find out just how deadly that lance could be.

Meanwhile, the sky, which only a short time before had been serene and cloudless, grew ever darker and more ominous. Suddenly, the thunder, which had been a distant rumble, grew louder and closer. There was a flash of lightning, and great sheets of rain mixed with hail swept across the piazza, soaking the logs and brushwood and leaving the crowd wet, bedraggled, and shivering. To some, this passing storm was a sign that God disapproved of the ordeal and did not wish it to take place. To others, the storm was evidence of Fra Girolamo's diabolical powers. "The air seemed filled with demons," said Fra Mariano da Firenze, the Franciscan chronicler. Many were convinced that Fra Girolamo had constrained those demons to loose rain and hail on the platform because he feared that the trial would expose his lies. Nevertheless, no one was willing to leave the piazza as long as there was the slightest chance the trial would take place. Only after the Signoria, having despaired of ever working out a compromise concerning the Host, dismissed the friars, did the crowd begin to disperse.

This was the outcome Savonarola had hoped for from the beginning, and he could tell himself that because the objections and the hesitations had come from the Franciscans, it was they who must be judged the losers. However, the crowd, which had waited without food since early morning and been drenched by the rain to boot, did not see it that way. Not only Fra Girolamo's opponents, said Jacopo Nardi, but also many of his devoted followers thought that rather than debate with the Franciscans, he and Fra Domenico should have ignored their quibbling and gone into the flames themselves to prove the truth of the prophecies. That they hadn't could only mean that Fra Girolamo had been deceiving them all along. In their rage and disappointment, they remembered every ugly name his enemies had used to describe him. "Hypocrite! Sodomite! Bigot! Excommunicate! Heretic!" they shouted. "Put down the Sacrament!"

Had Savonarola not been carrying the Host, Doffo Spini would later say, the *Compagnacci* would have made an end of him then and there. As it was, they mingled with the crowd so that not one of the friar's friends dared speak. Fearing that the troops of Marcuccio Salviati would not afford sufficient protection, Savonarola demanded an armed escort from the Signoria. Even with this escort on one side and Salviati's men on the other, the gibes did not let up, for the angry multitude followed them to San Marco. When at last the doors of the church closed behind them, the thousand or so women who for the past six hours had been praying for the friars crowded around them demanding to know what had happened. Since the failure of the ordeal was due to "the fraudulent and frivolous behavior of the opposing party," Savonarola told the women, the Dominicans must be accounted the victors. But even as he spoke, the hue and cry in the piazza reached into every corner of the church, and he knew how utterly beside the point the "victory" was. All the rest of the evening, said Violi, the *Compagnacci* "sought to further inflame the pleb by telling them that the Dominicans had sought to avoid the test." And no *Piagnone* dared show his face.

The next day was Palm Sunday—the Sunday of the Olive, it was called in the olive-rich valley of the Arno. On that day, which commemorates Christ's descent from the Mount of Olives into Jerusalem, Fra Girolamo awoke with the certainty that, like the Son of man, he must soon be delivered into the hands of his enemies. In a tearful sermon in San Marco, he all but announced his imminent tribulation. He was prepared to offer himself as a sacrifice to God and to suffer death for his flock, he told the reverent and loving congregation which had braved the taunts of the *Compagnacci* to come hear him. Motioning for them to kneel, he too sank to his knees, then turned to address the crucifix. "O Lord," he cried, "I thank Thee because in these times and very soon Thou desirest to make me in Thine image."

Meanwhile, the Franciscans were spreading the rumor that he had wanted to burn the Host—a rumor which Burlamacchi said was "easily believed by the pleb." Fearing that violence was inevitable, one *Piagnone* leader suggested that rather than wait for their enemies to attack, they take the offensive. But Francesco Valori thought it unseemly for the party of God to strike the first blow, and most of the others agreed with him. That afternoon, Fra Mariano Ughi was to deliver his customary post-vespers sermon in the cathedral. What Luca Landucci described as "quite a large congregation of men and women" awaited Mariano's arrival. Also awaiting his arrival were a number of armed *Compagnacci*. Seeing them there and perhaps fearing a repetition of the riot on Ascension Day, the priests announced that vespers would be postponed. One of the *Compagnacci* then made a flying leap on to the highest of the tiers where the *fanciulli* sat and began pounding on the flooring and shouting to the women to be gone, for the sermon had been canceled. Taking their cue from him, his comrades struck the backs of the seats in the women's section, saying, "Go away with God, you whining crybabies!"

Seeing the women abused thus, one of the *Piagnoni* drew his sword. The *Compagnacci* surrounded him shouting, "To arms! To arms! To San Marco!" In the ensuing turmoil, said Landucci, "Blessed was he who could find the door!" Those who did fled down the Via Cocomero, pursued by a mob of stone-throwing urchins in the pay of the *Compagnacci*. Fra Mariano Ughi, who had just come up the street with a large crowd of the faithful, was forced to turn back without having any idea what the commotion was all about. The *Compagnacci*, meanwhile, had split into small groups, which went through the city shouting, "To the friars! To the friars! To San Marco!" Soon, men, women, and children from every quarter of Florence were rushing toward the convent with stones. Unaware of the tumult in the making, one pious young man was on his way to the church of the Santissima Annunziata, chanting the psalms as he went, when he collided with a group headed for San Marco. "O the scoundrel," shouted someone, "still saying his prayers!" And the startled youth found himself pounced on from every side. He tried to make a run for the Annunziata, but he had gotten only as far as the Ospedale degli Innocenti when the mob caught up with him. There, on the steps of the foundling hospital, before the slender Corinthian columns of Brunelleschi's exquisite loggia, one of the *Compagnacci* ran him through with his sword, and the maddened crowd continued on its way.

At San Marco, about 600 people were still at vespers when the rioters began converging on the piazza. Hearing the uproar, a candle maker named Paolo went outside to see what was wrong. He was greeted by a shower of stones and cries of *"Pinzocherone!"* ("Bigot!") that forced him to beat a quick retreat. Never, it seemed to him, had he beheld such fury or heard such great shouts. The shouts so disturbed a spectacle maker who lived nearby, that, slippers in hand, he came out to remonstrate with the mob. Before he could finish speaking, one of the *Compagnacci* hit him over the head with his sword.

Without consulting either Fra Girolamo or Fra Domenico, Fra Silvestro, fearing an attack by the *Compagnacci*, had been collecting arms in a small storeroom. After locking the doors of the church, some of the younger friars headed for this storeroom. They were joined by about thirty men from the congregation, many of them members of Savonarola's bodyguard. The rest of the men and all of the women sought refuge in the cloisters. From there, an underground passage led to a building on the Via Lamormora known as the Sapienza, originally built to house the University of Florence but later purchased by San Marco. Many made their escape through this passage. Like Luca Landucci, the remainder left through a gate in the garden wall at the rear of the convent, then headed for the Porta San Gallo.

Francesco Valori, who along with Giovambattista Ridolfi and some of the other leaders of his party had also been at vespers, was not sure what he ought to do. As the mob outside grew ever larger, the cries of "To the house of Francesco Valori! Sack Valori's house!" grew louder and more insistent, and it seemed to him that he had an obligation to defend his own. Partly with the intention of doing so and partly with the intention of afterward returning to San Marco with a force large enough to disperse the mob, he too let himself out through the gate in the garden wall. He was immediately recognized and seized by two down-and-out members of the pleb, who doubtless expected a reward for his capture. Somehow or other, he managed to break free and reach his own house. But the violence he witnessed along the way so unnerved him that rather than defend his own, he decided to conceal himself in an attic until the fury of the mob had spent itself. He was not there very long when the *Compagnacci* and their plebeian allies surrounded the house. Seeing Valori's wife at a window, their leader ordered one of his men to aim his crossbow at her forehead. Meanwhile, the others broke down the door and set fire to the house of Valori's nephew, which was close by. From his hiding place, Valori could hear everything: the screams of his dying wife and the servant who came to her assistance, the ramming of the door, the smashing of the furniture, the cries of his great-nieces and -nephews. A little before nine, the invaders found him and turned him over to two mace bearers who had orders to conduct him to the palazzo.

When the party reached the shrine of the Virgin Mary at the intersection of Via Giraldi and Via Pandolfini opposite the tiny eleventh-century church of San Procolo, some people in the church called out to Valori not to be afraid. He was not afraid, he replied, for he was going before the Signoria, and he knew he was innocent. Just as he finished speaking, Vincenzo Ridolfi, a kinsman of that Ridolfi who had been beheaded for treason the summer before, and Simone Tornabuoni, whose kinsman Lorenzo had also been beheaded, came up behind him. Crying, "Valori, you will govern no more!" they cleaved his skull with a pruning hook. His corpse, despoiled of everything but a shirt, was dragged into San Procolo, where it lay on the pavement unattended until some friars from Santa Croce arrived to prepare it for burial.

"Many people believed that God wanted to punish him for having just a few months earlier denied an appeal from a death sentence to Bernardo del Nero and those other very respected citizens who had been his old friends and belonged to his own class," said Guicciardini.

But Machiavelli, to whom neither God nor class was as important as patria, found Valori's death "unfitting his life and goodness," for no country ever had a citizen "who more desired her good than he did or who was so much and with fewer scruples her defender." The proof of Valori's goodness and courage, as Machiavelli saw it, was that, although he had always held high office, he died poor.

At the time Valori had left San Marco, the friars were ringing the great brass bell known as La Piagnona in the hope of securing aid from the outside, and the defense of the convent was just getting underway. Wearing a helmet and a breastplate and carrying a sword and halberd brought from home, Paolo della Robbia, whose father Andrea had sculpted the blue and white medallions on the loggia of the Ospedale degli Innocenti, stood guard at the exit to the Sapienza with his friar brother, Luca, and a silkworker named Bartolomeo Mei.

Fra Benedetto, the convent miniaturist, went up to the roof where he spent the next few hours dropping tiles on the heads of the rioters. Paolo the candle maker and Fra Giovambattista della Serpe used the arquebuses they found in the storeroom to defend the church choir. Slipping a coat of mail he had found in the storeroom over his gown and brandishing a sword, Girolamo Gini, who normally sold notions in the Mercato Vecchio, joined a dealer in secondhand goods named Zanobi and fifteen or twenty other armed tradesmen and artisans in a foray into the piazza. Alessandro Pucci, who for some reason went into the piazza unarmed, picked up a handful of stones and proceeded to hurl them at the rioters. Panting like a bull, Francesco dell'Pugliese, the wealthy and influential patron of the artist Piero di Cosimo, brought his arquebus into the piazza and began firing into the crowd. The fire was returned, and a goldsmith who had come out with Zanobi fell to the ground.

Fra Domenico was by himself writing when he heard the shots. Dropping his quill, he began making the rounds of the convent urging all who had taken up arms to lay them down. They were going against the wishes of their superior and the teaching of the gospel, he told them. Rather than stain their hands with blood or seek help by ringing *La Piagnona*, it was necessary to remain calm and wait for things to quiet down.

While he continued to go from place to place seeking to pacify the others, Fra Girolamo was going through the dormitories with some of his friars, singing the litanies at the top of his lungs and begging those with him to let him give himself up. At one point, Fra Silvestro saw him in the first cloister near the entrance to the chapter room with a large group of friars and laymen, among whom Silvestro recognized Giovambattista Ridolfi. "Leave me go," Savonarola pleaded. "Because of me, this storm has arisen." Holding the cross before him, he seemed determined to go into the piazza. But his friars began to weep, and Giovambattista Ridolfi and the other laymen—most of them poor men, according to the class-conscious Silvestro—sought to restrain him shouting, "No, no, Father, they will tear you to pieces and what shall we do then?"

When the tumult had first begun, many people had rushed to the palazzo to warn the priors and the gonfalonier. Since by then one of the four *Piagnoni* priors had gone over to the *Arrabbiati*, the *Arrabbiati* had the plurality they needed to destroy their hated enemy. Over the protests of the three remaining *Piagnoni*, they issued an edict exiling Fra Girolamo and giving him twelve hours to leave Florentine territory. That done, they issued a second edict ordering all laymen then in San Marco to leave the convent within an hour or be considered rebels by the commune. When a mace bearer delivered the two edicts to San Marco, Fra Domenico and most of the other friars refused to believe that he had come from the Signoria. Until the very end, Domenico would say later, he was sure the Signoria disapproved of what was going on and would find a way to send help to the beleaguered convent. However, several of the laymen still in San Marco, including a member of the Eight, took the mace bearer at his word, and, after being given safe conducts, left through the gate in the garden wall.

By then, the *Compagnacci* had placed heaps of straw and other flammable material at all five entrances to the church and convent and ignited them. When the doors began to burn, Savonarola, who had done nothing to impede his friars' rush to arms, ordered them to put aside their weapons. Singing the litanies as he went, he led them and anyone else who wished to join him through the cloisters into the sacristy where he removed the silver ostensory containing the Host from its accustomed place and carried it with him into the choir. After setting it on the altar, he prostrated himself before it and motioned for the others to do the same. And there they remained hour after uncomfortable hour, constantly repeating the same pathetic prayer: "*Salvum fac populum tuum, Domine.* Lord, save Thy people," expecting at any moment to be hacked to pieces. And if anyone

looked behind him or missed a word, there was always someone to remind him: "*Orate, frater*. Pray, brother."

Although Savonarola felt obliged to set an example by fo-
cusing his thoughts on God and the need to prepare himself and
his brethren for eternal life, he could not remain oblivious to
the turmoil in the piazza. When the anxiety became more than
he could handle, he sought to ease it by asking those on either
side of him how their enemies were doing. But all anyone knew,
said Fra Domenico, was that there was a great deal of noise and
continual terror. Who was against them and who had come to
their defense, it was impossible to say. When some of the novices began to cry, Alessandro Pucci sought to console them by
telling them they would "sup with God."

Meanwhile, someone had brought three stone-throwing ma-
chines into the neighboring streets, and the stones catapulted
across the piazza striking friend and foe alike. At eleven that
night, Jacopo dei Nerli rode into the square with a large contingent of armed *Compagnacci*. While some of them fired at the
church, others went around to the Via Lamormora. Assisted by
the army of plebs which had followed them, they broke into
the Sapienza and raced through the underground tunnel leading
to the convent. After looting the infirmary and the kitchen, they
decided to break into the choir.

"Open the door, see who's there, and tell them not to make
such a racket," said Savonarola when he heard them in the sacristy. Crying *Viva Cristo!* and carrying torches and crucifixes,
three of his friars hastened to obey. Either because this was not
what the invaders had expected or because the torches blinded
them, they fled in panic. Their flight was the signal for all who
had put aside their arms to pick them up. Wearing a breastplate
over his long white tunic and carrying a sword, Fra Luca della
Robbia chased three of the invaders into the second cloister, then
confiscated their weapons and let them go. Fra Benedetto returned to the roof, where he let loose another barrage of tiles
and bricks. But the advantage this gave the besieged was only
temporary, for the long tongues of flame coming through the
doors were causing them to collapse. Seeing what was happen-

ing, Bartolomeo Mei went in search of a pail of water. Finding none, he rejoined the group praying in the choir.

Toward midnight, a company of rioters entered the church. When one of them started coming down the nave toward the choir, a novice named Marco Gondi picked up a heavy wooden cross and broke it over the rioter's head. While another novice sought to hold back the invaders by seizing their lances and breaking them with his bare hands, a German friar named Enrico went into the piazza in search of a weapon. Returning with an arquebus, he set it on the pulpit and began firing, crying, *Salvum fac populum tuum, Domine!* between shots.

Soon the choir was enveloped in a dense cloud of gunsmoke that threatened to suffocate Fra Girolamo and the sixty or so friars still prostrate before the Host. To dispel the smoke, one of the novices sent his lance hurtling through a window over the high altar. The rush of air helped the fire at the door, and the friars knew that if they were not to be incinerated, they must find some other refuge. First, however, Savonarola insisted that all attempts to defend the convent cease. Catching sight of Fra Benedetto, who, knife in hand, had just come down from the roof, he ordered him to put aside his weapon and take up the cross. After the other warring brethren had followed Benedetto's example, Savonarola removed the Host from the altar. Hugging it to him, he led his friars through the sacristy to the first clois-ter, then up the narrow staircase leading to the dormitories and along the cell-lined corridors to the stately colonnaded library which Michelozzo had built for Cosimo dei Medici.

The friars were on their knees before the Host when the *Compagnacci* sent their first delegation to the library. It was the wish of the Signoria that Fra Girolamo present himself at the palace, said their leader, a youth by the name of Guglielmo Alessandri. Still unwilling to believe that the Signoria was on the side of the rioters, Fra Domenico asked to see the order in writing. The Signoria did as the *Compagnacci* wished, said Ales-sandri. Nevertheless, he agreed to return with a written order. While waiting for him to do so, Savonarola delivered a last ser-mon to his friars. All that he had said had come to him from

God, he told them, and the Lord was his witness in heaven that he spoke no lie. Although he did not know whether those who were coming to arrest him would take his life, he did know that, once dead, he would be able to succor his brethren far better in heaven than it had been granted him to help them on earth. After bidding them take comfort and embrace the cross, he asked to receive that last communion, known as the viaticum. Hearing this, many of the friars began to sob. Instead of preparing for death, why shouldn't he try to escape by climbing over the garden wall, they asked. But Fra Malatesta objected. In times of stress, the shepherd ought to be willing to give his life for his sheep, he declared. For Savonarola, that ended the matter. Although Fra Benedetto did not protest, the exchange reminded him of a verse from Isaiah: "The treacherous dealer dealeth treacherously." And he asked himself if, in the approaching passion of Fra Girolamo, Malatesta was destined to play the role of Judas. The conviction that he was grew stronger when the *Compagnacci* returned with a written order for the arrest of Fra Girolamo, and Malatesta offered to negotiate the terms of surrender with them.

To Savonarola, his surrender was part of a preordained plan. He had always expected this to happen, he declared, "but not so soon or so suddenly." Like the "meekest of lambs," said Burlamacchi, he turned himself over to his captors and prepared to leave with them. "I too would come to this wedding feast," Burlamacchi had Fra Domenico say. Other chroniclers, however, said that there was an order for Domenico's arrest. Pretending to be a member of the party, Fra Benedetto sought to follow the arrested men, but the ruse did not work, and he was left to weep in the first cloister while his beloved pastors were led away.

The crowd in the piazza—"the great vile dogpack," Fra Benedetto called them in the poem he wrote later—had been waiting for the two friars a long time. When they finally appeared "with their hands tied behind their backs like malefactors," the roar that greeted them was loud and jubilant. Now they had him, the great impostor, the false prophet, the charlatan who had duped them for so long and deprived them of their spectacle. On every side, the bobbing torches showed drawn swords and faces askew with hatred, so that the officers of the Signoria, fearing that the prisoners would be killed before they reached the palazzo, raised a "roof of weapons" over their heads. If this kept the crowd from murdering them, it did nothing to stem the insults and the blows. "Thief! Traitor! Fra Cipolla! Go, wicked one!" they shouted. Some spat in Savonarola's face. Some kicked him. Others punched him. One grabbed his finger and began twisting it. Another brought a torch up so close to his face that it singed the skin. "Prophesy who it is that has struck you!" cried one of those who hit him. And when Savonarola reached the postern gate, a kick in the backside sent him over the threshold.

To Paolo Somenzi, who saw Savonarola and Fra Domenico handcuffed and led off to prison, the sight was the culmination of all he and Ludovico had worked for. Now it was possible to say that this matter of the friar had been brought to a satisfactory conclusion, Somenzi told Ludovico.

X

IN TE DOMINE SPERAVI

In Thee, O Lord, do I put my trust; let me
never be ashamed; deliver me in Thy right-
eousness.

Psalm 31

 few feet below the slender, tapering buttresses of the crenellated gallery which, like a heaven-kissing bloom on an earthbound stem, sits atop the tower of the Palazzo della Signoria, a pocket-sized opening on the side facing the piazza marks the location of a small, spare room known as the Alberghettino, or "little hotel." Because of its inaccessibility, this little hotel was reserved for potentially dangerous political prisoners. There, in 1433, Cosimo dei Medici had been held after his arrest by the oligarchy. There, in the early hours of Holy Monday, 1498, the officers of the Signoria deposited the chained and handcuffed Savonarola. Fra Domenico was put in another cell. Later that morning Fra Silvestro, who had gone into hiding during the assault on San Marco, was turned over to the Signoria by Fra Malatesta and also imprisoned.

"Although by then weapons had been laid aside," said Luca Landucci, "people never tired of crying 'Thief' and 'Traitor,' and no one dared say a word for the friars or they would have been killed.

To keep popular resentment at this feverish pitch, the *Compagnacci* stacked all the weapons they had found in San Marco in a cart. Without bothering to separate what had belonged to the defenders of the convent from what they themselves had brought in, they then hauled the weapon-laden cart through the

streets shouting, "Behold the miracles of the friar and the to-
kens of his love for the people of Florence!"

Like the *Compagnacci* and the majority of the people, the
Signoria had resolved that all three friars should die. First, however, they must be made to confess their crimes. Had they been
laymen, there would have been no problem about using torture
to extract confessions from them. Since they were priests, they
could neither be tried nor tortured without the pope's consent.
In a letter to Bonsi written immediately after the arrest of Fra
Silvestro, the Signoria urged the ambassador to secure that consent as quickly as possible. Because there were still so many
other matters to be settled before the examination could begin,
the Signoria then convened a *pratica*. The *pratica*, which was
composed exclusively of *Arrabbiati*, recommended that a sev-
enteen-member commission be appointed to examine the three
friars, that the examination be secret, and that the examiners
have full power to use any means they saw fit, which was another way of saying they could use torture.

Since the members of the Eight of the Ward and the Ten of
Balia were known to be sympathetic to Savonarola and could
not be depended on to cooperate with the commission, the
pratica also recommended that the Great Council elect a new
Eight and a new Ten. Such an election was, of course, illegal,
for the terms of the incumbents had not yet expired. However,
the *Arrabbiati* were too bent on eliminating the friar and his
party to let so trivial a thing as the law stop them, and the
Piagnoni were in no position to protest. Valori was dead; many
of their other leaders were being held for questioning, and those
who weren't were afraid to show their faces for fear of being
jeered at and called hypocrites.

The day after the *pratica* made its recommendation, the
Great Council elected a new Eight and a new Ten. In recognition of the key role the *Compagnacci* had played in the friar's
downfall, Doffo Spini was elected to the Eight. Benedetto dei
Nerli, whose brother Jacopo had lost an eye in the assault on
San Marco, was elected to the Ten. The following day, both Spini
and dei Nerli were also assigned to the commission which would

examine the friars. Fourteen of the remaining fifteen members were equally rabid enemies of Fra Girolamo. The fifteenth, a man by the name of Domenico Zati, refused to serve because, as he put it, he did not wish to be a party to this murder.

Even before the commission was chosen, pressure from the *Compagnacci* and the people compelled the Signoria to change its mind about waiting for the pope's consent before examining the friars. At five o'clock on the evening of April 10, Luca Landucci saw two men carry Fra Girolamo to the Bargello "on their crossed hands because his feet and hands were in irons." Since the members of the commission had not yet been chosen, an ad hoc committee appointed by the Signoria examined him, first with words, later with threats, and finally with the strappado—a torture in which the victim's hands were crossed behind his back and attached to a rope on a pulley that hoisted him from the ground, then dropped him halfway down with a jerk.

The great martyrs of old had endured far worse without flinching. When Fra Girolamo's turn came, as he had always known it would, he was determined to prove worthy of that blessed company—to be one with Jesus and Jeremiah and all the others who had suffered and died for God's truth without retracting so much as a syllable. But always there had been the fear that he might be found wanting. He would never recant, he had once told his congregation; if he were forced to recant, however, they must not believe what he said. "See how those who are innocent are accused!" he had cried on another occasion. "And you by your tortures make them confess to that which they did not do."

Landucci said that during the friar's first examination, he was given three turns of the rope. Paolo Somenzi told Ludovico that there were four. One printed summary of the trial puts the number at three and a half. Another says that there were three and a half and then another three and a half. Whatever the actual number, Savonarola found it more than he could bear. "Take me down," he begged, "and I will write you my whole life."

Burlamacchi said that in his agony the friar fell back on the words of Elijah when he went into the wilderness after fleeing from Jezebel: "O Lord, take away my life." However, after being lowered to the ground and returned to the Alberghettino, he grew calmer, and in his written confession, he conceded nothing. Whether he was a prophet or not was no concern of the state, he told the newly elected commission of sixteen when they examined him the next day. If he said he was, they wouldn't believe him. If he said he wasn't, he would be telling a lie.

But having once broken down under torture, it was perhaps inevitable that he should break down again. Between April 11 and April 17 he was examined daily, and each day, said the commission, he changed his mind on various points, sometimes speaking one way, sometimes another. Most of the reversals concerned the truth of his prophetic mission. Questioned without the use of torture, he would refuse to answer, as he had done on April 11, or would give ambiguous replies. If the matter of his prophetic mission was from God, He would give them manifest proof of it, he told the examiners on April 12. If it wasn't, it would fall.

Once suspended from the rope, however, he would confess that he was no prophet nor had God spoken to him as He spoke to his holy prophets, that in fact all he had said had been said out of a desire for earthly glory, all his talk of supernatural signs and miracles a way of giving credit to his enterprise. What was at work here was not simply his inability to withstand pain but all the doubts of his prophetic mission that had been with him from the first, doubts that were exacerbated by the sudden reversal in his fortunes and God's inexplicable silence. Unlike Cosimo dei Medici, who had spent most of his time in the Alberghettino dispensing bribes to city officials, Savonarola spent most of his time praying to God—imploring Him to give some sign that would bolster His servant's wavering belief or perhaps apologizing to Him for needing one.

The notary who transcribed his testimony each day and then presented it to him for his signature was Doffo Spini's right-hand man, Ser Ceccone. Like Spini and the other members of the commission, Ceccone was aware of the urgent need to present the people with a statement establishing the friar's guilt. Because one had not yet been forthcoming, Ceccone's own *Com-*

pagnacci were threatening to again take the law into their own hands; and the *Piagnoni* were saying that neither by the rope nor by any other torture had Fra Girolamo's examiners been able to find any crime in him. Ceccone's task, for which he was paid 14 florins, was to sift through the friar's amorphous and contradictory testimony and, by eliminating a little here and adding a little there, "put together and set in order" a confession that would give the lie to those who complained that the examiners were dragging their feet and at the same time discredit Fra Girolamo with his followers.

Florentine law required that a confession be in the handwriting of the accused. Since this one wasn't, Savonarola would have to approve what had been written by affixing his signature to it. The process of persuading him to do so began on April 18 when the pared-down and rearranged version of his testimony was read to him for the first time. Although until then he had changed his mind every day, the examiners noted that when questioned "without torture or bodily lesions," he "confessed and affirmed" that everything in the aforementioned testimony was true. And it was more or less true; it just wasn't the whole truth. But to point that out to the examiners was to risk further torture, and by then his left arm was in spasm from repeated turns of the rope.

Two high prelates and six friars of San Marco, including Fra Malatesta Sacramoro, were in the Sala Superiore of the Bargello the next morning when the prisoner's testimony was again read to him. With what the trial record called "humane and comforting words," the examiners then overcame any objections he may have voiced and persuaded him to affix his signature to what had been read to him. After his friars had also affixed their signatures, he asked for and received permission to speak to them.

Although he had, in effect, just admitted that he was a fraud, he began as if he were still their spiritual leader, speaking to them in the chapter room of San Marco. Only after bidding them follow the rules of right living and recommending the novices to them did he mention his own predicament. "Because God has taken the spirit [of prophecy] from me," he told them, "pray for me."

But after hearing his confession, his brethren no longer wished to have anything to do with their fallen prophet. "At thy word I believed, and at thy word I no longer believe," said Fra Malatesta.

Custom decreed that the accused read his confession to the people. At the end of Savonarola's confession, however, he declared that when asked if he wished to read it in public, he had said that he feared being stoned. That he should be reluctant to face the people after having denied his prophetic gift is, of course, understandable. But to say that he feared being stoned was to surrender his last shred of dignity, and it doesn't ring true. Rather, it seems like a further attempt to discredit him—someone else's version of how the accused ought to feel after his confession. It may very well have been another of Ser Ceccone's little additions, inserted either because the examiners feared that, face to face with the people, there was no telling what Fra Girolamo might say, or because the strappado had made him unpresentable.

In his absence, Ser Ceccone read the confession for him, being careful to emphasize the friar's reason for not reading it himself. Although, said Guicciardini, there were a number of important points against the friar, beginning with his admission that "the things he had predicted were not from God, revelation, or any divine source but were his own invention," other parts of Fra Girolamo's confession were "rather in his favor, for they showed that, except for pride, he had no vices whatsoever and that he had been completely alien to lust, avarice, and such sins." But those who had followed him for eight years in the belief that he was God's chosen prophet could not be so objective. A prophet was never supposed to deny his calling. If he did, he was a false prophet, a son of Satan, and nothing could compensate for that. For three days after hearing the confession read aloud, Fra Benedetto remained "stupefied." Then, "like a thrush struck to the ground," he made his way to the convent of Santa Maria della Quercia in Viterbo to seek repose for his troubled spirit.

His equally troubled brethren at San Marco decided to save their own skins. To that end, they dispatched a letter to the pope. Pen could not write nor tongue express the gratitude they owed after God to His Holiness for the fatherly solicitude with which he had delivered them "from the depths of the darkness of error" into which they had been plunged by "the crafty and cunning deceits" of Fra Girolamo, they told the Holy Father. "Let the friar suffer the punishment, if there is one sufficiently grave for such a crime. We erring sheep take refuge around our true shepherd, who is Your Holiness." The Signoria also urged the pope to have mercy on the innocent flock which had been so easily duped by the crafty friar. On behalf of the parents of those blameless dupes, many of them from the best families in the city, the Signoria begged the Holy Father to leave intact all the rights and privileges he had conceded to San Marco.

What with the discovery of Fra Girolamo's plan to summon a council and all the other provocations that year, Alexander had greeted the news of the friar's arrest with glee. As a reward for the measures the Signoria had taken "to repress the mad folly of that son of iniquity," the pope readily consented to the examination and torture of the three friars and all or any of their accomplices of whatever dignity. At the same time, he granted a plenary indulgence and remission of their sins to those who had attended the excommunicated friar's sermons, as well as full absolution to those who had taken part in the assault on San Marco. All that the Holy Father asked in return was that the three friars be sent to Rome as soon as the examiners had finished with them. One reason he was so eager to have them in Rome was his fear that if a *Piagnone* Signoria were elected for May and June, the friars would go unpunished. Another was the strong suspicion that Fra Girolamo's plan to convene a council had had the blessing of certain members of the College of Cardinals, notably the pope's archenemy Giuliano della Rovere—the future Pope Julius II—and the Holy Father's onetime friend and confidant Oliviero Caraffa. But the Signoria did not find it consonant with the city's honor to act as a sheriff. Besides, sending the friars to Rome could be dangerous, for who knew what secrets they might reveal once they were there? On the other hand, Florence was just then seeking the right to impose a tithe on church property, and antagonizing the pope was not the way to get it. A *pratica* convened on April 13 suggested finding some excuse for not sending the friars to Rome just then, all the while holding out the possibility that they would be sent later and continuing to insist on the tithe.

By far the most plausible excuse was that further time was needed to examine them. Since the Signoria really did wish to know more about Fra Girolamo's involvement in politics, what came to be known as his second trial began on April 21. It did not last as long as the examiners would have liked, for on April 24, in response to a demand that he reveal everything he had not yet told them about his political dealings with various citizens, the friar announced that he had nothing more to say. "And having said things which make me deserve death a thousand times over," he continued, "do not think that I am holding back other things which are far less serious. The truth is that I have a very poor memory for details, as my friars will testify. Hence, you must not be surprised that I don't tell you everything after one turn of the rope. If I remember anything else, I will tell it to you without holding anything back."

The same tone of wry desperation was evident the next morning when he again apologized for his poor memory. It really hadn't been worth their while to torture him, he told the examiners, for he would have said as much without torture if they had just given him the time. And there certainly wasn't any need to torture him again. They were in the Great Hall where he had been brought to ratify his deposition—not in the presence of witnesses as on April 19, but in secret. From beginning to end, this new deposition was a pastiche of false and misleading statements, many of them in the form of marginal notes added by Ser Ceccone. But the friar was even more unstrung than he had been when he signed his first confession, and though he referred to the notes, he did not take exception to them.

Later that day, the signed confession was read aloud before the Great Council. The examiners had also thought to make Fra Domenico's confession public, but in the end decided not to. All in all, Domenico had proved a most unsatisfactory witness, for neither by the strappado nor by the still more excruciating torment of the boot—a torture in which the prostrate victim had the bare heel of his right foot placed between two concave iron dies which were then pressed together until he began to scream—could he be persuaded to renounce his mentor. And when the examiners told Domenico that Fra Girolamo himself had denied his prophetic gift, Domenico cried out to God and "became stupid in this matter." Although by then his arms were totally useless, especially his left arm, which had twice been dislocated by the rope, the examiners insisted that he put his opinion of Fra Girolamo in writing. Because this written opinion did not satisfy them, they again subjected Domenico to the strappado in the hope that he would be persuaded to alter what he had written. But to no avail. "I have never perceived nor had the least occasion to suspect that my Father, Fra Girolamo, was a deceiver or that he acted falsely in any wise," Domenico wrote after being let down. "On the contrary, I have ever held him to be a thoroughly upright and most extraordinary man." Domenico assured them that if he had known of any duplicity on Savonarola's part, he would have openly revealed and protested it. But none had ever come to his attention.

Unlike Domenico, Fra Silvestro Maruffi had at first considered Savonarola's prophetic gift "an astute deception of the devil." Although he had later changed his mind, from time to time the old misgivings would surface. But to acknowledge those misgivings was to risk having to surrender his privileged position at San Marco, and like a true son of the Florentine *popolo minuto*, Silvestro had relished being on equal terms with Francesco Valori and all the other wealthy *cittadini principali* who had chosen him as their confessor. After his arrest, Silvestro's chagrin at having outfoxed himself made him readily admit all his doubts of Fra Girolamo to the examiners. When they questioned him about the affairs of the convent—the citizens who had come there, the subscription or joint letter to the pope so many of them had signed, and the armed defense of San Marco on Palm Sunday—he just as readily supplied them with long lists of names.

When the officers of the Signoria had arrested the three friars, those officers had promised amnesty to all the other friars and laymen in San Marco. Two days later, however, Paolo the candle maker was arrested and tortured; within a fortnight eighteen others were also detained. On April 27 Luca Landucci reported that "all the citizens arrested for this cause [of Fra Girolamo] were scourged, so that from 11 A.M. till evening there were unceasing cries at the Bargello."

Because the gonfalonier was unsure of what to do next, he sought the advice of a *pratica*. In addition to considering the fate of the nineteen citizens who had been arrested, the *pratica* considered what ought to be done about all the other citizens who had been implicated by either Fra Silvestro or Fra Girolamo. Had they all been as poor and insignificant as Paolo the candle maker, there would have been no problem. But many of them were *cittadini principali,* and their fellow aristocrats feared that once the people began shedding the blood of citizens like those, there was no telling where the matter would end. To Bernardo Rucellai, it seemed wiser to remove all guilt from the citizens and heap it on the friars. Punishing large numbers of citizens was not conducive to public tranquility, said Guidantonio Vespucci. Let the commune find a more profitable way to settle the matter. Even the normally vindictive Doffo Spini favored tempering justice with mercy.

Since as usual the city was in dire financial straits, the Great Council voted to impose financial amends on those who could afford to pay. Because silencing the *Frateschi* was also a consideration, in many cases those who were fined faced curtailment of their political rights. Thus, Francesco dell'Pugliese, who had defended San Marco with an arquebus and had also induced a friend to speak to the king of England about convening a council, had to pay a fine of 500 florins and was deprived of his seat on the Great Council for two years. Domenico Mazzinghi, whose letter to the Florentine ambassador at the court of Charles VIII had been intercepted by agents of Ludovico Sforza, had a choice between paying 300 florins and being deprived of his rights for two years or paying 100 florins and being deprived of his rights for eight years. On the other hand, Paolantonio Soderini, who had gone to Lucca to avoid being implicated, managed to keep his seat on the council but had to lend the commune 3000 florins, with no guarantee that he would ever see the money again. With the other fines and loans extracted from the friar's adherents, the commune found itself 12,000 florins richer. Satisfied with the way the matter had been handled, the Signoria sent all the arrested citizens home. "And," said Luca Landucci, "only the three poor friars remained."

After Fra Girolamo signed his second confession, there was no longer any need to carry him to the palace of the Bargello for questioning each morning. Alone in the ponderous gloom of the Alberghettino, he had ample time to confront the stranger within, the stranger who had recanted at the first turn of the rope, the stranger whose pusillanimity he could neither control nor condone. In his desperate need for some outlet for his anguish at having failed both his God and himself, he began a commentary on the fifty-first psalm, the so-called *Miserere*. "O unhappy wretch that I am, forsaken by all, who have offended heaven and earth, whither shall I go?" he asked."I dare not raise my eyes to heaven. On earth I find no refuge, for I have given cause for scandal. What shall I do? Shall I despair? No, truly God is merciful, my Savior is full of pity. I come therefore to Thee, most merciful God, I come full of melancholy and grief, for Thou alone art my hope, Thou alone my refuge."

He begged the Lord to sustain him with the force of His spirit so that no fear would cause him to separate from Christ, no torment or affliction weaken him. The case of Saint Peter had given him insight into human frailty, he confided. If Peter had lacked the fortitude to remain constant when questioned by a mere servant girl, what would he have done had he seen the whips brought out? No doubt he would have done anything to save himself. "Therefore," said the friar, "since Peter to whom Thou gave so many gifts and favors fell so miserably, what could I do Lord—I who never saw you in the flesh and never tasted your glory on the Mount or saw your miracles?

Feeling that he had scored a point, he pleaded with God to work some last-minute miracle that would allow him once again to teach the ways of Christ to the impious. Though he tried to keep to the same self-abasing tone in which he had begun and begged the Lord not to attribute his request to undue boldness, inevitably the vision of all he could still accomplish if only he were given the opportunity drew forth some of the old vehemence. Soon he was assailing the Lord with great baskets of words, much as he had once assailed his congregation in Santa Maria dei Fiore. "O Lord, I beseech Thee, look on Thy church and behold how in these days more infidels than Christians are numbered in its fold....Hell is filled, Thy church desolate," he wrote. And as he had done in his sermon to the women on March 17, he bade the Lord arise. "Why sleepest Thou, O Lord?" he asked. "Rise up and do not reject us forever....Where now is the glory of the apostles, the strength of the martyrs, the fruit of the preachers, the holy simplicity of the monks, the virtue and the works of the early Christians?...Do unto me I pray what must be done so that Thou mayest receive me as a sacrifice to justice, as an offering to holiness, as a holocaust to the religious life."

The *Miserere* was finished on May 8; he must have smuggled it out of the Alberghettino immediately, for it was published soon afterward. Perhaps it was while he was still beguiled by the hope of a miracle that he composed "A Rule for Leading the Good Life" for his jailer. But in the face of God's unrelenting silence, he soon lost heart. In a commentary on the thirty-first psalm—*In Te Domine Speravi*—he pictured Despair's repeated onslaughts on his faith in the very existence of a benign deity:

Do you believe what faith teaches? [Despair whispered in his ear.] Do you want to see that it's nothing but human invention?...If God made Himself man and was crucified for men, how can His great pity leave without consolation a man struck down by such an immense sorrow, a man who invokes Him with tears? If, as they say, His infinite goodness made Him come down from heaven to be crucified, why doesn't He come down now to console the wretched?... Believe me, all is governed by chance and nothing exists but what we see. Our spirit dissolves like smoke. Who has ever come back from hell to tell what happens to the soul after death? All that [talk of an afterlife] is nothing but fables for servingwomen. Arise! Have recourse to human aid so that leaving this prison, you may live without forever suffering in vain, deceived by your hope.

If Hope had not come to his rescue, Despair would have surely carried him off to her country. But the comfort that Hope brought was short-lived. Though the friar prayed to be delivered from the harsh servitude of Despair, she appeared once more, preceded this time by the banner of Justice—the officials responsible for carrying out the death penalty—and followed by an innumerable army. "O miserable one," she cried. "Do you think that God's mercy is greater than his justice?" And she cautioned him against seeking consolation in the stories of Mary Magdalene, the good thief, Peter, and Paul. "What makes you think you can be admitted to this small number?" she asked. "You who have offended heaven and earth.…Better for you to die.…Choose death, and if no one gives it to you, kill yourself with your own hand." Whereupon her entire army echoed her words like a Greek chorus, all crying in unison, "Death is your only refuge!"

At the sound of their voices, the friar fell to earth, imploring God not to abandon him, crying out to Hope to come to his rescue. Once again, however, the surcease that Hope provided was only temporary. God had placed him in the midst of the people even as if he had been one of the excellent, Despair reminded him. He had taught others but failed to learn himself. He had cured others but was himself still diseased. His heart was lifted up at the beauty of his own deeds, and through this he had lost his wisdom and was and would become to all eternity nothing. Didn't he know that God rejects the prideful? Like Lucifer, who told himself that he would go to heaven, he would surely be dragged down to hell. The moth beneath him would be his bed, the vermin his quilt. That being the case, why continue to delude himself with vain hope? Rather than being held back by shame, let him imitate the prostitute: "Eat and drink, for tomorrow we die."

But as Fra Girolamo had pointed out over and over again in his sermons, such arguments were the stock in trade of the Evil One, waiting to snare the sinner as he stood trembling on the brink of eternity, and he dared not allow himself to succumb. As in the *Ars Moriendi*—the manuals on the art of dying so popular at the time—in the end, Hope was made to triumph. Although she too blamed his fall on pride, she assured him that he was not forsaken. "Else why has God called upon you to repent? Is it not to make you worthy of divine grace and to lead you to eternal life?"

Filled with gladness, the friar used the words of the psalmist to reaffirm his faith in the Lord: "The Lord is my light and my salvation; whom shall I fear? the Lord is the strength of my life; of whom shall I be afraid?" But fear such as his, he soon discovered, was not so easily vanquished.

At the end of April when the friar had signed his second confession, the pope had still been adamant about having him and his two codefendants sent to Rome. The Holy Father would not even discuss the tithe until they arrived. Soon afterward, however, Alexander learned that the Signoria elected for May and June was even more solidly *Arrabbiati* than the previous one and just as bent on executing the friars. That being the case, he no longer saw any reason to insist on trying them in Rome. In response to the Signoria's plea that he allow them to be executed "in the place where they had deluded the populace for so long," he agreed to send two apostolic commissioners to Florence "to examine into the iniquity of those three children of perdition."

Because at this time he also allowed the city to impose a tithe on church property for three consecutive years, many of those who still loved Fra Girolamo declared that, like the Savior, he had been sold for thirty pieces of silver. For, they told themselves, three times ten equal thirty.

The apostolic commissioners who were to examine him entered the city on May 19. Gioacchino Torriano, the director general of the Dominican order, was there because it was necessary for one of the friar's superiors to be present at his trial by an ecclesiastical court. Rather than entrust the conduct of the trial to Torriano, however, the pope had entrusted it to the director general's much younger colleague, Francesco Remolines, bishop of Ilerda and auditor to the governor of Rome. Remolines, or Romolino, as the Florentines called him because he had come from

Rome, was a close friend of the pope's son Cesare. "My dearest chum," Cesare had called him when the two were studying canon law together at the Sapienza of Perugia. Like Cesare, Romolino was intelligent, ruthless, and amoral. And it was undoubtedly because of his Spanish birth and his friendship with the pope's son that this swaggering young man, who, said Cesare, "had no inclination for the sacerdotal life," had gone so far so fast.

"We shall make a good bonfire; I have the verdict already here in my bosom," he told a delegation of *Arrabbiati* who came to visit him that first day. To help him pass his nights agreeably, one of the visitors had brought him a beautiful girl dressed as a boy. His appreciation of this thoughtful gift may have had something to do with his decision to allow five representatives of the Florentine government to be present at the trial.

Like the friar's two previous trials, this one was held in the Sala Superiore of the Bargello, where the instruments of torture were kept. Because Romolino had brought his own secretary from Rome, there was, however, no need of Ser Ceccone's services. Consequently, the minutes of this third trial are more complete and more reliable than the minutes of either of the previous trials. It began on May 20. As Romolino had made clear, there was no question about the verdict. The friar was being cross-examined not to ascertain his guilt but to discover who had known of his proposed letter to the princes and how far negotiations for a council had progressed. Like all examiners, Romolino could be expected to use torture to elicit the truth.

Although Savonarola knew this, in the extremity of his fear he apparently convinced himself that if only he were accommodating enough, he would make its use unnecessary. Hence, he readily affirmed the truth of his two previous confessions and made a great show of having repented. But to no avail. After commanding him to tell the whole truth and nothing but the truth, Romolino ordered him stripped for the rope. Whereupon, said the trial record, "he, showing the greatest fear," knelt before the examiners. "Now hear my words!" he cried. "O God, Thou hast caught me! I confess I have denied Christ. I have told lies. O Signori of Florence, I have denied Him out of fear of being tortured. If I must suffer, let me suffer for the truth: that which I have said I have received from God himself. God, Thou givest me this penance for having denied Thee. I have denied Thee for fear of being tortured!"

Completely beside himself, he offered no resistance when the officers of the court made him rise so they could strip him. No sooner were they done, however, than he sank to his knees once more. Pointing to his dislocated left arm, he kept repeating, "I denied Thee, Lord, for fear of being tortured." When he was attached to the rope and drawn up, he called out to Jesus to help him.

Why had he spoken thus, Romolino asked the half-naked, trembling little man as he hung suspended from the rope. "To appear good. Do not torture me; I will tell you the truth, for sure, for sure," Savonarola replied.

"Why did you deny everything only a minute ago?"

"Because I am crazy."

At the sight of the strappado, he lost all control, he explained after being let down. But when he was in a room with a few well-intentioned people, he behaved better. Was the record of his previous examination true, asked Romolino. It was true, and because it was true he would affirm it always, the friar replied.

He had been a wicked man, and now he wished to clear his conscience, he told the court. But there were times during his cross-examination when the horror of his situation overwhelmed him, and he could not continue. "O friar, to what a pass you have come!" he cried after Romolino threatened to use the strappado if he did not tell all concerning his plans to convene a council. And he began to weep and lament and to wonder out loud how he had come to enter on this affair which now seemed to him like a dream. Then, regaining control of himself, he proceeded to describe his plan for convening a council.

Romolino had hoped that he would implicate Cardinal Caraffa. When he didn't, he was again menaced with the strappado. In his terror, he admitted having had dealings with the cardinal. Still not satisfied, Romolino ordered him stripped and given one turn of the rope, then asked him to confirm his testimony. Later, he was given another turn of the rope and asked to confirm it again. Although he did so, the knowledge that no confessor could absolve him if he implicated an innocent man gave him no peace; and when he was returned to the Alberghettino, he burst into tears.

Everything he had said was true except his testimony about Cardinal Caraffa, he told the court the following evening. If they doubted him, let them speak to his former secretary Nicholas of Milano, who had never sent any letter to the cardinal. Or let them question Fra Domenico and Fra Silvestro, who had both been party to this "fantasy" of his. Realizing that it would be pointless to pursue the matter further, Romolino had one of the papal process servers ask him if he would be present the next day to hear sentence pronounced. "I am in prison; if I can, I will appear," Savonarola replied.

Before being handed the day's testimony to sign, he was cross-examined concerning an outbreak of possession by spirits among the nuns of Santa Lucia, a convent under the jurisdiction of San Marco. Remembering how one of the sisters had snatched the crucifix from his hand and flung it to the ground, calling him *frataccio* and refusing to let go of his cloak, he began to laugh.

Although the ecclesiastical court had heard neither Fra Domenico nor Fra Silvestro, they too were to be sentenced that evening. Because Romolino believed that Fra Domenico's excessive simplicity had made it easy for Savonarola to deceive him, the commissioners had at first thought to spare his life. However, when someone pointed out that if Domenico were spared, he would undoubtedly do his utmost to keep Fra Girolamo's doctrines alive, thus negating all the work that had gone into stamping them out, Romolino was perfectly willing to drop the matter. "One friar more or less, what difference does it make?" he is supposed to have said.

He and Torriano found all three friars to be heretics and schismatics and to have preached innovations, and sentenced them to be degraded (that is, deprived of their habits) and consigned or in truth left in the hand of the secular judges—in this case the Signoria and the Eight.

At a *pratica* convened a few days earlier, the *Arrabbiato* law-

yer Agnolo Niccolini had proposed that Fra Girolamo be imprisoned for life and allowed to write so that the world might not lose
the fruit of his learning. But the majority of the *pratica* did not
trust future Signorias to keep him in prison. Under one of them,
he would certainly be restored to liberty and again cause disturbance in the city, whereas "a dead enemy fights no more." Because "many feared to see their country ruined, little by little,
under his prophetic teaching," said Machiavelli, "no ground for...
reunion could be discovered, unless his light divine continued
to increase, or unless by a greater fire it was extinguished."

Seated around the massive, intricately carved oaken table in
the Sala delle Udienze on the second floor of the palazzo, with
the marble statue of Justice over the doorway to remind them
of their responsibility, the Eight found the friars guilty of "abominable crimes." Just what those crimes were was not made clear.
They were judged sufficiently heinous, however, to warrant con-
demning all three friars "to be each and all hanged and their
bodies burned that the soul may be separated from the body in
public and on the square of their magnificent lordships [the
Signoria]."

While the sentence was being drawn up, a delegation of five
citizens paid an unexpected call on Fra Girolamo. They were
accompanied by Ser Ceccone and another notary, and they
wished the friar to explain more fully what he had promised to
reveal concerning the affairs of the city. After he had answered
their question at some length, they asked him by what means
he had planned to extricate himself if those temporal gains
which he had promised to Florence "presto" did not material-
ize. The means were not lacking, Savonarola replied, all the more
so because the "prestos" of the good Lord could be stretched
out indefinitely.

He had been praying when they arrived. As soon as they left,
he resumed his colloquy with the Almighty. Not long afterward,
he was told that he must die the following morning. Perhaps
because he had taken this verdict for granted, he showed no dis-
tress, nor did he ask in what manner he was to die.

*   *   *

Among the numerous confraternities, or charitable associations, in Florence was the Compagnia di Santa Maria della Croce al Tempio, known also as the Compagnia dei Neri because of the long black robes and black hoods worn by its members. To ease the loneliness and the terror of the condemned's last hours, one of the Neri remained with him from the moment the verdict of the Eight was announced until the moment it was carried out. When Jacopo Niccolini, the member assigned to Savonarola, brought him his supper, the friar refused it. He wished to prepare his soul to receive death, he told his comforter, and not be occupied with digesting food. Somehow or other, just how is not clear—Burlamacchi insisted it was by revelation—he learned that Fra Domenico wished to be burned alive and that Fra Silvestro intended to proclaim their innocence from the scaffold. Because the friar thought his brethren guilty of that same pride which he had come to deplore in himself, he asked Niccolini if he could arrange a meeting with them before the execution. Although Niccolini had no power to do this, he agreed to speak to those who did. When the black-robed comforter appeared at the door of the private apartments of the Signoria, the two priors who admitted him were at first reluctant to grant the request. Niccolini persisted, and in the end the priors allowed the condemned men to meet in the Great Hall.

As described by Burlamacchi, their meeting seems cold and formal, with Savonarola immediately assuming the role of a stern spiritual mentor with the others. "Know you not that it is not permitted to choose one's manner of dying?" he asked Fra Domenico. "Who knows whether you will be able to bear that which is made ready for you, as that depends entirely on God's grace?"

As for protesting to the people, he told Silvestro, not even Christ published his innocence from the cross; hence, it behooved them to keep silent, for every act of Christ was an example to them. Fra Domenico could be expected to bow to the will of his former chief. What is surprising is that after being reprimanded, Silvestro too knelt to receive his blessing. The three of them spent the rest of that night in the dark, empty hall, each retiring to a different corner with his comforter. Resting his head against Niccolini's knees, Savonarola fell asleep. Niccolini, who watched him attentively while he slept, was amazed to hear him talk in his sleep and occasionally laugh out loud.

When the first light of dawn made the preparations for the auto-da-fé visible from the two windows in the long eastern wall facing the piazza, the comforters and their charges moved to the chapel of the Signoria. In that tiny chapel where, on the day of the ordeal by fire, Fra Francesco da Puglia and Fra Giuliano Rondinelli had lain prostrate before the altar, Savonarola once again held the sacrament in his hands and addressed a final prayer to the Lord. In essence, this prayer was one long cry for forgiveness; forgiveness of his sins from the day he had received baptism, forgiveness for anything he had done to offend the city and the people in temporal matters, forgiveness from all present in the chapel. "Pray God for me," he implored, "that He may give me strength at my last end and that the Enemy may have no power over me."

Afterward, he gave the viaticum to himself and his brethren, and, together with their comforters, the three friars headed for the staircase that led to the piazza.

As on the morning of the ordeal by fire, so again on that bright blue morning of May 23, 1498, a narrow, raised walkway beginning at the *Marzocco* extended some 90 feet into the piazza in the direction of the Tetti dei Pisani. At the far end of this walkway, on the very spot where the pyramid of vanities had twice stood, was yet another *capannuccio*—a circular wooden platform heaped high with brooms, wood, and other combustibles from whose center emerged a wooden column some 23 feet high. Close to the summit of this column, a carpenter had nailed a transverse beam from which dangled three nooses and an iron chain designed to keep the friars' bodies suspended after the nooses burned. Because this transverse beam made the gibbet look like a cross, the Signoria had ordered the carpenter to saw off as much of each arm as he possibly could. Nevertheless, the resemblance persisted, remarked on by some, dismissed by others as unimportant, and a source of secret satisfaction to the many *Piagnoni* in the vast multitude that crowded around the gibbet.

The march to the scaffold began at the *ringhiera* where the friars had to appear before three tribunals. The first, which was next to the statue of Judith to the right of the palace door, was presided over by the bishop of Vasona. Even before the apostolic delegates had set out for Florence, the pope had assigned this bishop the task of degrading the friars. The ceremony of degradation was long and humiliating, for their clerical vestments had to be removed one by one while a priest murmured the appropriate formulas. When the last garment was removed, and the barefoot friars stood before the tribunal in their loose, white, woolen undertunics, the bishop had to separate them from the church militant. For most bishops, this would have presented no problem, but Vasona had once been a friar of San Marco. When Savonarola appeared before him, he grew so flustered that he declared him separate "from the church militant and triumphant." Savonarola could, of course, have ignored this slip of the tongue. But despite his professions of humility, pride clung to him like a barnacle to a ship. In a voice loud enough for everyone in the crowd pressing around the *ringhiera* to hear, he called attention to the bishop's error: "From the church militant, yes; from the church triumphant, no. That is God's affair, not yours."

After the bishop had corrected himself, the friars moved on to the tribunal in the center of the *ringhiera*, which was presided over by the apostolic commissioners. There they knelt on the marble pavement while Romolino pronounced them heretics and schismatics and consigned them to the tribunal of the Eight.

The Eight, of whom only seven were present, were seated on either side of the gonfalonier at the far end of the *ringhiera* beside the *Marzocco*. After one of them read the death sentence aloud, the friars were directed to the walkway. To one side of each friar was his black-robed comforter holding aloft an image of the Savior for him to gaze on. On the other side was his confessor, also in black. Earlier, some boys had concealed themselves under the walkway, and as the friars passed, the boys stuck pointed sticks through the crevices into their bare feet and legs. To the crowd's disappointment, the friars seemed oblivious of the pain. When they reached the gibbet, the hangman took hold of Fra Silvestro and, mounting the ladder leading to the summit, suspended him from the arm facing outward toward the great ribbed dome of the cathedral. As he felt the executioner's hand push him forward, Silvestro cried out in a loud voice, "*In manus tuas Domine commendo spiritum meum*, Into your hands, O Lord, I commend my spirit." Because the rope did not draw tight or run well, he suffered for some time, repeating *Jesu* over and over until he died.

Fra Domenico had wanted to sing the *Te Deum* aloud at the foot of the gibbet, but his comforter, fearing a riot, had persuaded him to sing it quietly to himself. He was suspended from the arm facing toward the palace, and he too kept repeating *Jesu* as he died.

Savonarola had asked for a cord with which he might tie his tunic about his legs so the crowd would not see his private parts when he mounted the ladder. But the request was refused, and this refusal may very well have troubled him more than the prospect of dying, to which he had, after all, grown accustomed. Repeating the words of the little Credo to himself, he followed the hangman up the ladder. At the summit, he paused and turned his head from side to side for one last look at the crowd below.

There were many in that crowd who were waiting for some word or sign from him, something that would give them cause to go on believing. But his thoughts were of his Savior on the cross at Calvary. Faithful to his decision to emulate Christ, he silently offered his neck to the hangman. He was hanged between his two companions with his face looking toward the palazzo.

In a nearly contemporary painting by an unknown artist, the three friars, in their white tunics, look like rag dolls suspended from the gibbet, and the flames have not yet reached them.

EPILOGUE

Thou hast borne me, a man of strife and a man
of contention to the whole world.
Jeremiah 15:10

nd so he was dead. But his death, which was supposed to remove the last obstacle to Florentine participation in the Holy League and make the French think twice about launching a new invasion, did nothing of the sort.

By one of those ironic coincidences beloved of Clio, the muse of history, Charles VIII had suddenly and unexpectedly died on the very day that the failure of the trial by fire made Savonarola's own death inevitable. Charles was at his castle at Amboise, where, as befitted a young ruler who did not think of dying, he had started the greatest building project that any king had undertaken for a century. While he and his queen were on their way to watch a tennis match in the castle moat, the nearsighted little monarch struck his head against the door leading to one of the galleries. It was in that gallery—"the filthiest place in the castle, for everyone pissed there," said Comines—that he died. The royal physicians attributed his death to apoplexy, but many modern scholars suspect that it was syphilis that killed him. Because he left no children, his crown went to his distant cousin, Louis of Orleans.

Louis's maternal grandmother was the daughter of Giangaleazzo Visconti, duke of Milan. As part of her dowry, she brought the house of Orleans the right of succession to her father's duchy. After Giangaleazzo's death, however, his condottiere, Francesco Sforza, who had married the duke's illegitimate daughter Bianca, made himself ruler of Milan. Louis's father, the poet-prince Charles of Orleans, did not consider the duchy worth fighting for. Louis, on the other hand, had nothing better to do with himself. And while he was at it, he decided that he might as well retake Naples, which he claimed by virtue of his connection with Charles. At his coronation at Rheims, he made his intentions clear by calling himself Louis XII, by grace of God king of France, Sicily, and Jerusalem, and duke of Milan.

At the time he assumed these titles, Ludovico and the pope were trying to persuade Venice to turn Pisa over to Florence. Rather than agree to do so, the Venetians sought an alliance with Louis, hoping thereby to keep Pisa and receive a share of the spoils when the new king conquered Milan. Although Alexander sent an envoy to France to warn Louis not to attack either Milan or Naples, the pope must have realized that the defection of Venice made a new invasion inevitable. As if this were not bad enough, King Frederic of Naples, who as a member of the Holy League should have been helping the pope, was secretly helping his rebellious barons. Alexander was still trying to decide what to do about this when Louis's envoy in Rome brought the pope a most interesting proposal.

The marriage of Anne of Brittany to Charles VIII had given the French control over the semi-independent appanage of Brittany. To retain that control, Louis wished to marry his predecessor's widow. Unfortunately, the king already had a wife: Anne's sister-in-law Jeanne de Valois, a woman so ugly and deformed that Louis swore he had never consummated his marriage with her. Were the pope to give him a dispensation to divorce Jeanne and marry Anne, the king promised to raise the county of Valence to a duchy and bestow it on the pope's son Cesare, who was then seeking to be relieved of his cardinal's hat. Louis also agreed to do his best to find a suitable wife for Cesare.

Alexander was a practical man. Rather than continue to depend on Ludovico Sforza and King Frederic, neither of whom the pope trusted and neither of whom trusted him, he decided to make capital out of Louis's marital difficulties. That July, the pope concluded a secret agreement with the French. Soon afterward, he appointed a judicial commission to examine Louis's request for a divorce. On August 17, when Cesare surrendered his cardinal's hat, he received Louis's royal patent investing him with the duchy of Valentinois. When he sailed for France that October, he took with him a papal *dispensa* allowing Louis to divorce Jeanne and marry Anne. The following April, the alliance of Venice and the pope with France was published. The years of scheming to be rid of Savonarola had served no purpose: the Holy League was all but dead; and Alexander, who had worked so hard to keep the French out of Italy, was an ally of the French king, prepared to countenance a new invasion in exchange for a duchy for Cesare and Louis's help in subduing the rebellious vassals of the papal states.

In July 1499, French troops crossed the Alps and headed for Milan, capturing fortress after fortress as they went. Ludovico had expected the emperor Maximilian and King Frederic to help him hold on to his duchy. But Maximilian was busy fighting the Swiss, and Frederic was too appalled by the French victories to do anything. Realizing that it would be folly to face the invaders alone, Ludovico fled to the Tyrol. Although he had posed as a friend of Florence, wooing the Florentines with promises of Pisa, few regretted his downfall. When the city heard that Louis had taken the citadel of Milan and was in possession of the whole duchy, the "joybells" rang out, bonfires appeared in every piazza, and the towers of the Palazzo della Signoria were illuminated. The following April, when Ludovico was captured by French troops after having retaken Milan, the *ringhiera* was festooned with draperies; a crown was set on the brow of the *Marzocco*, and a beautiful figure of the Savior was placed at the entrance to the palace.

Ludovico spent much of the rest of his life in one of the subterranean dungeons of Louis's fortresslike castle at Loches. Having derived no benefit from his machinations against Savonarola, he soon came to regret them. When a group of Florentine merchants visited him, he is supposed to have asked them to tell their countrymen that Fra Girolamo had been right and that he was a true prophet.

Another of the friar's erstwhile enemies who later had a

change of heart was Doffo Spini. He had never seen or heard Fra
Girolamo until after his arrest, Spini told Simone Filipepi, but
if he had heard him, he would have been a greater partisan of
the friar than Simone himself.

Spini's change of heart, however, in no way affected either
his way of life or that of his *Compagnacci*. During the first midnight mass on the Christmas following the friar's death, the *Compagnacci* brought an old horse with a thick pole stuck up its
rear end into Santa Maria dei Fiore and chased it up and down
the aisles, slashing it with their swords and poking it with sticks
until the poor beast collapsed on the steps of the cathedral, where
it remained all of Christmas day, torn to pieces and dying.

"They did this because, the friar being dead, it seemed as if
they were at liberty to commit every kind of sin, he by his
preaching having put a stop to all such things," said Giovanni
Cambi. And Luca Landucci praised God for having allowed him
to see "that short space of holiness," that is, the days of Fra
Girolamo.

However, such opinions had to be expressed cautiously, for,
said Jacopo Nardi, "in those days, it seemed as if no vice was
more shameful and reprehensible than to have believed in the
friar."

Less than two months after the incident of the horse, Francesco Mei, the procurator of the Dominicans, issued an order
forbidding anyone "to speak of Fra Girolamo either in praise or
blame." Nor were there to be any disputations as to whether he
had erred. Preachers were neither to criticize his life and habits
nor to defend his prophecies. The psalm *Quam Bonus*, which
had been his favorite, would no longer be sung, and under no
circumstances was anyone to keep any relics of the dead friar.

The battle to prevent the people from collecting relics had
begun immediately after his death. As soon as the friar's corpse
and those of his codefendants had been reduced to ashes and
the post from which they had been hanged burned to the ground,
the hangman and those whose business it was to dispose of the
remains had stirred up the fire so that the very last piece was
consumed. When some women disguised as servants approached
carrying urns, pretending that they wanted the ashes to wash

clothes with, the same boys who had earlier stoned the corpses broke the urns, and the soldiers drove the women away with the flat of their swords. The executioner and his helpers then fetched carts and, accompanied by the mace bearers, "they carried the last bit of dust to the Arno by the Ponte Vecchio, in order that no remains should be found." That night, however, some of the friar's more intrepid followers went to the riverbank with nets to gather the floating ashes "in fear and secrecy, because," said Landucci, "it was as much as one's life was worth to say a word, so anxious were the authorities to destroy every relic."

Three days later, women were found kneeling in the piazza on the spot where the friar had been burned. Soon afterward, the papal envoy ordered everyone who had any of the friar's writings to bring them in to be burned on pain of excommunication. To the envoy's mortification, nothing heretical was found in any of the works, and the people poked fun at the whole procedure.

Fearing that the friar's party was reviving, the Eight deprived many citizens who had entered the Great Council in Valori's time of their posts, declared some of the friar's former supporters incapable of bearing arms, and had some of the less important *Piagnoni* flogged. Still not content, the Signoria decided to exile *La Piagnona*, the great brass bell which had had the effrontery to summon the faithful to the defense of San Marco. On June 30, the bell was placed on a cart and paraded through the streets while the hangman whipped it for its part in the disturbance; it was then led through the San Niccolò gate and presented to the Franciscan community of San Miniato. The entire Dominican order protested the exile of the bell; the pope himself spoke up in its favor, as did Ludovico, but the only concession the Signoria would make was to reduce the period of exile from fifty years to ten.

Savonarola had been another Antichrist, insanely given over to the power of Satan, said Giovan Francesco Poggio Bracciolini, a canon of the cathedral and student of canon law, and it was as the Antichrist that the friar was depicted in the *Last Judgment* which Luca Signorelli painted for the cathedral of Orvieto in

1499. But with the coming of the French later that year, Fra Girolamo was again acclaimed as a true prophet, for had he not predicted another invasion, and weren't the French those *nuovi barbieri*, those new barbers, of whom he had warned?

A month after Louis took Milan, Giovambattista Ridolfi, who had had to go into hiding when Savonarola was arrested, was elected gonfalonier. Ridolfi was determined to punish Doffo Spini for his part in the friar's downfall. To that end, said Piero Parenti, the new gonfalonier and his followers "pretended that Spini had committed sodomy with a young man of the Antinori family." But the *Arrabbiati* protested, and the *Compagnacci* threatened to take up arms if their leader was indicted. A year later, however, the *Piagnoni* were strong enough to secure the exile of Giovan Francesco Bracciolini, the canon who had called Savonarola the Antichrist and had also had the audacity to insist that the Pisans had as much right to their freedom as the Florentines.

Among the many *Piagnoni* dismissed from the civil service during the *Arrabbiati* heyday that had followed Savonarola's arrest was Alessandro Bracci, the elderly, corpulent secretary of the second chancery, whom the pope had called a fat man with "a mighty thin commission." As Bracci's replacement, the Great Council chose the young, slender Niccolò Machiavelli. That July, Machiavelli was also made secretary to the Ten. The principal concerns of the Ten during his fourteen years in office were much the same as they had been in Savonarola's time: the return of Pisa and the alliance with France. What did change, however, was the cast of characters with whom the republic had to deal: Louis XII in place of Charles VIII, Louis's ally Cesare Borgia, and, after the death of Alexander VI and Cesare's subsequent downfall, Pope Julius II.

To punish the Venetians for refusing to turn over certain cities of the Romagna to him, Julius invited the kings of France and Spain and the emperor Maximilian to join him in the League of Cambrai. In 1509, when the armies of the League defeated the Venetians at Agnadello, Pisa finally surrendered to Florence.

Not long afterward, however, Julius decided that the French were trying to reduce him to being their king's chaplain, whereas he meant to be pope. With the cry of "Out with the barbarians!" he called on the states of Italy and the king of Spain to join him in a new Holy League which would expel the French. Rather than do as the pope asked, Florence chose to remain neutral. But Cardinal Giovanni dei Medici, who had become head of the family after his brother Piero drowned in the river Garigliano in 1503, decided to support Julius. In 1512, when Swiss mercenaries in the pay of the Holy League succeeded in ridding Italy of the French, the Congress of Mantua called for the return of the Medici; Spanish troops sacked Prato; Piero Soderini, the permanent gonfalonier the Florentines had elected in 1502, was forced to resign; Cardinal Giovanni and his brother Giuliano entered Florence at the head of a large army; a *parlamento* supervised by their troops abolished the Great Council; and Machiavelli was out of a job.

Although he was still a republican at heart, Machiavelli had a wife and four children to support. Like many other career diplomats of modest means, he hoped to eventually be rehired by the Medici. As luck would have it, however, his name was found on a list of republican sympathizers compiled by two young men who confessed that they had been planning a coup d'état. He was arrested and given six turns of the rope, a punishment which he bore with such stoicism that he "thought the better of himself for it," then sentenced to pay a fine for his unwitting part in the conspiracy. Since he did not have the money, he was confined to the Stinche until such time as he found it. By then, however, Pope Julius was dead. On March 11, 1513, Cardinal Giovanni became Pope Leo X, and, in the general amnesty following his election, Machiavelli was released.

He remained in Florence for a month, hoping that, as he told a friend whom he asked to help him, his "master" (that is, the Medici) would find something for him to do. But his imprisonment had made him persona non grata. Because he could not continue to live in Florence without an income, at the end of April he took his family to a small farm he owned at Sant'Andrea in Percussina, a hamlet 7 miles south of Florence. There, in the unwelcome leisure that had been forced on him, he wrote *The Prince* and the other books that would make the name of this transparently good man a byword for evil. In those books and in the letters he sent to his friends during the years at Sant'Andrea, he returned over and over again to the question of the friar.

Why had Fra Girolamo been able to make the people believe that he held converse with God although they had seen no extraordinary manifestations that should have made them believe it? And why in the end had he failed? "It was the purity of his life, the doctrines he preached, and the subjects for his discourses that sufficed to make the people have faith in him," Machiavelli concluded in *The Discourses.*

But if it is easy to persuade the people of something, it is difficult to keep them persuaded. "Thus, it comes about that all armed prophets have conquered, and unarmed ones failed," he wrote in one of the most famous passages in *The Prince.* As an example of an unarmed prophet, he cited Fra Girolamo, "who failed entirely in his new rules when the multitude began to disbelieve in him, and he had no means of holding fast those who had believed or of compelling the unbelievers to believe."

Like Moses, Savonarola understood the necessity of putting to death a great many persons "who opposed his designs under the instigation of no other feelings than those of envy and jealousy," said Machiavelli in *The Discourses.* Though the friar lacked the power and authority to put his ideas into practice, "he was not remiss in doing all he could, for his sermons abounded with accusations against the wise of this world, for it was thus he styled the opponents of his doctrines."

But in those cool and dispassionate appraisals of Fra Girolamo there was no jot of sympathy for the man, only an earnest desire to understand the realities of the political process. And despite a certain respect for the purity of the friar's life and his recognition of the need to crush envious opponents, from the references to Savonarola elsewhere in Machiavelli's work, it is clear that he continued to see him as an adroit dissembler who had "adjusted himself to the times and shaded his lies."

There is, for example, the passage in *The Discourses* in

which, as was mentioned earlier, Machiavelli wrote that the friar's failure to demand the right of appeal for the five citizens convicted of treason manifested his "ambitious and partial spirit."

There is also the passage in *The Prince* in which, without mentioning the friar by name, Machiavelli disparaged his prophecies. Speaking of the conquest of Italy by Charles VIII he said:

> Those who said it was due to our sins spoke the truth, but it was not the sins they meant, but those I have related. And because they were sins by the princes, the princes have paid the penalty for them.

Florence was a magnet for all the imposters in the world, Machiavelli told his friend Francesco Vettori in a letter describing a brother of Saint Francis who, "to get more belief for his preaching, claimed to be a prophet." And when the consuls of the wool guild asked him to persuade the chapter general of the Franciscans meeting at Carpi to send Fra Giovanni Gualberto da Firenze to preach in the Duomo, Machiavelli gave his dear friend Francesco Guicciardini a description of the sort of preacher he thought suitable for the Florentines:

> I should like to find one who would teach them the way to go to the house of the Devil...one crazier than [Fra Domenico da] Ponzo, more crafty than Fra Girolamo, more of a hypocrite than Fra Alberto [in the *Decameron*] because it would seem to me a fine thing and worthy of the goodness of these times that all we have experienced in many friars should be experienced in one, because I believe the true way of going to Paradise would be to learn the road to Hell in order to avoid it.

And in the same ironical vein in which he spoke of the goodness of the times, he called the friar "so great a man" and said that his writings showed "his learning, his prudence, and the vigor of his intellect."

It is one of the numerous paradoxes to be found in Machiavelli that, although he was repelled by the decadence of the church—"the evil example of the court of Rome has destroyed all piety and religion in Italy," he wrote in *The Discourses*—he was also repelled by Fra Girolamo's immoderate attacks on the pope. Nor, as far as is known, did he ever express any sympathy for Martin Luther.

Four years after Machiavelli moved to Sant'Andrea, Luther posted his ninety-five theses on the door of the castle church at Wittenberg. In 1523, when his break with the church was complete, he wrote the preface for a new edition of Savonarola's exposition of the *Miserere*. In his preface, Luther hailed the friar as a precursor of Protestantism and a martyr of the Reformation, a man put to death "solely for having desired that someone should come to purify the slough of Rome." And in the memorial to Luther at Worms, Savonarola sits at the master's feet along with Wycliffe and Hus. But does he belong there? Was the friar a precursor of Protestantism or, in fact, of anything else? Exactly where ought we to place him?

Like Luther, Savonarola was a preacher of the millenium who combined religious fervor with the promise of earthly rewards. Like Luther, he declared that a pope could err, and emphasized the superior authority of scripture. Like Luther, he wished to summon a council and was excommunicated by the pope. But when the Imperial Diet at Worms called on Luther to recant, he replied that he could not and would not recant, for to go against his conscience was neither right nor safe, a reply that in the printed version became, "Here I stand, I can do no other." Savonarola, by contrast, seemed incapable of taking a firm stand on anything. Instead, as Machiavelli was quick to point out, he "adjusted himself to the times," attacking the pope one day and backtracking the next, calling for a law of appeal when it suited his political allies and making no effort to see that it was enforced when it didn't. And whereas the program of the Reformation was concrete and limited, the friar's program was vague and all-encompassing: a great hodgepodge of the natural and the supernatural that included, among other things, the moral reform of Italy, a more democratic government for Florence under the kingship of Jesus Christ, as well as wealth and glory for its citizens, the recovery of Pisa, a second invasion by Charles VIII, the reform of the church, and the advent of an angelic pope. Because Savonarola's program was so diffuse and because he was so unclear about where he stood, it has been possible for wildly disparate groups to claim him for their own and for wildly divergent opinions of what he stood for to gain acceptance.

During the third Florentine republic, which lasted from the expulsion of the Medici in 1527 to their return in 1530, the contemporary historian Benedetto Varchi wrote that "the belief revived, nay multiplied a thousandfold, that Fra Girolamo had been a saint and a prophet." When the troops of the Medici pope Clement VII and the emperor Charles V besieged the city, the people remembered Savonarola's prophecy that Florence would be scourged and then renovated. And Guicciardini attributed their obstinate resistance to "their faith that they cannot perish according to the prediction of Fra Girolamo of Ferrara."

During the nineteenth-century movement for the unification of Italy known as the Risorgimento, a group which called itself the New *Piagnoni* met in San Marco. Like their Renaissance forebears in 1527, the New *Piagnoni* believed that Savonarola had been a saint and a prophet, and they considered his teachings as valid for the Risorgimento as they had been for the second and third Florentine republics. Their contemporary, the Swiss historian Jacob Burckhardt, on the other hand, thought Savonarola "at bottom the most unsuitable man who could be found for the reorganization of the state....He stood in no more relation to mundane affairs and their actual conditions than any other inhabitant of a monastery."

Mussolini, beguiled no doubt by Savonarola's organization of the boys, is supposed to have considered him the first Fascist. In the 1950s a man by the name of Warman Welliver wrote an article in which he compared Savonarola to Senator Joseph McCarthy. Although the Italian Communist leader Antonio Gramsci believed that "it was the revolutionary class of the time, the Italian people and nation, the citizen democracy, which gave birth to Savonarola," he found the friar's program "abstract and cloudy compared with the realistic one of Machiavelli."

"Savonarola was the last ray of a past that was setting on the horizon; Machiavelli was the dawn, the forerunner of modern times," said the Italian literary critic Francesco De Sanctis. "One was the last of his kind of medieval man; the other, the first representative of modern man." To Savonarola's biographer Pasquale Villari, however, it was the friar who was the first modern man, "the first man of the fifteenth century to realize that the human race was palpitating with the throes of a new life....He endeavored to conciliate reason with faith, religion with liberty."

But are modern man and medieval man so very different, and does the past ever set on the horizon? Machiavelli did not seem to think so. "Human events ever resemble those of preceding times," he wrote in *The Discourses*. "This arises from the fact that they are produced by men who have been, and ever will be, animated by the same passions, and thus they must ever have the same results."

Almost 500 years after the death of Savonarola and over 200 years after the Enlightenment, fundamentalist preachers all over the world—the majority of them neither as sincere nor as lofty of soul as the friar, but all of them with the same mixture of religious fervor and worldly ambition, the same love of power—are exhorting their followers to turn their backs on the modern world. Taking their text now from the Book of Revelation, now from the Koran, now from the apocalyptic books of the Old Testament, they paint a picture of the final days every bit as lurid as the one with which Savonarola terrified the Florentines. Like him, they do not hesitate to impose their morality on others, to insist that their way is God's way. Like him, they do not hesitate to mix religion and politics. Like him, they are more concerned with the life hereafter than the life here on earth. Like him, they are harbingers of upheaval and dissension. Their revolt against history serves as a reminder that men and women have not changed as much as we would like to think since the days when Fra Girolamo inflamed all Italy from the pulpit of Santa Maria dei Fiore. In the words of D. H. Lawrence, the Apocalypse is "still a book to conjure with." Perhaps more so than *The Prince*.

NOTES

PROLOGUE

2. "Praise be to God": Ridolfi, *Life*, p. 288; *Vita*, vol. 2, p. 234, n. 6; Filipepi, *Cronica*, p. 507.

CHAPTER I

5. "Men were crazy": Landucci, *A Florentine Diary*, p. 49.

6. "Florence is full of all imaginable wealth": Rubinstein, *Beginnings*, p. 213.

11. "If the lowest orders": Gage, *Life in Italy*, p. 101.

12. "The wise and the well-to-do": Guicciardini, *Florence*, p. 2.

13. Rather than being governed: Burke, *Tradition and Renovation*, p. 268.

16. "*Quant'é bella giovenezza:* Rowden, *Lorenzo*, pp. 88–89.

19. "Whoso wants to do": Ross, *Lives*, p. 223.

21. After studying such matters: Guicciardini, *Ricordi*, p. 72.

22. To the church: Origo, *Merchant*, pp. 353–354; Staley, *The Guilds*, p. 195.

25. "I am yours, O Medici!": Moorehead, *The Villa Diana*, p. 47.

28. God, said Pico: Burckhardt, *The Civilization*, pp. 263–264.

31. And, continues this same biographer: Burlamacchi, *La vita*, p. 17.

CHAPTER II

32. "And since as the prophet Amos says": Weinstein, *Savonarola*, pp. 68–69.

34. In the sonnet *De Ruina Mundi:* Ibid., p. 79.

34. "Remaining in this uncertain state": Burlamacchi, op. cit., p. 8; Weinstein, op. cit., p. 81.

37. "In Ferrara I have often been told": Ridolfi, *Life*, p. 28.

37. In *De Ruina Ecclesia:* Lucas, *Fra Girolamo*, p. 8.

39. "People were in a mood": Landucci, op. cit., p. 37.

40. That Savonarola shared their anxiety: Ridolfi, *Life*, p. 18.

42. On this lovely little isle: Renan, *Histoire*, pp. 377–379.

44. In a sermon preached at Genoa: Reeves, *The Influence*, p. 354.

46. If he could always have: Savonarola, *Scelta di prediche e scritti*, p. 174; Villari, *Life*, p. 381.

46. He would later say: Lucas, op. cit., pp. 53–54; Klein, *Le Procès*, pp. 158–159.

46. He also criticized: Weinstein, op. cit., p. 96; Reeves, op. cit., p. 435, n. 3.

47. "The poor are oppressed": Villari, *Life*, p. 126.

50. The tyrant was wont to occupy the people: Lucas, op. cit., pp. 77–78; Villari, *Life*, p. 129.

57. "Everyone is terrified": Ridolfi, *Studi*, p. 263.

57. Although it seemed clear to Poliziano: Ross, op. cit., pp. 336–341; Ridolfi, *Studi*, pp. 265–267. The letters reproduced in these two works disprove the account of Lorenzo's meeting with Savonarola described in Villari, *Life*, Chapter 9.

CHAPTER III

61. "The prettiest thing": Ross, op. cit., p. 271.

61. Lorenzo feared: Ibid., p. 216.

61. "I owe you": Ibid., p. 221.

62. "The poor lad": Ibid., p. 273.

62. "They," said Lorenzo: Ibid., p. 264.

63. Even Lorenzo seemed troubled: Ady, *Lorenzo dei Medici*, p. 100; Picotti, *La giovinezza*, p. 44, n. 2.

63. If we believe Guicciardini: Nardi, *Istoria*, p. 22, n. 1.

65. "To pair people off": Guicciardini, *Florence*, p. 75.

66. To the French writer and diplomat: Philippe de Comines, *The History*, vol. 2, p. 107.

68. And he did not trust Ludovico: Ross, op. cit., p. 281.

68. In the letter of condolence: Picotti, op. cit., pp. 364–365, p. 390, n. 15.

70. The world was all depraved darkness: Villari, *Life*, p. 167; Lucas, op. cit., p. 95.

73. In his sermon the following morning: Ridolfi, *Life*, p. 56.

75. Spurred by his assurance: Burlamacchi, op. cit., pp. 41, 51.

76. To the end of Michelangelo's life: Condivi, *The Life*, p. 80.

77. "O Lord!" he cried that Advent: Villari, *Life*, p. 184.

78. The king understood so little: Desjardins, *Negociations*, vol. 1, pp. 234–244.

79. Neither Piero's *si*: Ibid., p. 347.

80. In the Piazza del Castello: Burckhardt, op. cit., p. 355.

82. Piero Capponi: Desjardins, op. cit., pp. 363–369, 392–394; Pitti, *Dell'istoria*, pp. 26–30; Delaborde, *L'Expédition*, pp. 354–355; Guicciardini, *Florence*, pp. 116, 119–120; Comines, op. cit., vol. 7, Chapter 5; Acciaiuoli, *Vita*, pp. 13–14.

84. Never had Ludovico: Ibid., p. 399.

85. Michelangelo: Condivi, op. cit., pp. 12–14.

88. In a letter to the Signoria: Desjardins, op. cit., vol. 1, pp. 587–588; Roscoe, *Leo the Tenth*, pp. 96–97.

88. The French who had asked: Ibid., p. 98; Delaborde, op. cit., p. 436.

89. "O Florence": Ridolfi, *Life*, p. 80; Villari, *Life*, p. 214.

92. Capponi's speech: Picotti, op. cit., p. 88; Gaddi, *Sulla cacciata*, p. 43 (but he attributes the speech to Tanai dei Nerli); Acciaiuoli, op. cit., p. 30.

92. As Capponi was walking home: Pitti, op. cit., p. 30.

CHAPTER IV

93. Rather than discuss: Weinstein, op. cit., p. 133; Parenti, *Storia fiorentina*, pp. 9–10.

95. To the contemporary historian Jacopo Nardi: Nardi, op. cit., pp. 31–32.

95. To Luca Landucci: Landucci, op. cit., p. 60.

95. Another chronicler: Filipepi, "Estratto," p. 455.

96. Piero Parenti: Nardi, op. cit., p. 32, n. 7.

101. Sensing the king's bewilderment: Comines, op. cit., vol. 2, p. 199.

102. The rebellion of Pisa: Ibid; Nardi, op. cit., pp. 28–29; Parenti, pp. 11–12.

106. "You may think": Landucci, op. cit., p. 65.

106. "Then too," said Guicciardini: Guicciardini, *Florence*, p. 99.

108. The cause of the revolutionaries: Weinstein, op. cit., p. 135.

110. When Domenico Bonsi: Nardi, op. cit., p. 39; Acciaiuoli, op. cit., pp. 31–32.

114. As a result of one of those sudden: Villari, *Life*, pp. 260–261; Ridolfi, *Life*, p. 91; Weinstein, op. cit., pp. 151–153.

115. December 14th sermon: Nardi, op. cit., pp. 47–48; Ridolfi, *Life*, pp. 91–92; Savonarola, *Scelta di prediche*, pp. 75–87; Weinstein, op. cit., pp. 155–156; Villari, *Life*, pp. 85–86, 261–264.

116. "What I told you yesterday in my sermon": Weinstein, op. cit., p. 156, n. 51.

117. Like Jesus, on whom: Ridolfi, *Life*, pp. 103–105; Savonarola, *Scelta di prediche*, pp. 87–102; Klein, op. cit., pp. 121–124.

119. "And this new head": Ridolfi, *Life*, pp. 94–95.

122. "You may know in your sorrows": Savonarola, *Scelta di prediche*, pp. 111–127; Villari, *Life*, pp. 331–334.

123. "This wretched friar": Landucci, op. cit., p. 80.

126. The *tiepidi:* Savonarola, *Scelta di prediche*, pp. 154–159.

128. In a letter: Gherardi, *Nuovi documenti*, p. 128.

130. Although this led Piero Parenti: Parenti, op. cit., p. 67.

CHAPTER V

136. "Italy ought to be left to the Italians": Woodward, *Cesare Borgia*, pp. 70–71; Negri, *Le missione*, p. 34.

138. Nor was the church his only target: Perrens, vol. 1, p. 158, n. 2; Savonarola, *Scelta di prediche*, pp. 164–170.

138. "To our well-beloved son": Villari, *Life*, p. 376.

140. In his farewell sermon on July 28: Ridolfi, *Life*, pp. 134–135; Savonarola, *Scelta di prediche*, pp. 170–178.

142. In a letter which he wrote: Ridolfi, *Lettere*, pp. 58–61.

143. In a letter which he sent the pope: Lucas, op. cit., pp. 186–187; Ridolfi, *Life*, pp. 138–139.

144. In the friar's sermon on October 11: Ridolfi, *Life*, pp. 139–140.

145. "Holy Father": Lucas, op. cit., p. 197; Ridolfi, *Life*, p. 148; Gherardi, op. cit., pp. 129–132.

146. So inveterate and ancient a custom: Nardi, op. cit., pp. 79–80.

147. Every street corner: Lungo, "Fra Girolamo Savanarola," p. 8.

147. On February 7: Landucci, op. cit., p. 101.

150. For this, his first sermon: Savonarola, *Scelta di prediche*, pp. 186–203; Ridolfi, XXX, pp. 153–154.

152. Two epigraphs: Nardi, op. cit., p. 72; Landucci, op. cit., p. 103; Oliphant, *Makers of Florence*, p. 345.

153. He chose as his text: Savonarola, *Scelta di prediche*, pp. 209–215.

153. "The Lord threatens Rome": Ibid., pp. 215–222.

154. "O you unbelieving ones": Ibid., pp. 222–228; Villari, *Life*, p. 412.

156. "Woe to the city": Trexler, *Public Life*, p. 481.

156. The complaint now was not of Fra Girolamo: Gherardi, op. cit., pp. 140–142.

157. "O Lord," he cried: Villari, *Life*, p. 419.

164. He went considerably further, however: Lucas, op. cit., pp. 212–213; Villari, *Life*, pp. 465–467; Ridolfi, *Life*, pp. 175–176.

165. "First laughter, now tears": Weinstein, op. cit., pp. 279–280.

CHAPTER VI

167. During the five and a half years: Guicciardini, *Florence*, p. 147; Klein, op. cit., p. 276; Villari, *Storia*, vol. 2, p. cclviii.

170. "Until then," said one chronicler: Parenti, op. cit., p. 155.

171. On January 17: Ridolfi, *Vita*, vol. 2, p. 178, n. 21; Parenti, op. cit., p. 157; Nerli, op. cit., p. 74.

174. But when a Venetian merchant: Burlamacchi, op. cit., p. 131.

175. "Should anyone regard this": Villari, *Life*, p. 490, n. 1.

175. Savonarola's sermon on Ash Wednesday: Savonarola, *Prediche sopra Ezechiele*, vol. 1, pp. 249–252.

177. "Florence, I have told you many things": Ibid., pp. 288–290.

179. "Come here thou ribald church": Villari, *Life*, pp. 517–518; Ridolfi, *Life*, p. 185.

180. On March 7 he sent a confidential letter: Lucas, op. cit., p. 225; Capelli, "Fra Girolamo Savonarola," #108 p. 375; Savonarola, *Le Lettere*, p. 118.

180. He was not alone: Ridolfi, *Life*, p. 188.

180. Bracci's meeting with the pope: Gherardi, op. cit., pp. 149–153.

184. "Because," said Guicciardini: Guicciardini, *Florence*, p. 130.

185. "Because," said Nardi: Nardi, op. cit., p. 98.

187. As the text for his sermon: Ferrara, pp. 321–329.

187. Reactions to the dropping of the alms box: Landucci, op. cit., p. 119; Parenti, pp. 185–186; Villari, *Storia*, vol. 2, p. xxxvii.

188. Virtually beside himself with rage: Guicciardini, op. cit., p. 126.

189. To Paolo Somenzi: Lungo, op. cit., pp. 18–19.

CHAPTER VII

191. To Piero Parenti: Parenti, op. cit., p. 189.

194. The papal brief: Nardi, op. cit., pp. 103–104.

194. The "Epistle against Surreptitious Excommunication,": Savonarola, *Le Lettere*, pp. 141–145; Lucas, op. cit., pp. 236–239.

195. God would not suffer: Savonarola, *Le Lettere*, p. 131.

196. Upon learning that his son: Burchard, *At The Court*, p. 147.

196. "No longer can we tolerate": Bedoyere, *The Meddlesome Friar*, p. 25.

197. Savonarola's letter to the pope: Lucas, op. cit., pp. 259–260; Villari, *Life*, p. 551.

199. "Because the pope refused to absolve Fra Girolamo": Parenti, op. cit., p. 201.

201. They saw nothing: Savonarola, *Le Lettere*, pp. 154–155.

201. "Our persecutions do not": Ibid., pp. 156–157.

202. The words "Thou art Peter": Villari, *Life*, p. 592.

205. Descriptions of those arrested: Guicciardini, *Florence*, pp. 130–131; Pitti, op. cit., pp. 42–50; Cerretani, *Storia fiorentina*, pp. 47–50; Nardi, op. cit., pp. 106–107; Parenti, op. cit., pp. 206–207.

208. "In the matter of the five citizens": Villari, *Storia*, vol. 2, pp. clxxxix–cxc.

208. He advised his friend: Savonarola, *Le Lettere*, pp. 178–179; Ridolfi, *Life*, pp. 210–211.

210. But he consoled himself with the thought: Landucci, op. cit., pp. 125–126.

210. In *The Discourses* Machiavelli wrote: Machiavelli, *Discourses*, p. 230.

210. Guicciardini too thought: Guicciardini, *Italy*, p. 126.

212. Savonarola's letter to the pope: Lucas, op. cit., pp. 267–268; Ridolfi, *Life*, p. 212.

213. Machiavelli's description of the procession: Tommasini, *La vita*, p. 162.

214. Luca Landucci, who had always: Landucci, op. cit., p. 129.

214. On February 1: Capelli, op. cit., p. 398.

214. He would later say: Villari, *Storia*, vol. 2, p. clxiii.

Chapter VIII

216. Comments on the friar's return to the pulpit: Guicciardini, *Florence*, p. 136; Nardi, op. cit., p. 112; Parenti, op. cit., p. 227.

217. The friar's first sermon: Savonarola, *Esodo*, vol. 1, pp. 1–36; Lucas, op. cit., pp. 272–279.

218. And here, wrote Lorenzo Violi: Lucas, op. cit., p. 277; Savonarola, *Esodo*, vol. 1, p. 29.

220. The meetings of Bracci and Bonsi with the pope: Gherardi, op. cit., pp. 177–182; Marchese, *Lettere inedite*, p. 170.

222. "We await the outcome": Capelli, op. cit., p. 399.

222. What was needed: Perrens, *Jerome Savonarole*, vol. 1, p. 492.

222. "O Lord I would": Lucas, op. cit., pp. 283–284; Savonarola, *Esodo*, vol. 1, pp. 95–96.

223. The *Compagnacci*: Cerretani, op. cit., pp. 54–56; Filipepi, op. cit., p. 480. Exactly when the *Compagnacci* first appeared is difficult to determine. Many writers assume that they were responsible for the Ascension Day riot. One reason for believing that they weren't is that none of the contemporary descriptions mention Doffo Spini. Moreover, Cerretani's account of the origin of the group, which is the most complete, comes immediately after the announcement of Domenico Bonsi's appointment as ambassador to Rome, which occurred at the end of 1497. Another reason for believing that the *Compagnacci* did

not exist until the end of 1497 is that Luca Landucci does not mention them until after that.

225. "Citizens of Florence": Oliphant, op. cit., p. 319; Villari, *Life*, p. 608.

225. In fact Parenti tells us: Parenti, op. cit., pp. 231–232.

226. The vanguard of the procession: Filipepi, op. cit., pp. 486–488; Parenti, op. cit., p. 232; Burlamacchi, op. cit., pp. 135–136; Tommasini, op. cit., p. 162; Landucci, op. cit., p. 132.

227. "O clergy, clergy": Ridolfi, *Life*, p. 223.

228. "If Fra Girolamo will prove": Gherardi, op. cit., pp. 183–184.

228. "Briefs have come from Rome": Ridolfi, *Life*, p. 223; Savonarola, *Esodo*, p. 144.

230. Savonarola's sermons on March 2 and 3: Savonarola, *Esodo*, vol. 1, pp. 146–203.

230. Machiavelli's letter to Ricciardo Becchi: Machiavelli, *Lettere*, pp. 21–25.

231. The letter which the Signoria: Gherardi, op. cit., pp. 187–188; Villari, *Storia*, vol. 2, p. liv; Marchese, op. cit., pp. 165–167.

232. Savonarola's letter to the pope: Ridolfi, *Life*, p. 226; *Vita*, vol. 2, p. 202, n. 34–35; *Studi*, pp. 193–194.

232. "Tell me Florence": Ridolfi, *Life*, p. 232.

234. The *pratica*: Lupi, *Nuovi documenti*, pp. 33–53; Villari, *Life*, pp. 629–635; Lucas, op. cit., pp. 308–316.

235. So uneasy was he: Savonarola, *Esodo*, vol. 2, pp. 247–248.

236. Savonarola's sermon to the women: Savonarola, *Esodo*, vol. 2, pp. 254–288; Perrens, op. cit., vol. 2, pp. 404–408; Klein, op. cit., pp. 64–69.

236. In his sermon the next morning: Savonarola, *Esodo*, vol. 2, pp. 291–329.

237. And, Paolo Somenzi told Ludovico: Lungo, op. cit., pp. 29–30.

238. In fact, said Guicciardini: Guicciardini, *Florence*, p. 137.

238. The moment of vengeance was come: Villari, *Life*, pp. 644–647.

CHAPTER IX

240. Fra Domenico Buonavinci da Pescia: Ridolfi, *Life*, p. 149; Lungo, op. cit., p. 30; Villari, *Storia*, vol. 2, p. cclix; Cerretani, p. 57; Burlamacchi, pp. 140–141.

242. In his sermon of March 27: Landucci, op. cit., p. 133; Villari, *Life*, p. 652, n. 2; *Storia*, vol. 2, pp. lxxi–lxxi; Marchese, op. cit., pp. 176–177.

242. It was astounding: Gherardi, p. 216.

242. He deeply regretted: Villari, *Storia*, pp. clxxii–clxxiii.

242. Those who guided: Violi, *La sesta giornata*, p. lxxiij.

246. To put an end: Ridolfi, *Due Documenti*, pp. 236–237; Burlamacchi, pp. 145–146; Villari, *Life*, p. 661.

246. That Savonarola shrank: Eliot, *Romola*, p. 536.

247. The day after he wrote his apology: Landucci, op. cit., p. 134.

248. Burlamacchi says: Burlamacchi, "Storia della controversia," p. 144.

251. All that week: Conti, "Storia della controversia," p. 372.

251. That morning great crowds of the faithful: Ridolfi, *Life*, p. 241; Burlamacchi, op. cit., p. 148.

253. One Franciscan chronicler: Conti, op. cit., p. 374.

253. Simone Filipepi: Filipepi, op. cit., pp. 482–483.

254. To Luca Landucci: Landucci, op. cit., p. 136.

255. The air seemed filled with demons: Conti, op. cit., p. 375.

255. Not only Fra Girolamo's opponents: Nardi, op. cit., p. 121.

256. He was prepared: Ridolfi, *Life*, pp. 244–245.

256. What Luca Landucci describes: Landucci, op. cit., p. 136.

258. Like Luca Landucci: Landucci, op. cit., p. 137.

259. Many people believed: Guicciardini, *Florence*, p. 141.

259. But Machiavelli: Machiavelli, *Collected Works*, vol. 3, p. 1438.

260. At one point Fra Silvestro: Villari, *Storia*, vol. 2, p. ccxxvj.

262. When the anxiety: Ibid. p. ccxliii.

262. Open the door: Burlamacchi, op. cit., pp. 158–160; Klein, op. cit., pp. 110–111.

264. The crowd in the piazza: Fra Benedetto, *Cedrus*, pp. 88–89.

265. To Paolo Somenzi: Villari, *Storia*, vol. 2, p. xcviij.

CHAPTER X

266. Although by then weapons had been laid aside: Landucci, op. cit., p. 138.

268. At five o'clock: Ibid. p. 138.

268. Savonarola's interrogation: Ridolfi, *Processi*, pp. 6, 36; Landucci, op. cit., p. 138; Burlamacchi, op. cit., p. 166; Villari, *Storia*, vol. 2, p. xcix.

269. Whether he was a prophet: Violi, p. cxviij; Klein, p. 235; Ridolfi, *Processi*, p. 28, n. 1.

269. Between April 11 and April 17: Villari, *Storia*, vol. 2, op. cit., p. cxlix; Klein, op. cit., p. 233.

271. Although, said Guicciardini, there were a number of important points: Guicciardini, *Florence*, pp. 143–144.

271. For three days after hearing the confession read aloud: Fra Benedetto, *Cedrus*, pp. 90–91.

272. But the Signoria did not find it consonant: Guicciardini, *Florence*, p. 144.

273. And having said things: Villari, *Storia*, vol. 2, p. clxxxiv.

273. Domenico's confession: Villari, *Life*, pp. 714–723; *Storia*, vol. 2, p. ccxv; Ridolfi, *Life*, p. 256.

274. Fra Silvestro: Ridolfi, op. cit.; Villari, *Storia*,, vol. 2, pp. ccxx–ccxxxj.

275. On April 27 Luca Landucci: Landucci, op. cit., p. 140.

276. The commentary on the *Miserere*: Ridolfi, *Life*, pp. 260–261; Savonarola, *Scelta di prediche*,, pp. 383–393; Ferrara, *Savonarola*, pp. 395–415; Villari, *Life*, pp. 734–736.

277. *In Te Domine Speravi*: Ibid., pp. 736–739; Klein, pp. 304–311; Ridolfi, *Life*, pp. 261–262; Savonarola, *Scelta di prediche*, pp. 390–393; Ferrara, *Savonarola*, pp. 416–437; Goukowski, "Response," pp. 222–227.

280. Savonarola's testimony: Villari, *Storia*, vol. 2, pp. cxcij–cxcvij.

282. At a *pratica* convened a few days earlier: Burlamacchi, op. cit., pp. 173–174.

283. Because many feared to see their country ruined: Machiavelli, *Collected Works*, vol. 3, p. 1448.

285. In essence this prayer: Burlamacchi, op. cit., p. 180; Ridolfi, *Life*, pp. 268–269.

287. As he felt the executioner's hand: Landucci, op. cit., p. 143: Burlamacchi, op. cit., p. 183.

EPILOGUE

289. The filthiest place: Comines, op. cit., vol. 2, p. 357.

291. When the city heard: Landucci, op. cit., p. 161.

292. He had never seen or heard: Filipepi, op. cit., p. 498.

292. They did this because: Landucci, op. cit., p. 153, n. 1.

292. for, said Jacopo Nardi: Nardi, op. cit., pp. 131–132.

295. He remained in Florence: Machiavelli, *Letters*, pp. 100–101.

296. It was the purity: Machiavelli, *Discourses*, p. 149.

296. "Thus it comes about": Machiavelli, *The Prince*, p. 22.

296. Like Moses: Machiavelli, *Discourses*, p. 499.

297. There is, for example: Ibid., p. 230.

297. There is also the passage in *The Prince:* Machiavelli, *The Prince*, p. 45.

297. Florence was a magnet: Machiavelli, *Letters*, p. 147.

297. "I should like to find one": Ibid., p. 198.

297. "So great a man": Machiavelli, *Discourses*, p. 149.

298. "the evil example of the court of Rome": Ibid., p. 151.

298. In his preface: Villari, *Life*, p. 740.

299. When the troops of the Medici pope: Roth, *The Last Florentine Republic*, pp. 210, 299.

299. And Guicciardini attributed: Guicciardini, *Maxims*, pp. 39–40.

299. Their contemporary, the Swiss historian: Burckhardt, *Civilization of the Renaissance*, p. 358.

299. Although the Italian Communist leader Antonio Gramsci: Gramsci, *The Modern Prince*, pp. 142, 163.

300. "Savonarola was the last ray": Garin, *Portraits*, Chapter 8.

300. To Savonarola's biographer: Villari, *Life*, p. 770.

300. "Human events ever resemble": Machiavelli, *Discourses*, p. 530.

300. The Apocalypse is: Lawrence, *Apocalypse*, p. 121.

BIBLIOGRAPHY

Acciaiuoli, Vincenzo: "Vita di Piero di Gino Capponi," *Archivio storico italiano*, vol. 12, part 2, 1853, pp. 13–40.

Acton, Harold: *The Pazzi Conspiracy*, Thames & Hudson, London, 1979.

Ady, Cecilia M.: *Lorenzo dei Medici and Renaissance Italy*, Collier Books, New York, 1955.

Armstrong, Edward: *Lorenzo de'Medici and Florence in the Fifteenth Century*, Putnam, New York, 1923.

Bedoyere, Michael de la: *The Meddlesome Friar and the Wayward Pope*, Hanover House, New York, 1958.

Benedetto da Firenze: "Cedrus Libani," *Archivio storico italiano*, Appendix, vol. 7, 1849, pp. 41 ff.

————: *Vulnera Diligentis*, Villari *Storia*, vol. 1, pp. lxxxiv ff.; vol. 2, pp. lxxxiii ff.

Berti, Luciano: *Florence: The City and Its Art*, Florence, Saverio Becocci, 1979.

Biagi, Guido: *Private Life of the Renaissance Florentines*, R. Bemporad & Sons, Florence, 1896.

Bisticci, Vespasiano da: *Renaissance Princes, Popes and Prelates*, Harper & Row, New York, 1963.

Brucker, Gene A.: "The Ciompi Revolution," in Nicolai Rubinstein (ed.), *Florentine Studies*, Northwestern University Press, Evanston, Ill., 1968, pp. 314–357.

Burchard, Johann: *At the Court of the Borgia*, Geoffrey Parker (trans.), Folio Society, London, 1963.

Burckhardt, Jacob: *The Civilization of the Renaissance in Italy*, Modern Library, New York, 1954.

Burke, Peter: *Tradition and Renovation in Renaissance Italy*, Great Britain: Fontana/Collins, 1974.

Burlamacchi, Fra Pacifico: *La vita del beato Ieronimo Savonarola. scritta da un anonimo del secolo XVI e già attribuita a fra Pacifico Burlamacchi*, Leonardo S. Olschki, Florence, 1937.

Calogero, Cassandra: *Gli avversari religiosi di Girolamo Savonarola*, Editrice Studium, Rome, 1935.

Capelli, Antonio: "Fra Girolamo Savonarola e notizie intorno il suo tempo," *Atti e memorie delle RR deputazioni di storia patria per le provincie modenesi e parmensi*, vol. 4, 1869, pp. 301–406.

Cartwright, Julia: *Beatrice d'Este*, E. P. Dutton, New York, 1899.

Cassuto, Umberto: *Gli Ebrei a Firenzi nell'età del Rinascimento*, Leonardo S. Olschki, Florence, 1955.

Cerretani, Bartolomeo: *Storia fiorentina*, in Joseph Schnitzer (ed.), *Quellen und Forschungen zur Geschichte Savonarolas*, vol. 3, Munich, 1904.

Chastel, André: "L'Antéchrist a la Renaissance," in *Cristianesimo e ragione di stato. L'umanesimo e il demoniaco nell'arte*, Atti dell'II congresso internazionale di studi umanistici a cura de Enrico Castelli Roma, Fratelli Bocca, 1953, pp. 177–186.

————: "L'Apocalypse en 1500. La Fresque de l'Antéchrist à la Chapelle Saint–Brice d'Orvieto," *Bibliothéque d'Humanisme et Renaissance*, vol. 14, 1952, pp. 124–140.

————: "Le Bucher des Vanités," *Cahiers du Sud*, vol. 44, no. 338, 1956, pp. 63–70.

Cinozzi, Fra Placido: "Epistola di fra Placido Cinozzi…" in P. Villari and E. Casanova, *Scelta di prediche e scritti di fra Girolamo Savonarola con nuovi documenti intorno alla sua vita*, Sansoni, Florence, 1898, pp. 3 ff.

Cohn, Norman: *The Pursuit of the Millennium*, rev. ed., Oxford University Press, New York, 1970.

Comines, Philippe de: *The History of Comines*, Thomas Danett Anno (trans. 1596), AMS Press, New York, 1967.

Condivi, Ascanio: *The Life of Michelangelo Buonarroti*, Herbert B. Horne (trans.), Marymount Press, Boston, 1904.

Conti, Augusto: "Storia della controversia di Girolamo Savonarola coi frati minori," *Archivio storico italiano*, vol. 13, part 1, 1871, pp. 367–375.

Dei, Benedetto: "Cronica fiorentina: descrizione della citta di Firenze," in Giuseppina Carla Romby (ed.), *Descrizione e rappresentazioni della città di Firenze nel XV secolo,* Libreria Editrice Fiorentina, Florence, 1976, Appendix 1, pp. 41–45.

Delaborde, Henri François: *L'Expédition de Charles VIII en Italie,* Librairie de Firmin Didot, Paris, 1888.

De l'Epinois, Henri: "Le Pape Alexandre VI," *Revue des questions historiques,* vol. 30, 1881, pp. 526–548.

Desjardins, Abel: *Négociations diplomatiques de la France avec la Toscane,* Imprimerie Imperiale, Paris, 1859.

Dorez, L.: "La Mort de Pic de la Mirandole," *Giornale storico della letteratura italiana,* vol. 32, 1898, pp. 360–364.

Durant, Will: *The Reformation,* in *The Story of Civilization,* vol. 6, Simon & Schuster, New York, 1957.

————: *The Renaissance,* in *The Story of Civilization,* vol. 5, Simon & Schuster, New York, 1953.

Eliot, George: *Romola,* A. L. Burt & Co., n.p., n.d.

Erlanger, Rachel: *Lucrezia Borgia,* Hawthorn, New York, 1978.

Ferrara, Mario: *Savonarola. Prediche e scritti commentate e collegate da un racconto biografico,* vol. 1, Leonardo S. Olschki, Florence, 1952.

Filipepi, Simone: "Estratto della cronica novamente scoperto nell'archivio vaticano. (Archivio segr. vaticano politicorum XLVII f338 e seg.)," in P. Villari and E. Casanova, *Scelta di prediche e scritti di Fra Girolamo Savonarola con nuovi documenti intorno alla sua vita,* Sansoni, Florence, 1898.

Frati, Ludovico: "La morte di Lorenzo de'Medici e il suicidio di Pier Leoni," *Archivio storico italiano,* 1889, pp. 255–260.

Gaddi, Agnolo, and Francesco: "Sulla cacciata di Piero de'Medici e la venuta di Carlo VIII in Firenze," *Archivio storico italiano,* vol. 12, part 2, 1853, pp. 41–48.

Gage, John: *Life in Italy at the Time of the Medici,* Putnam, New York, 1968.

Garin, Eugenio: *Portraits from the Quattrocento,* Harper & Row, New York, 1963.

Gautier–Vignal, L.: *Pic de la Mirandole,* Editions Bernard Grasset, Paris, 1927.

Gherardi, Alessandro: *Nuovi documenti e studi intorno a Girolamo Savonarola,* G. C. Sansoni, Florence, 1887.

Goldthwaite, Richard: *The Building of Renaissance Florence,* Johns Hopkins University Press, Baltimore, 1980.

Goukowski, M.: "Réponse à M. Robert Klein," *Bibliothèque d'Humanisme et de la Renaissance*, vol. 25, 1963, pp. 222–227.

Gramsci, Antonio: *The Modern Prince and Other Writings*, Lawrence and Wishart, London, 1957.

Guicciardini, Francesco: *The History of Florence*, Mario Domandi (ed. and trans.), Harper & Row, New York, 1970.

————: *The History of Italy*, Sidney Alexander (ed. and trans.), Collier, New York, 1969.

————: *Maxims and Reflections of a Renaissance Statesman*, (*Ricordi*), Harper & Row, New York, 1965.

Hale, J. R.: *Florence and the Medici*, Thames and Hudson, London, 1977.

Hibbert, Christopher: *The House of Medici: Its Rise and Fall*, Wm. Morrow, New York, 1975.

Klein, Robert: *Le Procès de Savonarole*, Le Club du Meilleur Livre, n.p., 1957.

Landucci, Luca: *A Florentine Diary from 1450 to 1516 (continued by an anonymous writer until 1542, with notes by Iodoco del Badia)*, Alice de Rosen Jervis (trans.), Books for Libraries Press, Freeport, N.Y., 1927.

La Torre, Ferdinando: *Del conclave di Alessandro VI Papa Borgia*, Leonardo S. Olschki, Rome, 1933.

Lawrence, D. H.: *Apocalypse*, Penguin/Heinemann, London, 1974.

Lucas, Herbert: *Fra Girolamo Savonarola*, Sands, London, 1906.

Lungo, Isidoro del: "Fra Girolamo Savonarola," *Archivio storico italiano*, vol. 18, part 2, 1863, pp. 3–45.

Lupi, C.: "Nuovi documenti intorno a fra Girolamo Savonarola," *Archivio storico italiano*, vol. 3, part 1, 1866, pp. 3–77.

McCarthy, Mary: *The Stones of Florence*, Harcourt Brace Jovanovich, New York, 1963.

Machiavelli, Niccolò: *Chief Works and Others*, vol. 3, Allen Gilbert (trans.), Duke University Press, Durham, N.C., 1965.

————: *History of Florence and the Affairs of Italy from the Earliest Times to the Death of Lorenzo the Magnificent*, Harper & Row, New York, 1960.

————: *Lettere di Niccolò Machiavelli a cura di Giuseppe Lesca*, Bompiani, Milan, 1945.

————: *Machiavelli: A Selection of His Letters*, Allen Gilbert (trans.), Capricorn, New York, 1961.

Maguire, Yvonne: *Women of the Medici*, Routledge, London, 1927.

Marchese, Vincenzo: "Lettere inedite di fra Girolamo Savonarola e documenti concernente lo stesso," *Archivio storico italiano*, Appendix, vol. 8, 1850, pp. 75–203.

Marks, Louis F.: "The Financial Oligarchy in Florence under Lorenzo," in E. F. Jacob (ed.), *Italian Renaissance Studies*, Telegraph Books, Norwood, Penn., 1960.

Mayor, A. Hyatt: "Renaissance Pamphleteers, Savonarola and Luther," *Metropolitan Museum of Art Bulletin*, October 1947, pp. 66–72.

Moorehead, Alan: *The Villa Diana*, Hamish Hamilton, London, 1951.

Nardi, Jacopo de: *Istoria della città di Firenze*, vol. 1, Le Monnier, Florence, 1858.

Negri, P.: "Le missione di Pandolfo Collenuccio a Papa Alessandro VI," *Archivio della Società romana di storia patria*, 1910, pp. 333–439.

Nerli, Filippo de: *Commentari dei fatti civili occorsi dentro la città di Firenze dall'anno 1215 al 1537*, Coen, Trieste, 1859.

Niccolini, G.: "Tre lettere di Girolamo Savonarola e una di fra Domenico da Pescia sull'unione dei conventi," *Archivio storico italiano*, 1897, pp. 116–125.

Nulli, Siro Attilio: *Ludovico il Moro*, Casa Editrice Ambrosiana, Milan.

Oliphant, Margaret: *The Makers of Florence*, Macmillan, New York, 1888.

Origo, Iris: *The Merchant of Prato*, Knopf, New York, 1957.

———: *The World of San Bernardino*, Jonathan Cape, London, 1963.

Parenti, Piero: *Storia fiorentina*, in Joseph Schnitzer (ed.), *Quellen und Forschungen zur Geschichte Savonarolas*, vol. 4, V. von Duncker & Humbolt, Leipzig, 1910.

Pastor, Ludwig: *The History of the Popes*, 5th ed., vols. 5 and 6, Routledge & Kegan Paul, London, 1950.

Perrens, F. T.: *Jerome Savonarole. sa vie, ses prédictions, ses ecrits*, 2 vols., Hachette, Paris, 1853.

Picotti, G. B.: *La giovinezza di Leone X*, Ulrico Hoepli, Milan, 1917.

Pieraccini, Gaetano: *La stirpe del Medici di Caffagaivolo*, vol. 1, Valecchi, Florence, 1924.

Pitti, Jacopo: "Dell'istoria fiorentina di Jacopo Pitti sino al 1529," *Archivio storico italiano*, 1842, pp. 1–309.

Randi, Luigi: "Fra Girolamo Savonarola guidicato da Piero Vagliente cronista fiorentino," *Rivista delle biblioteche*, 1893, pp. 49–63.

Reeves, Marjorie: *The Influence of Prophecy in the Later Middle Ages: A Study of Joachism,* Oxford University Press, London, 1969.

Renan, Ernest: *Histoire des origines du Christianisme,* vol. 4: *L'Antéchrist,* M. Levy Frères, Paris, pp. 1863–1883.

Ridolfi, Roberto: "Due documenti sopra la prova del fuoco," *La bibliofilia,* vol. 38, 1936, pp. 234–242.

————: "I Processi del Savonarola," *La bibliofilia,* vol. 46, 1944, pp. 3–41.

————: *The Life of Niccolò Machiavelli,* Cecil Grayson (trans.), University of California Press, Berkeley, 1963.

————: *The Life of Girolamo Savonarola,* Cecil Grayson (trans.), Knopf, New York, 1959.

————: *Studi savonaroliani,* Leonardo S. Olschki, Florence, 1935.

————: *Vita di Girolamo Savonarola,* Angelo Belardetti, Rome, 1952.

Roover, Richard de: *The Rise and Decline of the Medici Bank,* Harvard University Press, Cambridge, 1963.

Roscoe, William: *The Life and Pontificate of Leo the Tenth,* George Bell and Sons, London, 1888.

————: *The Life of Lorenzo de'Medici Called the Magnificent,* Henry G. Bohn, London, 1851.

Ross, Janet: *Lives of the Early Medici As Told in Their Correspondence,* Chatto and Windus, London, 1910.

Roth, Cecil: *The Last Florentine Republic,* Methuen, London, 1925.

Rowden, Maurice: *Lorenzo the Magnificent,* Weidenfeld and Nicolson, London, 1974.

Rubinstein, Nicolai: "Beginnings of Political Thought in Florence," *Warburg Institute Journal,* vol. 5, 1942, pp. 199–227.

————: *Florentine Studies,* Northwestern University Press, Evanston, Ill., 1968.

————: *The Government of Florence under the Medici, 1434–1494,* Clarendon, Oxford, 1966.

————: "Politics and Constitution in Florence at the End of the Fifteenth Century," in E. F. Jacob (ed.), *Italian Renaissance Studies,* Telegraph Books, Norwood, Penn., 1960.

Sachar, Abram Leon: *A History of the Jews,* 5th ed., Knopf, New York, 1964.

Salter, F. R.: "The Jews in 15th Century Florence and Savonarola's Establishment of a *Mons Pietatis,*" *Cambridge Historical Journal,* vol. 5, 1936, pp. 193–211.

Sanuto, Marino: *I Diarii*, vol. 1, V. Stefani, Venice, 1879.

Savonarola, Girolamo: *Le lettere di Girolamo Savonarola ora per la prima volta raccolte e a miglior lezione ridotte da Roberto Ridolfi*, Leonardo S. Olschki, Florence, 1933.

————: *Collected Works*, vols. 1 and 2: *Prediche sopra Ezechiele a cura di Roberto Ridolfi*, vols. 3 and 4: *Prediche sopra l'Esodo a cura di Pier Giorgi Ricci*, Angelo Belardetti, Rome, 1955–1956.

————: *Prediche e scritti commentati e collegati da un racconto biografico*, vol. 1, Mario Ferrara (ed.), Leonardo S. Olschki, Florence, 1952.

————: *Scelta di prediche e scritti di fra Girolamo Savonarola con nuovi documenti intorno alla sua vita*, P. Villari and E. Casanova (eds.), G. C. Sansoni, Florence, 1898.

————: "Sermons, poèmes et textes inédits présentés et traduits par Robert Klein et Georges Mounin," *Cahiers du Sud*, vol. 44, 1956, pp. 18–29, 43–62.

Schevill, Ferdinand: *Medieval and Renaissance Florence*, 2 vols., Harper & Row, New York, 1961.

Schnitzer, Joseph: *Savonarola*, 2 vols., Ernesto Rutili (trans. from the German), Treves, Milan, 1931.

Seligmann, Kurt: *The History of Magic*, Pantheon, New York, 1948.

Soranzo, Giovanni: *Il tempo di Alessandro VI Papa e di fra Girolamo Savonarola*, Societa Editrice Vita e Pensiero, Milan, 1960.

Spini, Giorgio: "Introduzione al Savonarola," *Belfagor*, July 1948, pp. 414–428.

Staley, Edgcumbe: *The Guilds of Florence*, Benjamin Blom, New York, 1967.

Steinberg, Roland M.: *Fra Girolamo Savonarola, Florentine Art and Renaissance Historiography*, Athens University Press, Athens, Ohio, 1977.

Symonds, John Addington: *Renaissance in Italy*, vol. 2, Modern Library, New York, 1935.

Tommasini, Oreste: *La vita e gli scritti di Niccolò Machiavelli*, vol. 1, Ermanno Loescher, Rome, 1883.

Trexler, Ricard C.: *Public Life in Renaissance Florence*, Academic Press, New York, 1980.

Villari, Pasquale: *The Life and Times of Girolamo Savonarola*, Linda Villari (trans.), Fisher and Unwin, London, 1899.

————: *La storia di Girolamo Savonarola e di suoi tempi. narrata da P. Villari con l'aiuto di nuovi documenti*, 2 vols., Successori Le Monnier, Florence, 1910.

—— and E. Casanova (eds.): *Scelta di prediche e scritti di fra Girolamo Savonarola con nuovi documenti intorno alla sua vita*, G. C. Sansoni, Florence, 1898.

Violi, Lorenzo: "La sesta giornata," in Villari, *La storia de Girolamo Savonarola...*, op. cit., vol. 2, doc. xxi, pp. cviij–cxxxj.

Weinstein, Donald: *Savonarola and Florence. Prophecy and Patriotism in the Renaissance*, Princeton University Press, Princeton, 1970.

Welliver, Warman: "La demagogia del Savonarola," *Il Ponte*, vol. 12, 1956, pp. 1197–1201.

Wilde, J.: "The Hall of the Great Council of Florence," *Warburg Institute Journal*, vol. 7, no. 3, 1944, pp. 65–74.

Woodward, William H.: *Cesare Borgia*, Chapman and Hall, London, 1913.

Yates, Frances: *Giordano Bruno and the Hermetic Tradition*, Vintage, New York, 1964.

GLOSSARY

Accoppiatori
Officials who placed the names of those citizens considered eligible for office in the appropriate purses or *borse*. Following the overthrow of the Medici in November 1494, twenty *Accoppiatori* were named to purge the eligibility lists of Medici sympathizers. During the year it was expected to take for the *Accoppiatori* to complete their task, they would handpick the Signoria. However, pressure from the people and from Savonarola forced the *Accoppiatori* to resign long before the year was up.

Alberghettino
The small room in the upper reaches of the tower of the Palazzo della Signoria in which Savonarola was imprisoned after his arrest.

Arrabbiati
A political faction opposed to Savonarola.

balià
The word *balià* means "extraordinary powers." In Florence a *balià* was a commission set up to deal with a crisis. Usually, the commission existed only a short time. During that time it was not bound by constitutionally defined procedures.

Bargello
The palace in which the bargello, or sheriff, resided. In Savonarola's time the Palace of the Bargello was at the beginning of Via Gondi adjoining the Customs House. Later this building became part of the Palazzo della Signoria. What is now known as the Palace of the Bargello was originally the Palace of the Podesta. It did not become the residence of the sheriff until 1502.

Benedetto	Friar of San Marco and the convent miniaturist. Author of the *Cedrus Libani*, an account of Savonarola's life written in verse, and of the *Vulnera Diligentis*, which relates Savonarola's life in dialogue form.
Bigi	A political faction which favored the return of the Medici.
borse	Purses in which the names of those eligible for office were placed.
Burlamacchi	Life of Savonarola based on an anonymous *Vita Latina* written by a friar of San Marco between 1520 and 1530. The life was erroneously attributed to Fra Pacifico Burlamacchi, who entered San Marco in 1499. It is sometimes called the pseudo-Burlamacchi.
capannucci	Great wooden trees or wooden infrastructures around which were heaped great quantities of wood, faggots, old brooms, and other combustibles, which were then ignited.
Careggi	The Medici villa 2 miles northwest of Florence where Lorenzo died.
Cerretani, Bartolomeo	Florentine aristocrat who was opposed to Savonarola. Cerretani's *Storia fiorentina* is a history of Florence during the Savonarola years.
Cinozzi, Placido	A friar of San Marco during the Savonarola years and the author of the first biography of Savonarola.
cittadini principali	Principal citizens of Florence.
ciompi	Wool carders. Leaders of the 1378 rebellion which drove the incumbent Signoria out of the palazzo, installed a barefoot carder whose wife and mother sold vegetables in the Mercato Vecchio as gonfalonier, and organized three new guilds: the guilds of the dyers, the doublet makers, and the *ciompi*.
Compagnacci	Literally, the "boon companions," an organization of 300 young men, many of them from the best families in Florence, and all of them committed to making life miserable for the friar and his supporters.
Council of Eighty	A council appointed by the Great Council to advise the Signoria and select ambassadors and commissaries. All proposals approved by

the Signoria had to be discussed and passed upon by the Eighty before being submitted to the Great Council for final approval.

Duomo	The cathedral of Santa Maria dei Fiore
Eight of the Ward	At first the Eight were responsible only for investigating, tracing, and capturing political prisoners. Later they were given the responsibility of administering justice in all criminal cases. Still later they were made responsible for the military preparedness of the city and entrusted with the surveillance of military outposts. After 1494 they served for 4 months.
fanciulli	Male children between the ages of 5 and 18.
Filipepi, Simone	A friar of San Marco during the Savonarola years and the brother of Sandro Botticelli. Filipepi was the author of another early biography of Savonarola.
Frateschi	One of the names used to describe those who supported Savonarola.
giovani	Males between the ages of 24 and 30. Until Francesco Valori became gonfalonier in 1497, *giovani* could neither vote nor hold office. Valori was responsible for a law which lowered the age of eligibility for membership in the Great Council to 24.
gonfalonier	The standard-bearer of the republic and its chief officer. To be eligible for the office of gonfalonier, a citizen had to be 40 years old and belong to one of the seven major guilds. Like the priors, the gonfalonier was chosen by lot, but the names of those eligible for the office were placed in a separate purse. The gonfalonier served for 2 months.
Great Council	A council of 3,100 citizens modeled after the *Consiglio Grande* in Venice. Although the Great Council could not initiate legislation, it had to approve every bill by a two-thirds majority before it could become a law. For the council to meet and pass on legislation, a quorum of 1,000 was needed. Since there was no meeting place in Florence large enough to hold such a crowd, a new hall was built over the courtyard of the Customs House in the Palazzo della Signoria.

Guicciardini, Francesco	Florentine historian, lawyer, and author of *The History of Florence* and *The History of Italy*. Guicciardini was 8 years old when Lorenzo died and 15 when Savonarola was executed. The Guicciardini family was numbered among the *cittadini principali*. Guicciardini's father Piero was a supporter of the friar and a member of the Signoria which condemned the five citizens accused of having helped Piero dei Medici.
guilds	The guilds were of two types: the seven greater guilds and the fourteen lesser guilds. However, each guild had many subsidiary guilds; the sellers of fish, for example, belonged to the butchers guild, and many people joined a guild which had nothing to do with their actual profession or trade just to have a political voice. Thus Lorenzo dei Medici was enrolled in the silkworkers guild and Dante Alighieri belonged to the guild of doctors and druggists.
Machiavelli, Niccolò	An unemployed *giovane* during the Savonarola years; secretary to the second chancery and secretary of the Ten of Liberty and Peace from 1498 to 1512. Author of *The Prince, The Discourses,* and numerous other works.
Madonna dell'Impruneta	A miraculous painting of the virgin Mary in the church of Santa Maria dell'Impruneta 7 miles south of Florence. In times of crisis the Signoria would order the tabernacle containing the picture carried in solemn procession from its resting place in the church into the streets of Florence to hear the prayers of the people and receive their gifts.
Marzocco	Stone lion seated on its haunches with the shield of the commune emblazoned with the Florentine lily under its paw. The Marzocco was the symbol of the republic. During Savonarola's time, a Marzocco sculpted by Donatello was at the northern corner of the Palazzo della Signoria directly in front of the *ringhiera*. A copy of Donatello's statue is now in the National Museum of the Bargello.
Mercato Nuovo	The New Market where the Guild of Bankers and Moneychangers had its palace and the money changers had their tables. The present

Loggia of the *Mercato Nuovo* was built in the sixteenth century.

Mercato Vecchio

The old marketplace of the city where everything from produce to notions to clothing was sold. The marketplace was demolished at the end of the nineteenth century when it was replaced by what was then called the Piazza Vittorio Emanuele and is now called the Piazza della Repubblica.

Miserere

The fifty-first psalm, which begins *"Miserere mei Deus"* (Have mercy upon me O God).

Monte delle Dote

The dowry fund.

Palazzo della Signoria

Now known as the Palazzo Vecchio. Residence of the Signoria during its 2-month term of office and seat of government.

palle

The balls in the Medici coat of arms. Those who supported the Medici were sometimes called *Palleschi* and used the word *palle* as a battle cry.

Parenti, Piero

Ardent supporter of the friar, later became an equally ardent *Arrabbiato*. He was a member of the committee which examined the friar after his arrest. Parenti's *Storia fiorentina* is an account of events from the death of Lorenzo to shortly after the execution of Savonarola.

parlamento

A meeting of the entire adult male population (women had no voice in the government). A *parlamento* was usually convened to approve some innovation or to grant *balià* (extraordinary powers) to a commission set up to deal with a specific crisis.

Pazzi

Family of Florentine bankers who headed an unsuccessful conspiracy to get rid of Lorenzo dei Medici.

Piagnoni

The most commonly used pejorative to describe Savonarola's followers. Its literal meaning is "weepers."

popolo grasso

Literally, the "fat" or "well-fed people." A term used to describe the well-to-do who were usually, but not always, members of the seven greater guilds.

popolo minute   Literally, the "little people," who comprised more than half the population of Florence. This included the poorer artisans and tradesmen who belonged to the fourteen lesser guilds, as well as apprentices, laborers, servants, porters, messengers, and all the others who lacked the property qualifications necessary for guild membership.

pratica   An ad hoc committee called into being to advise the Signoria or some other governing body on an important issue. Usually a *pratica* was composed of leading citizens; sometimes it also included representatives of each of the districts of Florence.

prior   A member of the Signoria. For method of election, see Signoria.

ringhiera   The three-step platform and railing which began at the front entrance to the Palazzo della Signoria and continued around the front and north sides of the palazzo. It was used for haranguing the people and was demolished in 1812 when the present platform and steps were erected.

scrutiny   Not every citizen eligible for office could expect to have his name placed in a *borsa*, or purse. A scrutiny was the process by which those names which were to be put in the *borse* were chosen. During the Medici era the names of the men elected were drawn not from the regular *borse* but from much smaller ones in which only a few names had been placed.

Ser   Title of a notary.

Signore   The lord or head of a state, no matter how small.

Signoria   The chief executive branch and deliberative body of the Florentine state and the only one with the right to initiate legislation. The Signoria could also issue ordinances on its own authority and had wide power in foreign affairs. Each of the four *quartiere*, or districts of Florence, was represented by two priors. After 1343 six of the priors had to come from the major guilds, leaving only two priors to represent the more numerous minor guilds.

The gonfalonier of the republic, who was the ninth member of the Signoria, also had to come from the greater guilds. So much for democracy in Florence.

six beans

Both the Eight of the Ward and the Signoria could condemn a man by a plurality of six votes. Since voting was done with beans, a black bean signifying yes and a white bean no, a vote of six beans was another way of saying a vote that determined a man's fate.

sottoposti

Wage earners who worked in the shops of the members of the wool, silk, and *calimala* guilds but were denied a voice in the running of either the guilds or the government because they lacked the necessary property qualifications. They were also called the "people of God" because their only voice was in the celestial body politic.

Stinche

The prison located on the site of the present Teatro Verdi.

strappado

Torture in which the victim's hands were crossed behind his back and attached to a rope on a pulley that hoisted him from the ground and then dropped him halfway down with a jerk. Each drop was referred to as a "turn of the rope."

Ten of War

Before 1494 it was called the Ten of *Balià*. After the overthrow of the Medici, it became the Ten of Liberty and Peace. The members of the Ten were elected as needed for a six-month term. The Ten were responsible for waging wars, procuring supplies and soldiers, and conducting foreign affairs in wartime.

tiepidi

Literally the "lukewarm," by which Savonarola meant the bad priests and monks, whom he accused of preparing to wage war with him. At times he extended the definition to include his lay enemies.

La Vacca

The great bell atop the tower of the Palazzo della Signoria. It was called *La Vacca*, "the Cow," because of its low mooing sound and was used to summon the people to a *parlamento*.

Via Larga	Now the Via Cavour. The street on which the Medici palace (now the Palazzo Medici-Riccardi) was located.
Violi, Lorenzo	The notary who transcribed Savonarola's sermons. Author of *Giornate*, a series in dialogue form in which he gives his reminiscences of Savonarola.

INDEX